AF560863

POST-COLONIAL WOMEN WRITERS

NEW PERSPECTIVES

Sunita Sinha

Published by

ATLANTIC

PUBLISHERS & DISTRIBUTORS (P) LTD

7/22, Ansari Road, Darya Ganj,
New Delhi-110002
Phones : +91-11-40775252, 23273880, 23275880, 23280451
Fax : +91-11-23285873
Web : www.atlanticbooks.com
E-mail : orders@atlanticbooks.com

Branch Office
5, Nallathambi Street, Wallajah Road,
Chennai-600002
Phones : +91-44-64611085, 32413319
E-mail : chennai@atlanticbooks.com

Printed in India at Glorious Printers, A-13, D.S.I.D.C., Jhilmil Industrial Area, Delhi-110095

Dedicated to My Grandfather

Dr. R.K. Sinha

M.A. (Pat.), D. Phil (Oxon),
Professor Emeritus, Head, Department of English,
Patna University

Foreword

When Pressurized Belongings Give Way to
Felicitous Becomings

The scope of *Post-Colonial Women Writers: New Perspectives* is remarkably vast. Dr. Sunita Sinha has commented on women writers from a great variety of regions and nationalities in a single work of literary criticism. In this respect, *Post-Colonial Women Writers* is impressively comprehensive. Yet the vastness to which I am referring extends well beyond the ingenuity and resourcefulness with which Sinha productively puts into conversation so many significant voices. Inclusive in the vastness is the openendedness to which her study points. On the horizon of post-colonial women writers are more women writers with different experiences to share and stories to tell, all moving under pressures, undergoing becomings, and venturing new belongings, and they take on these challenges not necessarily as a departure from real or imaginary lacks but rather, apparently driven more by desires than needs, in the directions of accumulations and excesses. This may be indicative, and mutually so, of the fact that Post-Colonial Studies is no longer an emergent discipline but instead a legitimated and accomplished discipline that has changed expressions as its subject matters of investigation have transformed.

From the beginning and throughout its development, Post-Colonial Studies has been most concerned with the oppression of people by colonizers; thus, most of the work has been dedicated to giving voice to the oppressed and exposing the injustices perpetrated by their oppressors. The political purport of this undertaking is immediate and has been championed within the academy because in many ways it represents the cultural-activist apex of scholarly interventions into discourses within and outside of academia on social history, politics, and foreign affairs. Needless to say, this approach is still going strong insofar as colonialization and imperialism continue to be enacted and suffered. But Post-Colonial Studies has also expanded, with new perspectives, to account for recent phenomena in the articulations of colonization and, more poignantly, of the ramifications of liberation, diaspora, immigration, and assimilation.

The works discussed in *Post-Colonial Women Writers* both represent and engage with what I would call the articulatory space of post-colonial discourse of which Sinha's study is indeed a contributing amalgamation of elements as well as a timely manifestation.[1] Articulatory spaces are the multifaceted areas where discourses and performances negotiate and amass meanings. They continually redefine their boundaries and strategies, orbit subjects of critical speculation, and furnish connectivity to otherwise disparate elements. They create clusters of coherence out of multiple ideas, objects, subjects, and people. Articulatory spaces emerge in effect of individual and collective actions sometimes consciously and sometimes inadvertently performed both diachronically and synchronically and at varying degrees of affective presence, in other words, more or less influentially—emotionally and conceptually—at a given moment and location. For instance, consider the effects of the war in Iraq—of "Iraq-warspace"—for people in different parts of the world, with different ideologies, perspectives, and sensibilities, which is to say, for people occupying radically different subjective territories. Subjective territories, the official territories and societies that commonalities among subjective territories together make up, are the deeper preoccupations of the identity politics that fuel the plots of many of the works analyzed by Sinha. To illustrate some of the changes in "post-colonial (studies) space"represented by *Post-Colonial Women Writers*, I want to discuss briefly the Pulitzer Prize winner Jhumpa Lahiri's novel, *The Namesake*, which Sinha analyzes in chapter fourteen, "The Sense of Exile, Alienation and Assimilation in Jhumpa Lahiri's Fiction."

While comfortably reading a collection of short stories by Russian writer Nikolai Gogol on a train in India, preferring to read about experiences elsewhere rather than pursue them himself, Ashoke Ganguli's subjective territory is suddenly forced to expand and reconfigure as he is catapulted transversally, that is, beyond what is rationally processable within the established parameters of his subjective territory. This happens when the train crashes horribly. His subsequent becomings, which is to say, his wilful endeavours to experience and become alternatively to how he imagines himself, takes him to the United States and away from his Hindu Bengali roots. It is in the United States that he, and later also his wife Ashima, negotiate their efforts to assimilate into Bostonian culture with their Bengali ties and affinities, and thus they must reconcile with the comings-to-be that are often symptomatic of attempts at assimilation and emulation, especially when under such divergent identitarian pressures.

Unlike becomings, comings-to-be occur when someone becomes more of or like someone or something else than anticipated or desired. Put differently, Ashoke and Ashima experience pressurized belongings as opposed to the more insular belongings characteristic of the cultural homogeneity from which they departed when they left India. For comparison, consider that when a fluid is added to a container already full of a fluid, some fluid must be expelled or the container must expand. This is the same for subjective and official territories. Exposure to alternative perspectives and aesthetics, for instance, encourages exterior thought and expansion within the established subjective territory. These usually occur through subjunctive movements in the forms of contemplation of the "as ifs" and "what ifs" that life and death may or may not have to offer. If this exposure happens, physically speaking, in a strange territory, then interaction with foreign molecules and organisms come into play as well. All this puts pressure on subjective territories and the belongings defined by identifiable material or abstract connections that associate people and are requisite for maintaining community and society, which are the official territories (with structure, codes, and ideology) that laminated and organized subjective territories comprise.

The complexity of pressurized belongings in processes of becomings and comings-to-be that the novel explores is further complicated when Ashoke and Ashima have children in the United States. The principle of pressurized belongings still applies. Their children, Gogol and Sonia, are perceived by themselves and others both as belonging to American culture and as foreigners indelibly marked as alien by their darker skin, and this situation persists despite their becomings and comings-to-be American and/or Bengali, which can be seen in their changing and often confused or conflicted alliances with people and the cultures they represent. This can be seen in Gogol's shift from loving to rejecting his white American girlfriend Maxine. But at different junctures—the emotional and conceptual highpoints in their respective narratives—their pressurized belongings become felicitous insofar as their reflexive-consciousness about their social identities and performances enables them to achieve heightened awareness of their affective presence in both American and immigrant Bengali communities. Sonia's crystallizes through her mother's acceptance of her love for and marriage to a white American. In Gogol's case, the transition begins with the sudden death of his father and is perpetuated by his relationships and break-ups with Maxine and the Bengali Moushumi, among other experiences such that they seem never-ending. His life at the novel's conclusion, as Sinha eloquently puts it is all-too ready for felicitous becomings.

The omission of a concrete ending serves as a final reminder of Lahiri's focus on the tension between the past and present. Thus, the story of Gogol develops progressively through the novel into the allegorical saga of diasporic decentredness. With penetrating insight, Lahiri reveals not only the defining power of names and expectations bestowed upon us by our parents but also the means by which we slowly redefine ourselves. What we reclaim was our past, what we can claim is our present. Where we live, we do not belong and where we belong we can not live.

Through reclaiming and claiming, living but not belonging, belonging but not living, with special emphasis on a subjunctive imperative because Gogol is actively, processually future-going,

The Namesake, like Sinha's collection of thematically interwoven critical essays on some of the most compelling (post-colonial) writings ever produced, calls for and surrenders to the generation of experiences and the post-colonial (studies) space they ineluctably inform. The novel along with Sinha's essays are themselves testimonies to the fact that becomings can be felicitous even when under the pressure of belongings.

Bryan Reynolds
University of California, Irvine

Note

1. For detailed discussion on articulatory space and the related terms used below (pressurized belongings, insular belongings, affective presence, transversal movement, becomings, comings-to-be, subjunctive movement, reflexive-consciousness), see Bryan Reynolds, *Becoming Criminal: Transversal Performance and Cultural Dissidence in Early Modern England* (Baltimore: Johns Hopkins University Press, 2002); *Performing Transversally: Reimagining Shakespeare and the Critical Future* (New York. Palgrave Macmillan, 2003); and *Transversal Enterprises in the Drama of Shakespeare and His Contemporaries: Fugitive Explorations* (London: Palgrave Macmillan, 2006).

Acknowledgements

I am humbled when I think about all the love, support and cooperation extended to me during the entire writing process. There have been many people along the way who have helped me and got me to this point, which I want to acknowledge in print.

I suppose, my list of acknowledgements must begin with Sudhanshu, my husband, who provided me with the impetus for this project and demonstrated as well as made me aware of the potentials of the computer, the websites and above all in myself. Further, my mother, Dr. Manju Rani Sinha, retired Principal, Magadh Mahila College, Patna, has been the source of my constant support, encouragement and approval. Sharing both my excitement and paranoia she always spurred me on with her angelic smile. I am thankful to my brother-in-law Himanshu, who extended his valuable support in ways more than one. I also wish to thank Ishaan, my son. Despite my negligence of his tutorial guidance, he has been a source of delight and pride rather than of concern.

I can go no further without thanking Professor Bryan Reynolds, Head of Doctoral Studies, Department of Drama, University of California, Irvine, for writing a sensitive foreword which has indeed, added a balance to this book.

Above all, I would like to acknowledge my grandfather, Dr. R.K. Sinha, for being my source of inspiration and knowledge. To him, most reverently, I dedicate this book.

I am thankful to Dr. K.R. Gupta, Chairman, Atlantic Publishers and Distributors (P) Ltd., New Delhi for the confidence evinced in me and for seeing the book through the Press.

Sunita Sinha

Preface

Today's women
Born yesterday
Dealing with tomorrow
Not yet where we're going
But not still where we were

Adrienne Rich

"The appearance of woman in the field of literature is a significant fact.... The advent of female literature promises woman's view of life, woman's experience; in other words a new element."

George Henry Lewes

Within the present cultural-theoretical discussion, the post-colonial discourse has gained much visibility and influence. Ever since the collapse of colonialism, cultures that were formerly European colonies can be seen working to define themselves outside the boundaries of colonialism. Focusing on critical discourses like postmodernism, feminism and multiculturalism which rise from the specifically western socio-political content, the post-colonial theory enables us to pose questions related to identity, race, gender and ethnicity.

As the post-colonial discourse seeks to "reinstate the marginalised in the face of the dominant," the acknowledgement of women's experience, the focus on the indifference towards gender issues and the quest for identity become significant aspects of post-colonial thought and fiction. Feminism and post-colonialism share a common concern for voicing the position of the subaltern in society and engendering feminist consciousness in reaction to male paradigms of female experience. As Rosalind

Miles remarks, "The task of interpretation of women's experience cannot be left to male writers alone, however sympathetic they may be. The female perspective, expressed through women's writings of all kinds is more than a valuable corrective to an all male view of the universe."

Though women have been official storytellers to generations, much of world literature had been dominated by a canon that dismissed women's writings as inconsequential a few centuries ago. Women writers whether post-colonial or not have always been marginalised and excluded from the literary canon. They are treated as "colonies" in a male-dominated value system. Their work has been undervalued due to patriarchal assumptions about the superior worth of male experience because they were presumed to write within the enclosed domestic space and women's perceptions of their experience within it and therefore, rank below the works of male writers who deal with weightier themes. However, with the collapse of colonialism and focus on feminist discourse we can see the emergence of several counter canons, resulting as a reaction against this exclusion, which has helped to establish women's writing in mainstream literature. Women writers today, reveal the disconnection between what the women said and what they wrote, between their spoken words and their silences, between women as the subject matter of writing and women subjects and writers, between language, literature and social movements and the emergence of women's voices. Thus, their fiction aims at developing new definitions of power and stresses that "women's values, centered around life giving, must be revalued."

Contemporary women writers through their fiction have chosen to talk back, "Moving from silence into speech is for the oppressed, the colonized, the exploited and those who stand and struggle side by side, a gesture of defiance that heals, that makes new life and new growth possible. It is that act of speech, of 'talking back,' that is no mere gesture of empty words, that is the expression of a movement from object to subject—the liberated voice."

Post-Colonial Women Writers: New Perspectives celebrates the excellence, originality and diversity in women's writings which is rapidly flourishing in the global market and creating waves. It offers an inclusive analysis of a number of relevant post-colonial and feminist writers whose critiques open up a new set of questions concerning post-colonialism and its related issues like hybridity, otherness, orientalism, multiculturalism, diaspora, globalisation and feminism. Conceptualised around a series of topics like quest for identity and self-definition, the problems of exile and displacement, the agony of alienation and issues of racism and "otherness," the book covers a wide spectrum of issues which constitute the "terrains of post-colonial world literature."

In almost all the literatures of the world, the women writers are transcending the boundaries and making their presence felt on the international stage. Hence, the book is a humble effort to present the exemplary canon of women's writings which includes not only English women, but women writings in English in several national traditions including African, American, Australian, Canadian, South Asian and the British. The distinctive women writers discussed in this book are highly acclaimed and celebrated authors who have also been the recipients of prestigious literary prizes and have been drawn from New Literatures the world over. The brilliant constellation of women writers includes Doris Lessing, the Nobel Laureate for Literature 2007 and Nadine Gordimer, the Nobel Prize winner in 1991, both from Africa; Toni Morrison, the Nobel Prize winner in 1993 from America; Jane Austen from Britain, whose *Pride and Prejudice* topped a survey of the greatest women writers; Margaret Atwood, the Booker Prize winner for the year 2003 and many more in the earlier years; Margaret Laurence, Alice Munro, the distinctive women writers dominating the literature of Canada; and Inez Baranay from Australia. It also includes Indian women writers, namely Kiran Desai, the Man Booker Prize winner in 2006; Manju Kapur, the winner of Commonwealth Prize; Jhumpa Lahiri, the winner of year 2000 Pulitzer Prize for Fiction; Anita Desai, thrice shortlisted for the Booker Prize; Shashi Deshpande, the Sahitya Akademi winner in 1990 and Anita Nair who has been tipped as the most promising young writer of the time. The book also includes the controversial

Bangladeshi novelist Taslima Nasrin, who has also received many awards; Monica Ali, also from Bangladesh, who has been judged the winner of Granta's Best of Young British Novelists; Bapsi Sidhwa, "Pakistan's finest English language novelist" and the recipient of Sitara-i-Imtiaz and Tehmina Durrani, another Pakistani writer who won the Italian Marrissa Bellasario Prize.

Post-colonial literature is writing at the margin and has similarities to contemporary European thought, for example feminism, post-structuralism and even hypertext theory. Post-colonial Feminist Literature has unravelled the layers of misinterpretations of traditions and religions. The more traditional a post-colonial society is, the more problematic the question of women's emancipation is and therefore, more passionate its women writers are and their works can be characterised as feminist treatises. The book contains the illuminating views of women writers with a distinctive feminist stance and as interpreters of exile, dislocation and racism.

The first female writer in this collection does not chronologically belong to the post-colonialism constellation of women writers but she is too significant to be excluded from the 20th century feminist canon. Though a seemingly unlikely feminist, Jane Austen's fiction, with its emphasis on the reality of women's lives reveals the subservient position of women and explores the issues of gender that explore the male and female power. In the recent years Austen has been valued particularly by the feminist critics who have appreciated the high intelligence of her heroines. The arrival of feminist criticism has led to a re-examination of Jane Austen's novels which establishes her as a protofeminist—a forerunner of feminism. The epicist of female experience, Doris Lessing's fiction rests on her treatment of women in modern life, and presents women with whom one can identify complex, intelligent, questioning women who are not content with the status quo and rebel against the established order. Doris Lessing deals with every significant issue of twentieth century ranging from racism, communism and feminism to psychology and mysticism in every post-modernist fictional form like magic realism, metafiction, surrealism, fantasy and space fiction.

Canadian literature is remarkable for the prominence of women writers like Margaret Atwood, Margaret Laurence and Alice Munro. Margaret Atwood's fiction reveals no exquisite definition of feminism but her fiction has been seen as a barometer of feminist thought. Her protagonists are female characters who are forced to remake themselves, to achieve courage and self-reliance in their attitudes. Margaret Laurence has emerged as a predominant shaper of post-war Canadian Literature. Her novels portray strong women striving for self-definition while immersed in the daily struggle to make a living in a male-dominated world. One of the major female voices of Canadian literature, Alice Munro's novels explore complexities in what appears to be effortless anecdotal recreations of everyday life. Munro may be regarded as a feminist, but one who fights small quiet battles instead of loud ones.

Recent Indian writers depict both the diversity of women and the diversity within each woman, rather than limiting the lives of women to one ideal. The novels emerging in the twenty-first century furnish examples of a whole range of attitudes towards the imposition of tradition, some offering an analysis of the family structure and the caste system as the key elements of patriarchal social organization. They also re-interpret mythology by using new symbols and subverting the canonic versions. In conclusion, the work of Indian women writers is significant in making society aware of women's demands, and in providing a medium for self-expression. Manju Kapur's fiction stresses on the woman's need for self-realisation. Displaying a mature understanding of the female psyche, Manju Kapur beautifully explores the various issues of woman in her political, sexual and domestic milieu. Shashi Deshpande too, deals with the quest for the human self within the woman and fights for recognition of women as individuals. Anita Nair's *Ladies Coupe* has been hailed as one of the most important feminist novels to come out of South India. The first Indian writer based in India, to be on the Picador USA select list for Spring 2000, Anita Nair, in *Ladies Coupe*, answers the questions that every woman would have faced in her life—the questions relating to her place in society. Nayantara Sahgal is one such prominent Indian English novelist who has tried to depict women suffering due to sexist bias in patriarchal society and she envisions a world which should be based on equality and harmony between the two sexes. Placed within the context of the writing of the fifties and sixties, Sahgal displays a highly developed consciousness of the gendered nature of morality and social structures. She is primarily seen as a feminist and her feminism is rooted in the larger framework of human rights—of personal freedom and right to body.

The changing images of women in south Asian novels, from the suffering women to the assertive ones, redefining self and defying traditional mores, are beautifully documented in the novels of Taslima Nasrin and Bapsi Sidhwa, who have opened up areas for new exploration and debate in post-colonial feminist studies. The emergence of Taslima Nasrin's feminist writings inaugurates one of the most controversial moments in the scene of Bangladeshi literature. Bapsi Sidhwa emerges as one of the most prominent Anglophone novelists of South Asia. Stylistically dextrous and liberally laced with humour, her fiction offers a sensitive insight into the complexities of life in the subcontinent with particular focus on the lives of women. A chronicler of the history of the Indian subcontinent, Sidhwa's novels reflect her personal experience from the days of the Raj, to the partition of India, the rise of religious fundamentalism and the impact of the modern ideas of Mahatma Gandhi on the traditions of colonial India. Tehmina Durrani's writings too, represent a distinctive and original contribution to all the oppressed voiceless classes of women around the world and provide an extraordinary insight into the vulnerable position of women caught in the complex web of patriarchal society, establishing new directions for the women's movement in South Asia. Whether the spokesperson is Taslima Nasrin or Tehmina Durrani, building a strong case for indictment against marriage, Vedic diktats, and social mores for women, lusty Pirs and holy men, the essence of all they want to speak is not much different to what Jonathan Swift has said: "We have just enough religion to make us hate, but not enough to make us love one another."

Across the world, the diasporic women writers have carved their distinct niche. Kiran Desai, the youngest ever women writer to win the Man Booker Prize, 2006, for *The Inheritance of Loss*, combines in herself the naturalness of Tolstoy and depth of Dickens with post-modern ambivalence. From the sweet-natured playfulness of her first novel, *Hullabaloo in the Guava Orchard* to the exploration of almost every contemporary international issue of globalisation, multiculturalism and terrorist violence in *The Inheritance of Loss*, Kiran Desai has expanded her reach to the global arena. Jhumpa Lahiri's *The Interpreter of Maladies* won her a Pulitzer and established the presence of the Indian women writers on the international scene. Lahiri successfully explores the sense of exile, alienation and assimilation experienced by the immigrants in *The Namesake* and brings out rather successfully the predicament of the Indians who trapeze between and across two traditions, one inherited and one left behind, and the other encountered but not necessarily assimilated. She has emerged as an interpreter of exile in its varying nuances and manifestations. Monica Ali, through her fiction, brilliantly explores the complex issues of colonialism and immigration and illuminates the pangs of exile and displacement. Ali has extended the migrant voice in British fiction, particularly through her representation of gender and focus on history and dislocation.

The legacies of colonialism are invariably tied up with racism. The economic and political legacies of colonialism have radically changed the "racial" and ethnic make-up of societies, in Europe and North America, bringing with them problems of white ethnocentrism, ethnic conflict and racism that feminists must address. Toni Morrison, the Nobel Prize winner, broke through the barriers for women and blacks and beautifully evoked the legacy of displacement and slavery in her various novels. Her novels fuse the universal themes in the particularity of the African-American experience and define the beauty and brutality of human life. For Nadine Gordimer, the Nobel Prize winning South African writer, apartheid was the dominant theme and her works articulated key issues for white South Africans, presenting the true face of racism in all its human complexities. With her restless energy and prodigious talent,

Gordimer is able to enter into the existence of others whether they be black or white, men or women.

Post-colonialism has become one of the most exciting, rapidly expanding and challenging areas of literary and cultural studies today. Hence, the book includes an introductory chapter on post-colonialism and its key issues, discusses the themes, the meaning and boundaries of post-colonialism. Dealing with the major women writers in English across centuries and spaces, the book aims at fascinating the readers with a broad spectrum of perspectives which have much contemporary relevance in the arena of post-colonial literature today. Since most of the authors included in this collection are prescribed in the English syllabus in the universities of India, both the teachers and the students will find it useful in their scholarly pursuits.

I am thankful to Dr. K.R. Gupta, Chairman, Atlantic Publishers and Distributors (P) Ltd., New Delhi for the confidence evinced in me and for seeing the book through the press.

Sunita Sinha

Contents

Introduction

1

> Post-Colonial theory is a discussion of "migration, slavery, suppression, resistance, representation, difference, race, gender, place, and responses to the influential master discourses of imperial Europe...and the fundamental experiences of speaking and writing by which all these come into being."
>
> —Bill Ashcroft, Gareth Griffiths, and Helen Tiffin
> The Empire Writes Back:
> Theory and Practice in Post-Colonial Literatures

Unlike the other "post-isms," post-colonialism does not reject what it contains; it does not signify a closure of colonialism, rather, it opens a world of inquiry and understanding. In 1970s, having gained prominence perhaps with Edward Said's influential critique of Western constructions of the Orient in his book, *Orientalism*, the term "post-colonial" remains "a relative newcomer to the jargon of Western social science. Although discussions about the effects of colonial and imperialist domination are by no means new, the various meanings attached to the prefix "post" and different understandings of what characterizes the post-colonial continue to make this term a controversial one."[1] Post-Colonialism appeared in the context of decolonisation that marked the second half of the twentieth century and has been appropriated by contemporary critical discourse in a wide range of domains. From a strictly historical definition, the concept of post-colonialism has stretched to the more encompassing and controversial sphere referring on the one hand, to the status of a land that ceases to be colonised and has regained its political independence and on the other hand denouncing the new forms of economic and cultural oppression that have succeeded modern colonialism. Though these two senses are intimately linked, they foreground different aspects of a single process: the cultural homogenizing of ever larger areas of the globe as disparate as those of White settler colonies such as Australia and Canada and of the Latin American Continent, whose independence battles were fought in the 19th century and countries such as India, Nigeria, or Algeria that emerged from very different colonial encounters in the Post-World War Two era. Nevertheless, "What the concept *may* help us to do is to describe or characterize the shift in global relations which marks the (necessarily uneven) transition from the age of Empires to the post-independence and post-decolonisation moment."[2]

Despite a basic consensus on the general themes of post-colonial writing, however, there is an ongoing debate regarding the meaning of post-colonialism—"The term post-colonialism—according to a too-rigid etymology—is frequently misunderstood as a temporal concept, meaning the time after colonialism has ceased, or the time following the politically determined Independence Day on which a country breaks away from its governance by another state, Not a naïve teleological sequence which supersedes colonialism, post-colonialism is, rather, an engagement with and contestation [sic] of colonialism's discourses, power structures, and social hierarchies.... A theory of post-colonialism must, then, respond to more than the merely chronological construction of post-independence, and to more than just the discursive experience of imperialism."[3]

Many critics propose that the term should be expanded to include the literatures of Canada, the United States and Australia. In his essay discussing the nature and boundaries of post-colonialism, Simon During offers an inclusive definition, "the need, in nations, or groups which have been victims of imperialism to achieve an identity uncontaminated by Universalist or Eurocentric concepts or images."[4] Deepika Bahri's essay on post-colonialism reveals that the diversity of definitions of post-colonialism exists because the term post-colonial is used both as a literal description of formerly colonial societies and as a description of global conditions after a period of colonialism. Bahri holds that post-colonial as a literary genre connotes meanings that are completely separate from a historical moment or time period. Post-Colonial literature is concerned with the political and cultural independence of peoples formerly subjugated in colonial empires, and the literary expression of post-colonialism. What each of these literatures has in common beyond their special and distinctive regional characteristics is that they emerged in their present form out of the experience of colonisation and asserted themselves by foregrounding the tension with the imperial power, and by emphasizing their differences from the assumptions of the imperial centre. It is this which makes them distinctively post-colonial.

Post-Colonialism is the study of the interactions between European nations and the societies they colonised in the modern period for several centuries. The sheer extent and duration of the European empire and its disintegration after the Second World War have led to widespread interest in post-colonial literature and criticism in our own times. Thus, the term 'post-colonial' covers all the culture affected by the imperial process from the moment of colonisation to the present day and is concerned with the world as it exists during and after the period of European imperial domination and the effects of this on contemporary literatures.

Post-Colonial studies allows for a wide-ranging investigation into power relations in various contexts: The formation of empire, the impact of colonisation on post-colonial history, economy, science and culture, the cultural productions of colonised societies, feminism and post-colonialism, agency for marginalised people, and the state of the post-colony in contemporary economic and cultural contexts are some broad topics in the post-colonialism. It essentially focuses on the persistence of colonial forms of power in contemporary world politics, especially how the social construction of racial, gendered and class differences uphold relations of power and subordination. It addresses issues such as identity, gender, race and ethnicity:

the challenge of developing a national identity in the wake of colonial rule, the ways in which knowledge of colonised people has served the interests of colonisers, and how knowledge about the world is produced under specific power relations, repetitively circulated, and finally legitimated, to serve certain interests. Post-Colonial theory is also built around the concept of resistance, of resistance as subversion, or opposition which can carry with it ideas about human freedom, liberty, identity, individuality, etc.

One of the most disputed terms in post-colonial studies, **hybridity** commonly refers to "the creation of new trans-cultural forms within the contact zone produced by colonisation."[5] It emerges an important concept in post-colonial theory, referring to the integration of cultural signs and practices from the colonizing and the colonized cultures. The assimilation and adaptation of cultural practices, the cross-fertilization of cultures, can be seen as positive, enriching, and dynamic, as well as oppressive. "Hybridity" is also a useful concept for helping to break down the false sense that colonized cultures—or colonizing cultures for that matter—are monolithic, or have essential, unchanging features.

Where as in Jean Rhys' *Wide Sargasso Sea*, to be a Creole or a 'hybrid' was essentially negative but according to Ashcroft, most post-colonial writing has focused on the hybridized nature of post-colonial culture as strength rather than as a weakness. It is not a case of the oppressor obliterating the oppressed or the coloniser silencing the colonised. In practice, it stresses that the mutuality of the process and the clash of cultures can impact as much upon the coloniser as the colonised. In his piece entitled *Cultural Diversity and Cultural Differences*, Bhabha too, stresses the interdependence of coloniser and colonised.

Post-Colonial theory is built in large part around the concept of **otherness**, which includes doubleness, both identity and difference, so that every 'other,' every different than and excluded by is dialectically created and includes the values and meaning of the colonising culture even as it rejects its power to define. In general terms, the 'other' is anyone who is separate from one's self. The existence of others is crucial in defining what is 'normal' and in locating one's own place in the world. "The colonised subject is characterised as 'other' through discourses such as primitivism and cannibalism, as a means of establishing the binary separation of the coloniser and colonised and asserting the naturalness and primacy of the colonising culture and world view,"[6] remarked Ashcroft. In colonial discourse, the subjectivity of the colonised is continually located in the gaze of the imperial Other, the 'grande-autre.' Through a reading of novels by Naipaul, Gordimer and Morrison, Bhabha invites us to imagine "world literature" as the study of the way in which cultures recognize themselves through their projection of 'otherness.'

Edward Said's evaluation and critique of the set of beliefs known as **Orientalism** forms an important background for post-colonial studies. The beginning of post-colonial studies in history, literature, philosophy, anthropology and the arts can be traced back to the publication of Edward Said's *Orientalism* in 1978. An eminent scholar in post-colonial studies, Said focusses on the interplay between the "Occident" symbolising the West and the "Orient" symbolising the romantic Middle East and Far East. According to Said, the West has created a culture, history and future promise to the Orient's, who, backward and unaware as they were, of their history and culture are viewed with racism and prejudice. Here, Said examines the ways through which the 'Orient' was and continues to be constructed through the lens of Europeans. Orientalism could be seen as a Western style for dominating, reconstructing and having authority over the Orient. Said's work highlights the inaccuracies of a wide variety of assumptions as it questions various paradigms of thought which are accepted on individual, academic, and political levels. The Orient signifies a system of representations framed by political forces that brought the Orient into Western learning, Western consciousness, and Western empire. The Orient exists for the West, and is constructed by and in relation to the West. It is a mirror image of what is inferior and alien ("Other") to the West. As Said remarks, "The Orient is not only adjacent to Europe; it is also the place of Europe's greatest and richest and oldest colonies, the source of its civilizations and languages, its cultural contestant and one of its deepest and most recurring images of the Other."[7]

The special post-colonial crisis of identity concerns itself with the development or recovery of an effective identifying relationship between self and place. A valid and active sense of self may have been eroded by dislocation, resulting from migration, the experience of enslavement, transportation, or 'voluntary' removal for indentured labour. **Diaspora** cannot be separated from colonialism, as it was this historical condition that led to the displacement of people across the world under different circumstances or forms of compulsion. Whether or not the people of the diaspora were settlers, migrants, transported convicts, slaves, or labourers, what is more apparent is the capacity of colonialism to produce so many varied forms of power that compel people to move. Consequently, the culture produced by diaspora cannot but contain so many resonances of the movement, the imagination of their homelands, sense of tradition, the circumstances of their removal, and the reaction to the places they currently live: "The descendants of the diasporic movements generated by colonialism have developed their own distinctive cultures which both preserve and often extend and develop their originary cultures."[8]

Like many of the other terms in post-colonial theory and discourse that popularly suggest detachment from metropolitan or local spaces, **Exile** has been deployed as a concept beyond simply a forced removal from a given physical location. Exile in everyday use invokes images of individual political dissidents sent overseas or large groups of people banished to distant lands, forming various Diasporas. In these cases there is sometimes a presumption that the exiled are different from casual migrants who forget their original homelands and form new allegiances with the places in which they settle. Exiles retain a sense of (be)longing to for a real or imagined homeland. One doesn't need to be physically removed from the "homeland" in order to be exiled. Exile can take place in different cultural spaces, especially through processes like modernisation. What is important to grasp in post-colonial exile is, therefore the profundity of the impact of colonialism and ongoing imperialism.

The term itself has to be over determined so as to suggest the magnitude of cultural transformations inflicted by colonialism, the type of consciousness exile produces, and the responsibility that exile should uphold.

Displacement is a key term in post-colonial theory which applies to all migrant situations concerning people who have left their homes to settle in countries or cultural communities which are initially strange to them. Colonialism often creates a setting which results in the migration of large numbers of people, either within the colonies or from them to the "imperial centre" though, not all migration takes place in a colonial setting, and not all post-colonial literature deals with migration. Migrant literature, has commanded growing interest within literary studies since the 1980s and focuses on the social contexts in the migrant's country of origin which prompt them to leave, on the experience of migration itself, on the mixed reception which they may receive in the country of arrival, on experiences of racism and hostility, and on the sense of rootlessness and the search for identity which can result from displacement and cultural diversity. It refers both to physical displacement and a sense of being socially or culturally out of place.

Many contemporary women writers who live in strong patriarchal cultures, language and the ability to write and communicate, represent power and draw a relationship between post-colonialism and **feminism**. Some of these writers, for example, have noted that since the language of British-ruled colonies is English, literature written in English has often been used to marginalise and constrain female points of view. In the post-colonial period, however, language, and the ability to speak, write, and publish, has become an enabling tool for post-colonial authors. Feminism and post-colonialism have both been concerned with language because of its importance to identity formation and also its use as a weapon to subvert patriarchal and colonial powers. Many post-colonial feminists argue that oppressions relating to the colonial experience, particularly racial, class, and ethnic oppressions, have marginalised women in post-colonial societies. They challenge the assumption that gender oppression is the primary force of patriarchy. Moreover, post-colonial feminists object to "the perceived portrayal of women of non-Western societies as passive and voiceless victims, as opposed to the portrayal of Western women as modern, educated and empowered."[9] Post-Colonial feminists do not present a united front on feminist issues, but can be described as "feminists who have reacted against both universalising tendencies in Western feminist thought and a lack of attention to gender issues in mainstream post-colonial thought."[10]

"Post-Colonial feminists today struggle to fight gender oppression within their own cultural models of society rather than through those of the West,"[11] says Talpade. In 1984, Black American feminist Barbara Smith spoke warmly of being part of a Third World feminist movement: "And not only am I talking about my sisters here in the United States—American Indian, Latina, Asian American, Arab American—I am also talking about women all over the globe.... Third World feminism has enriched not just the women it applies to, but also political practice in general."[12] More often, the silenced objects of Western analysis, Third World women are making their voices heard and are beginning to change the face of feminism in the West. Post-Colonial feminism in the new millennium now accepts a crucial point, long self-evident to Third World women, that racism, colonialism and its legacies are not just the province of non-white, non-Western women. Feminist and post-colonialist theories share much common ground due to their examination of the voice, and the position of, the subaltern in society. Their critiques of, and struggles against, domination by the white male has led to their alignment and relevant discussions about their similar problems, affects and strategies. Atwood's *Surfacing* for example, presents the analogous nature of patriarchy, cultural imperialism and geographical colonisation and how this combined colonial experience has left the victim with feelings of displacement and disconnectedness from their language, history and culture, which in turn has led to a fractured sense of self and a desperate need to regain and reclaim identity.

Post-Colonial literature often focuses on race relations and the effects of **racism** and usually indicts white and/or colonial societies. Colonised countries have been profoundly affected by the exploitative, racist nature of the interrelation which was and remains economic, political and cultural. In Europe and North America, the economic and political legacies of colonialism have radically changed the 'racial' and ethnic make up of societies, bringing with them problems of white ethnocentrism, ethnic conflict and racism that feminists must address. As in the colonial period, the legacies of colonialism are invariably tied up with racism and the works of literature that are defined as post-colonial often record racism or a history of genocide, including slavery, apartheid, and the mass extinction of peoples, such as the Aborigines in Australia. In her novel *The Bluest Eye* (1981), Toni Morrison graphically depicts the effects of the legacy of nineteenth-century classical racism for poor black people in the United States. The novel tells of how the daughter of a poor black family, Pecola Breedlove, internalises white standards of beauty to the point where she goes mad. Her fervent wish for blue eyes comes to stand for her wish to escape the poor, unloving, racist environment in which she lives. For a long time mainstream white Western feminism paid scant attention to the question of race. Racism was seen as secondary to patriarchy and, at best, the problem of non-white women. Many white women took a liberal, colour blind position which claimed not to see difference or act upon it. It took a long, hard struggle by black women to have racism included on the feminist agenda. The strong tendency of white women to disregard racism was an effect of white privilege—a point that women of colour were forced to make repeatedly: "As Third World women we clearly have a different relationship to racism than white women, but all of us are born into an environment where racism exists. Racism affects all of our lives, but it is only white women who can 'afford' to remain oblivious to these effects. The rest of us have had it breathing or bleeding down our necks."[13] The idea of a cultural hybridity that can challenge existing binary oppositions and hierarchies has become a popular one in post-colonial theory. It is seen by some women of colour as a profound and empowering effect of diasporic experience. Thus, Black British feminist Heidi Safia Mirza writes: "Cultural hybridity, the fusion of cultures and coming together of difference, the 'border crossing' that marks diasporic survival, signifies change, hope of newness, and space for creativity. But in the search for rootedness—a 'place called home'—these women, in the process of self-identification, disidentify with an excluding, racist British colonising culture. They articulate instead a multi-faceted discontinuous black identity that marks their difference."[14]

Yet, while it is not only Black Women who reject racist, colonising cultures, white women, who *de facto* benefit from such exclusions, need to be more vocal in contesting them. They need to work to establish new forms of identity and ways of being, that are inclusive and that respect and celebrate difference. Some recent writing by Black and Third World Women in the West has argued that the diasporic experience of women of colour can create the conditions for breaking down traditional binary categories and liberating difference. Another key question in post-colonial feminism is who speaks for whom and whose voices are heard in discussions of Third World women's issues. The question of voice was raised by Gayatri Spivak in her influential essay *Can the Subaltern Speak*? (1988) in which she analyses "the relations between the discourses of the West and the possibility of speaking of (or for) the subaltern woman."[15]

A feminist approach to environmental ethics, Ecofeminism, or ecological feminism is a term coined in 1974 by Françoise d'Eaubonnet who sought to describe the epic violence inflicted on women and nature as a result of male domination. Her early analysis has since been expanded upon and refined, based in part on new conceptions of the history and character of our species. It is a philosophy and movement born from the union of feminist and ecological thinking, and the belief that the social mentality that leads to the domination and oppression of women is directly connected to the social mentality that leads to the abuse of the environment. Ecofeminists believe there are interconnections between the oppression of women (sexism), the oppression of the Other (racism, classism, ageism, colonialism, etc.) and the domination of nature (naturism). They argue that a relationship exists between the oppression of women and the degradation of nature, and explore the intersectionality between sexism, the domination of nature, racism, speciesism, and other characteristics of social inequality. Ecofeminism believes that patriarchal society is built on four interlocking pillars; sexism, racism, class exploitation and environmental destruction. Ecofeminist analysis reveals that it's not only women who are portrayed as being 'closer to nature,' oppressed races and social classes have also been closely associated with nature. In Western society women are treated as inferior to men, 'nature' is treated as inferior to 'culture,' and humans are understood as being separate from, and often superior to, the natural environment. "Women have had no real power in the outside world, no place in decision-making. Intellectual life, the work of the mind, has traditionally not been accessible to women—due in part to society's either/or mentality, coupled with a valuing of the spiritual over the natural. Women have been generally passive, as has been nature. Today, however, ecology speaks for the earth, for the 'other' in human and environmental relationships; and Ecofeminism, by speaking for the original others, seeks to understand the interconnected roots of all domination, and ways to resist and change."[16]

Today many female nature writers and feminists lay claim to a connection or oneness with nature. In her poem "Wild," Mary Donahoe becomes a creature of the wild, roaming the woods and "communing" with nature. In an excerpt from Woman and Nature Susan Griffin, a noted feminist and nature writer, plainly states this idea that women have some level of communion with nature that men cannot attain. "He says that woman speaks with nature.... He says he is not part of this world, that he was set on this world as a stranger. He sets himself apart from woman and nature.... We are women and nature. And he says he cannot hear us speak."[17] Not only women writers men too, have had the notion that women somehow have a special connection with nature. According to many of them some deep rooted instinctive connection exists between woman and that which is nature. A short survey of some of the poetry we read in my writing class proves my point. S.T. Coleridge said of nature, "she is the preserver, the treasure of our joys." E.E. Cummings, in his poem "O sweet spontaneous," portrays nature as a sweet young innocent hounded by the dirty old men of philosophy, science, and religion. In his poem "To Autumn," John Keats compares spring and summer to a fair maiden who flitters about the fields and takes naps on the granary floor.

"The goal of ecofeminist environmental ethics is to develop theories and practices concerning humans and the natural environment that are not male-biased and that provide a guide to action in the prefeminist present,"[18] said Karen Warren. The primary aims of ecofeminism are not the same as those typically associated with liberal feminism. Ecofeminists do not seek equality with men as such, but aim for liberation of women as women. Central to this liberation is recognition of the value of the activities traditionally associated with women; childbirth, nurturing and the whole domestic arena. Some feminists have criticised ecofeminism for reinforcing oppressive stereotypes and for its tendency toward essentialism.

The notion of **multiculturism** and the "plural society" has quite a specific usage in the study of colonial and post-colonial societies and features high on the political agenda of most states today since most states incorporate a variety of ethnic, religious and other diversities. The problem has become exacerbated in recent decades because of the increased influx of immigrants into the advanced capitalist states. During the colonial period and after the achievement of political independence, individuals from the colonies and former colonies migrated to the metropolis and led to a surge of multiculturism. Multiculturism sees culture as open-ended, permeable, and continuously (re)produced by cross-cultural encounters; a borderland topos where the lives of people from a multiplicity of backgrounds are constantly intersecting and crisscrossing and thereby producing "a polyvalent assemblage of new cultural meanings."[19] As Cornel West reminds us, analysing multiculturalism from a contemporary philosophical perspective means situating oneself within hybrid culture and giving up on the "quest for pure traditions and pristine heritages."[20] Multiculturalism represents a new kind of universalism where integration of individuals into the state is not predicated on a total disengagement from particularistic community ties. It cherishes cultural diversity and envisions a society in which different communities forge a common identity while retaining their cultural provenance and acknowledges the existence of diverse communities, but what is more important is that it accords positive value to the collective identities of all ethnic communities.

Thus, grappling with the legacy of colonial rule, the post-colonial constellation is marked by the confrontation with neo paracolonial dependencies on industrialised countries and the thematisation of conflicts and problems related to their cultural tradition and their attempts at modernisation.

NOTES AND REFERENCES

1. Kandiyoti, Deniz: In an article entitled "Post-Colonialism Compared: Potentials and Limitations in the Middle East and Central Asia."
2. Hall: 1996, p. 246.
3. Gilbert, Helen and Tompkins Joanne: In Post-Colonial Drama: Theory, Practice, Politics.
4. During, Simon: In an essay on post-colonialism.
5. Ashcroft, G. Griffiths and H. Tiffin: *Post-Colonial Studies: The Key Concepts*. London: Routledge, 2003, p. 118.
6. *Ibid.*
7. Said, Edward: Orientalism, New York: Vintage, 1979.
8. Ashcroft, G. Griffiths and H. Tiffin: *Post-Colonial Studies: The Key Concepts*. London: Routledge, p. 70.
9. Mills, S.: "Post-colonial Feminist Theory," p. 106 in S. Jackson and J. Jones eds., Contemporary Feminist Theories (Edinburgh: Edinburgh University Press), 1998, pp. 98-112.
10. *Ibid.*
11. Talpade, Mohanty Chandra: 'Under Western Eyes' in Feminist Review, No. 30 (Autumn, 1988), pp. 61-88.
12. Smith, Barbara (1984): "Black Feminism: A Movement of Our Own." In Karen Kahn (ed.). Front Line Feminism, 1975-95.
13. Essays from Sojourner's First 20 Years. San Fransisco: Aunt Lute Books, 1995, pp. 22-27.
14. Heidi Safia, Mirza: 1997, 16.
15. Spivak, Gayatri: In an essay, "Can the Subaltern Speak?" In Cary Nelson & Lawrence Grossberg (eds.). Marxism and the Interpretation of Culture. London: MacMillan, 1988, pp. 271-313.
16. Plant Judith, remarks in 'Women and Nature.'

17. Griffin, Susan: In an excerpt from Women and Nature.
18. Warren, Karen in Ecofeminst Philosophy (2000).
19. Peter McLaren, Critical Pedagogy and Predatory Culture (New York: Routledge, 1995), 57.
20. West, Cornel: "Diverse New World," in P.C. Debating, ed. Paul Berman (New York: Dell, 1992), pp. 326-27.

Reassessing Jane Austen: 'The Unlikely Feminist'

> "A feminist is a woman who does not allow anyone to think in her place."
>
> —*Michele Le Doeuff*

Despite the huge commercial success of modern authors such as J.K. Rowling, Zadie Smith and Helen Fielding, Jane Austen's bitter sweet social comedy *Pride and Prejudice* written in 1813 topped a survey of the greatest women writers. Scholars often cite Austen as an early example of feminism in her critique of courtship and in her creation of strong heroines. Julian Gough's *Juno and Juliet* which resonates with protofeminist ideas begins with an epigraph from *Northanger Abbey*—"Man has the advantage of choice, women only the power of refusal."[1] Placed firmly at the beginning of the 'Great Tradition' of British novelists by Dr. F.R. Leavis, Jane Austen perhaps is the only novelist before Charles Dickens to still command, a significant popular readership. Jane Austen has proved to be one of the most accessible and enduring legacies of Western culture in the last two hundred years. As a cultural icon as well as an object of serious intellectual investigation, Jane Austen has influenced the critical understanding and popular imagination around social relations and cultural rituals like the institution of marriage, the ideology of romantic relationship, the cultural imagining of class as well as larger historical pictures such as slavery, imperialism and feminism.

Nearly two hundred years after her works first appeared, she still has the distinction of being widely read all over the world and of being considered as one of the most important English language novelists. Though her social scene is circumscribed by the drawing rooms, assembly rooms, walks and gardens of the minor landed gentry and her concern is primarily with the correct assessment of character and with the right conduct, she remains a supreme innovator to whom all subsequent novelists should be indebted. Her fictional world seen as an idyllic bygone time and place, both unlike and preferable to the present, has entered into the mainstream of popular literary culture.

Content to depict a small slice of English life and concentrating on the landed gentry in rural England and the small triumphs and defeats of young women in their struggle for survival, Austen has been a writer of great prose but limited subject matter, writing only what she has experienced. The scene may be narrow, the action trivial but the condition is the human condition, because for Jane Austen, human kind was of first importance. Le Faye is quick notice her "ability to create the sensations that we are visiting genuine places and joining in the lives of genuine people."[2] In her intense concentration on the thoughts and feelings of a limited number of characters, Jane Austen creates as profound an understanding and as precise a vision of the potentialities of human spirit as the art of fiction has ever achieved. When Jane Austen's novels were published they were dismissed as 'too natural to be interesting,' yet their true to lifeness helped earn Austen her place in the literary canon.

Ironically, though considered to be England's first truly important novelist, Austen had difficulty in establishing a reputation for herself in her life time. "Men have had every advantage of us telling their own story. Education has been theirs in so much a higher a degree, and worst of all, the pen has been in their hands"[3]—protested Jane Austen.

The editors preferred to review novels with a didactic bent and perceived that novels oriented towards concerns of women were intrinsically less important than works oriented towards men. Hence, Austen's novels received relatively few reviews during her lifetime. It was Walter Scott who attempted for the first time to place Jane Austen's novels within the larger context of recent literature. As he remarked—"That young lady has a talent for describing the involvements of feelings and characters of ordinary life which is to me the most wonderful I ever met with."[4] After her death in 1817, however, she was praised for her "exhaustless invention"[5] and Richard Whately compared her to such acknowledged immortals like Homer and Shakespeare praising the dramatic qualities of her narrative in comparison with Shakespeare.[6]

Nevertheless, for the nineteenth century critics, Austen remained "a critic's novelist."[7] Her fiction failed to conform to the early Victorian English preferences which required a display of powerful emotion in writing. Charlotte Bronte criticised Austen for the absence of visible passion in her work: "the passions are perfectly unknown to her..."[8] and Elizabeth Barrett Browning complained that Austen's characters "lacked souls."[9] It was only James Edward Austen Leigh's *A Memoir of Jane Austen* that Austen was suddenly "invested with an attractive personality identity and a formidable literary reputation,"[10] and thus a daunting mass of commentary accumulated on Jane Austen. After the Second World War, Austen and her works were interpreted in the light of new social issues like feminism, class conflict and anti imperialism.

The advent of feminist criticism led to a re-examination of her novels. Beginning with Julia Prewitt Brown's, *Jane Austen's Novels: Social change and literary form* (1979) and Margaret Kirkham's *Jane Austen: Feminism and Fiction* (1983) to Claudia Johnson's Jane *Austen: Women Politics and Novel* (1988) and Deborah Koplan's *Jane Austen among women*, it became customary to approach Jane Austen not only as a great novelist but also as a representative of what critics, have called the 'feminist tradition' in the English novel. Though Austen may not be called a feminist in today's sense of the word, it can be argued that she was a protofeminist, a forerunner of feminism.

In the recent years, Austen has also been valued particularly by the feminist critics who have appreciated the high intelligence of her heroines and her discriminating writing. Thus, interest in Jane Austen was revitalized by the advent of feminist literary history. The question whether her novels advocate conservative Toryism or a more subversive position is one of the main planes along which one can divide Austen's scholarship.

In a bold and long overdue rescue of Jane Austen from the a historical school of moral criticism Margaret Kirkham properly places her in cultural and political history quite specifically in the climate of Post Enlightenment Feminism. Kirkham refreshingly demands that we rid ourselves of the assumption that Austen's moral interest is of purely personal nature, uncorrected with any general changes in the awareness of her time; we will then see the strong resemblance between Austen and Mary Wollstonecraft as feminist moralists—the exemplification of Austen heroines of "the first claim of Enlightenment Feminism that women share the same moral nature as men, ought to share the same moral status and exercise the same responsibility for their non-conduct and the fact that Austen everywhere is first a foremost a feminist."[11] Elegantly presented in an economical lucid prose, devoid of any jargon, Kirkham's argument focuses on the eighteenth century prelude and background to Austen's feminism and her irony as a feminist attack on the patriarchal refusal to understand woman as rational creatures. Margaret Kirkham concentrates on identifying affinities between Austen's thought as expressed in her novels with that of English Enlightenment feminists. She portrays Austen as a protofeminist who purposefully argued in her novels against the social, political and economic limitations placed on women by patriarchal society. Kirkham's book on Austen offers a new and different way of looking at Austen "lifting her from a rare female presence in a male dominated literary canon to one of a line of feminine moralists...called feminist since (she) was concerned with establishing the moral equality of men and women and the proper status of individual woman as accountable beings."[12] Kirkham's book is divided into four parts and the first part lays the foundation for the argument for Jane Austen as a feminist. The section explores the history and understanding of Enlightenment Feminism and in this light explores Austen as a feminist.

"In her own novels, Austen criticises the belief that women's problems are to be solved by benevolent patriarchs...her heroines, especially the later ones, solve their own problems before making marriages with men who see themselves in a fraternal, rather than a patriarchal relationship as husbands."[13] Mary Waldron in *Jane Austen and The Fiction of Her Time* (1999) presents Austen as a radical innovator who rejected the popular novelists of the time and developed new approaches to fiction as part of her reaction against them. However, Susan Friman differs and states that Austen's heroines towards the end are re-incorporated back into the patriarchal society though they are witty and intelligent.

Critics see Austen as the inheritor of Mary Wollstonecraft's Enlightenment Feminism: critiquing the limited education given to, and expectations of young women from the propertied classes. Austen's heroines always capable of thinking for themselves, criticizing themselves, referring themselves in tension with traditional patriarchal treatment of women as property or sentimental eighteenth century accounts of women's refined sensibility and essentially emotional, rather than rational culture; even if the outcome of their thought self criticism and reformation is an ultimate affirmation of the social status quo in which they live. In a scholarly article "A Feminist Connection: Jane Austen and Mary Wollstonecraft," Miriam Ascarelli situates Austen in the context of protofeminism and suggests that Jane Austen's novels echo ideas put forward by Mary Wollstonecraft. Although contemporaries, the two writers have contrasting lifestyles, attitudes and genres in which they write. However, a close reading of their books reveal that a lot of common material and the conviction of both writers that women are rational creatures and just as accountable for their actions as men. Both writers affect the development of women; Wollstonecraft wants to change society radically and win political rights for women; Austen is content to seek change from within. Whereas Wollstonecraft is strident and indignant in his her analysis of how important the education system was for women, Jane Austen too, advocates the importance of education lent in a comic vein and where Wollstonecraft's work engendered a history of feminist reasoning to answer its painful questions, Austen's work by contrast floated effortlessly to the height of narrative literary achievement while remaining uncompromisingly feminocentric. Thus, Austen's novels fit the paradigms of feminist argument only indirectly.

In all her novels she tells about the reality of women's lives, which meant that women in the eighteenth century were supposed to live in a straight jacket of propriety. Austen comes across as a realist, who presents women's lives as being tough and focusses on the reasoning skills women need to survive. Throughout her novels she portrays the disadvantageous position of women, presenting the issues of gender stereotyping and marriage in great detail thus fully exploring male power and female power in her novels. Though she harshly criticises the social structures of her era, she was not a revolutionary. It may be argued that she never proposed any alternatives to the strictures placed on women and lacked any open rebellion against patriarchal norms, there are areas in which she reveals the heart of a feminist forerunner. The agency with which Austen invests her female protagonists even under great social and material pressures is itself a feminist stance.

In all her novels, Austen portrays the lives of women wanting to be married. Austen's rejection of marriage, her personal independence and the portrayal of women in dominant roles in her novels present her as an early feminist who tried to hide it by the use of irony and satire. At the time when Austen was writing, it was considered to be a man's trade and an unfeminine thing for a woman to do. By writing Austen stated her independence to herself and to others but being a parish's daughter, she decided to publish anonymously in order to maintain an amicable reputation. However, Austen portrayed women as the aggressors—a subject quite questionable in her days. Her female characters hold dominant positions without offending the readers, and are thus strong, independent and aggressive. As Anthony Trollope rightly remarks—"Throughout all her works, a sweet lesson of homely household virtue is ever being taught,"[14] but once the question has been asked, it is not hard to see some feminist tendencies.

Though all of her heroines marry, not all marriages are good ones. Elizabeth Bennett's friend Charlotte Lucas for instance, knew an economic life raft when she saw one. Her marriage to Mr. Collins reveals Austen's clear eyed assessment of the economic underpinnings of marriage. Since marriage is the main theme in all Austen's novels her being called a feminist seems unpalatable to a few critics. Marilyn Butler in *Jane Austen and the War of Ideas*, said that Austen was a conservative propagandist because all her heroines got married and that she was endorsing the established social order. Mary Poovey in *The Proper Lady and Woman Writer* casts Austen as a defender of the status—a novelist who sees marriage "as the ideal paradigm for the most perfect fusion between the individual and the society."[15] But Austen always presents the view of marriage from the point of view of a woman, whether it is Elizabeth Bennett's point of view in *Pride and Prejudice*, Emma Woodhouse's in *Emma* or Marianne Dashwood's in *Sense and Sensibility*. Besides, her heroines are not only interested in marriage and children, even though this was the only acceptable career for women. Emma tells Harriet that she doesn't want to get married at all and that women with their own money are always respectable. Elizabeth who will be dependent on her family and at the mercy of Mr. Collins, who holds the entail to the family house, if she never marries, only wants to marry if she can find 'the very deepest love.' Fanny refuses Henry Crawford, a wealthy senior, inspite of family outrage. Elizabeth actually refuses the proposals—one from the pompous Mr. Collins and one from the very handsome, wealthy, Mr. Darcy. For example most of Jane Austen's heroines don't have anyone whom they can confide in, or whose advice they can rely on, about certain delicate matters. Thus, they must make their own decisions more or less independently. Similarly, in a letter of November 30th, 1814 to her niece Fanny Knight, discussing whether Fanny should engage herself to one Mr. Plumtre, Jane Austen wrote: "...you must not let anything depend on my own opinion. Your own feelings and none but your own, should determine such an important point."[16]

Such moral autonomy on the part of young women would by no means have been universally approved of in Jane Austen's day, as can be seen from Sir Thomas's diatribes in *Mansfield Park*, when Fanny Price is resisting his advice to marry Henry Crawford.

Sense and Sensibility (1811) registers the desperate situation of genteel women deprived of the where withal to sustain social dignity or nobility of mind and feeling. Mary Wollstonecraft argued in *A Vindication of Rights of Women* (1792) that this plight drove many women of the middle and upper class to courtly intrigue and ruin of domestic bliss. Austen doesn't protest anywhere in *Sense and Sensibility*, but her reticence accords with a post revolutionary programme—of "wild passiveness" which was better in the long run than rebellion. If Austen was a feminist, she was a post revolutionary one.

Pride and Prejudice (1813) one of the world's most popular novels is a humorous portrayal of the late eighteenth century and early nineteenth century England, concentrating chiefly on the courtship rituals of the English gentry. However, it is much more than a comedic love story, it also addresses economic, political and feminist themes. In the later decades of the twentieth century and into the early years of twenty-first century the most prominent trend in criticism of *Pride and Prejudice* have derived from the perspectives of literary feminism, including analysis of the novels view of female oppression, its portrayal of the patriarchal society of the time and its treatment of the possibility, fantasy and reality of female power. Feminist critics like Judith Lowder Newton have envisioned the novel as a triumphant fantasy of female autonomy. The opening lines of *Pride and Prejudice*—"It's a truth universally acknowledged that a single man in possession of a good fortune must be in want of a wife,"[17] clearly states that men "must be in want of woman" and not the other way around, thus supporting the feminist's view. Elizabeth Bennet is the moral centre of her family, at home with opinions and comfortable making judgments about character. Her disregard for male opinion is evident in the line—"What are men to rocks and mountains."[18] Here it is the heroine Elizabeth who is to educate Darcy and unlike Elizabeth it is Darcy who needs a radical readjustment to become a suitable companion for her. Elizabeth uses irony to disguise the fact that she being a woman is instructing a man who according to social norms should be superior to her in health and privilege.

As mentioned earlier, the question of Jane Austen's feminist credentials has long been a puzzling one for critics. Kirkham had identified Austen with the English Enlightenment feminists and Claudia Johnson has managed to read a feminist agenda into all Austen's work. Somehow, Kirkham and Johnson make only passing reference to the influence of Rousseau, seeing Austen following Wollstonecraft in rejecting Rousseau's idealization of female sensibility. It was due to popularity of Rousseau's work among women in England in late eighteenth century and also the affinities of his work *The New Eloise* and *Emile* to Richardson's novels—whom Austen is known to have admired, that critics read some influence of Rousseau in her works. In keeping with his view of the roles which nature has assigned to men and women, Rousseau denies the possibility of relationship between men and women—"Thus the whole education of women ought to relate to men. To please men to be useful to them, to make herself loved and honoured by them, to raise them when they are young to care for them when grown...these are the duties of women at all times and they ought to be taught from childhood."[19] Though *Northanger Abbey* adopted Rousseau's model for male female role-playing, *Pride and Prejudice* onwards Austen moves from novice to a mature author and from social apologist to independent and indeed feminist thinker. Austen directly contradicts Rousseau's dictum as presented in Emile that "Woman is made to please and be subjugated...and put up with little resistance."[20]

When Elizabeth is accosted to the dance floor she "looked archly and turned away." However, her refusal to conform to conventional female behaviour has a seductive power which wins her Darcy's love and inspires him to behave differently. Elizabeth's spontaneity and originality express her self confidence and self knowledge clearly. Elizabeth's resistance to Darcy, her determination to make judgments concerning character and events and her assumption of the role of female teacher to a male student, all estrange her from the stereotypical female. She insists that Darcy should assume many of its responsibilities, if he is to become her partner, thus leading to a democratic sharing of characteristics.

Mansfield Park (1814) too interrogates the relationship of power and gender—"Gender came to be seen as a construct of society, designed to facilitate the smooth running of society to the advantage of men,"[21] proving that men gained power throughout the socially constructed subordination of woman. Austen's writings are a form of oppressive ideology, in which women are kept in their socially and sexually subordinate place. In the society and culture that Austen depicts, man is regarded as norm, as the central position from which the female is defined. Women are defined by men, just as in *Mansfield Park* there is pressure on Fanny to meet—Sir Thomas' expectations of what a woman is and Fanny's personal identity is misrepresented by men, making her a female victim of male power and gender stereotypes. Thus through her, many gender issues are conveyed and men are able to demonstrate their authoritative power. Although Fanny is in love with Edmund, he talks about female identity and her looks in a condescending manner. He said that, "she is worth looking at" thus implying that she is an object of his sexual desire. Thus, Austen defines the role of the two sexes in which men give information and advice to women and also analyses sexual stereotypes in great detail and with deep observation. *Mansfield Park* shows the importance of being true to oneself. The main character, Fanny Price is being pressurized to marry for money alone but she rejects the proposal and even though it meant to upset her family she doesn't compromise herself for any camp. Austen was able to consistently portray her female characters in the dominant positions without the public objecting or taking offence. Women as the aggressors was a fairly untouched subject at the time, and also very questionable. Austen somehow manages in her novels to have her women strong, independent and aggressive. The female characters do all this, while keeping a spotless reputation just as Jane succeeded in doing during her life. It is clearly evident throughout each of her novels that Austen held women on a higher pedestal in her mind when compared to men.

Emma (1816) presents a handsome clever, rich protagonist Emma Woodhouse who is a slightly spoilt woman. Though vowing, she will never marry, she delights in making matches for others. In Emma Woodhouse Austen portrays, a very vain but also liberal and independent woman whose self realization helped her correct the flaws of her character, but that did not mean compromising who she was and what she stood for. Besides Emma, is as much a celebration of the power of love and conquest of the human heart as it is an assertion of the power of property in an age of Empire and Enlightenment feminism? In her novel, *Persuasion*, Austen returns to the silently suffering, stoical heroine disregarded by everyone who applies merely social criteria in judging others. It is interesting that the most explicit feminist protests by Jane Austen in her six novels all have to do with literature. In *Persuasion*, Anne Elliot debates Captain Harville on who loves longest, women or men: Captain Harville: "I do not think I ever opened a book in my life which had not something to say upon woman's inconstancy.... But perhaps you will say, these were all written by men." Anne Elliot: "Perhaps I shall.—Yes, yes, if you please, no reference to examples in books. Men have had every advantage of us in telling their own story. Education has been theirs in so much higher a degree; the pen has been in their hands. I will not allow books to prove anything."[22] There is a romantic shift in the feminist and individualistic ideology of Jane Austen's work as her career progresses. In *Pride and Prejudice* throughout the novel, Anne develops as this individual on her own, and by the time she finally marries Went Worth the marriage is not needed to complete her because she has already made her emotional transformation independent of marriage proposal. Whereas Elizabeth is representative of women being capable and worthy to reason in the world of men, Anne's individualism gives women something even more important in Austen's assertion of the validity and worth of female emotions.

Austen's *Northanger Abbey* though written in 1797-1798, was published posthumously. *Northanger Abbey* not only contains the "Defence of the Novel," but what has seemed to be a strong statement—Catherine Morland's faux-naïf declaration —"But history, real solemn history, I cannot be interested in... I read it a little as a duty, but it tells me nothing that does not either vex or weary me. The quarrels of popes and kings, with wars or pestilences, in every page; the men so good-for-nothing, and hardly any women at all—it is very tiresome."[23] The novel is said to consider "the authority of men and books, women's books in particular and suggest how the latter can illuminate and even resist the former."[24]

Thus, Austen may be said to respond to the sexual stereotypes in a highly controlled manner and this led to the emergence of a feminist perspective in her novels. Austen has remained a part of the twentieth century canon because "she is not merely a writer but also a critic."[25] In a chapter on Austen's feminism, Christopher Brooke remarks—"there is no overt feminist doctrine in Jane's novels," he asserts "but she knew a woman's worth."[26] Evidently meant to entertain and not offend, her novels concentrate on "the treatment of less privileged women—the treatment of women altogether."[27] Austen's fiction explores the relationship between men and women, the problems of women in her day one had some scathing criticisms of society—especially as it affected women. Examining the works of Jane Austen, the popularity of her novels can be based mainly on the universal themes she chose, her familiarity with the subject and her optimism. She has focused on themes that never die—As Gill Hornby comments—"Her novels are only about romantic love and family life and they are two of the few things that haven't changed in the world since she was alive. Both things still absorb us and annoy us in equal measure. If she'd written about Napoleonic Wars no one would have read her books."[28]

A living 'classic' Austen truly deserves the praise lavished on her by George Henry Lewes—"Her fame as we think, will endure. Such art as hers can never grow old, never be superseded.... Her place is among the immortals...in a quiet niche of a great temple."[29] Such a pronouncement is an arresting testimony to Austen's stature and her enduring significance as a novelist.

NOTES AND REFERENCES

1. Austen, Jane: *Northanger Abbey*, New York: Penguin, 1972.
2. Deirdre, Le Faye: Jane Austen: A Family Record.
3. Austen, Jane: Persuasion, New York, 1995.
4. Scott, Walter in his journal, 14th March, 1826, Quoted in Claire Tomalin's: Jane Austen—A Life, Alfred A. Knopf (New York 1997), p. 251.
5. The Edinburgh Review, Quoted in Waldron, "Critical Responses, Early," p. 89.
6. The Quarterly Review, January 1821, Quoted in Waldron "Critical Responses, Early," pp. 89-90.
7. Southam, Brian C: Jane Austen's Literary Manuscripts: A Study of the Novelists Development (London: Oxford University Press, 1964).
8. Bronte, Charlotte in a review article.
9. Browning, Elizabeth Barett in a review article, 1855.
10. Leigh, James Edward Austen: *A Memoir of Jane Austen*, London Richard Bentley, 1870.
11. Deirdre, David: University of Maryland in a review on Kirkham's Jane Austen Feminism and Fiction.
12. Jones, Amanda, on Margaret Kirkham's Jane Austen, Feminism and Fiction, p. 3.
13. *Ibid.*, p. 32.
14. Trollope, Anthony declared in 1870.
15. Poovey, Mary: *The Proper Lady and Woman Writer* (Chicago: The University of Chicago Press, 1984), p. 203.
16. Austen, Jane in a letter to her niece Fanny Knight, dated 30th Nov. 1814.
17. Austen, Jane: *Pride and Prejudice*, New York: Penguin, 1972, p. 1.
18. *Ibid.*, p. 190.
19. Rousseau, Jean Jacques: Emile, Trans. and Intro. Allan Brown, New York: Basic, 1979, p. 358.
20. *Ibid.*
21. Literary Theory: An Introduction, Terry Engleton (Blackwell Publishers Ltd., 1996), p. 114.
22. Austen, Jane: *Persuasion*, New York, 1995.
23. Morland, Cathrine's declaration.
24. Looser, Devoney in a review of Claudia Johnson's Jane Austen: Women, Politics and the Novel.
25. Gardiner, Ellen's essay, "Privacy, Privilege and Poaching in Mansfield Park," quoted in Dabundo Laura's review of Jane Austen and Discourses of Feminism.

26. Brooke, Christopher: Jane Austen: Illusion and Reality, 1999.
27. *Ibid.*
28. Hornby, Gill: Jane Austen: The Girl with the Magic Pen.
29. Lewes, George Henry remarked in an article published in Blackwood's magazine in 1850.

'The Real and Imagined Worlds' in Doris Lessing's Fiction

> "I myself have never been able to find out precisely what feminism is: I only know that people call me a feminist whenever I express sentiments that differentiate me from a doormat, or a prostitute."
>
> —*Rebecca West*

As an 'epicist of the female experience who, with skepticism, fire and visionary power has subjected a divided civilization to scrutiny,' Doris Lessing at eighty-seven, has been awarded with the Nobel Prize for Literature 2007, by the Swedish Academy. A deeply autobiographical author with deeper feminist engagement, Lessing emerges as the eleventh woman and the oldest one to be awarded with the prestigious Prize.

Crusading dexterously between the realms of fantasy and realism, Doris Lessing emerged as one of the most radical, controversial, and diverse writers of the twentieth century. Aptly described as, "one of the half dozen most interesting minds to have chosen to write fiction in English in this century,"[1] Lessing has been dubbed as an African writer, a mystic writer, a feminist writer, a psychological writer and also a science fiction writer. Her writings extend the boundaries of fiction, experiment with different genres, explore the worlds of Africa, Britain and of Space, as well as offer a socio-political and cultural commentary upon the post modern world. A chronicler of our age for nearly half a century, her novels range from social realism to science fiction, with brief excursions into speculative mysticism and fables of horror. Her works focus on a wide range of twentieth century issues, from the politics of gender which lead to her adoption of the feminist movement, to the role of the family and the individual in society, explored in her space fiction of late 1970s and 1980s. Her detailed descriptions, symbolism and imagery evoke a wide range of environment and moods and achieve what Edward J. Fitzgerald termed "tension and immediacy" in her work.

Lessing's fiction was realistic, in the tradition of the great contemporary novelists of the nineteenth century, particularly Stendhal and Balzac and also Turgenev and Chekhov. For Lessing, realist writing was the highest form, "higher than and out of reach of any comparison with expressionism, impressionism, symbolism, naturalism or any other 'ism.'"[2] As Mary Ann Singleton aptly remarks—"Not simply an artist, she is also a critic and a prophet, dissecting in minute detail the faults of society, ...and prophesying the calamitous results of those faults. At the same time she attempts to delineate possible solutions to the world's problems."[3] Having actively opposed colonialism, imperialism and institutionalized racism throughout her career, nearly all of her work is explicitly or implicitly critical of both literal and secondary or metaphorical colonialism. Her characteristic mode of fiction being a traditional one in which individual fates, caught in a tangle of social and political circumstances, were rendered with moral and psychological nuance.

However, Lessing's appeal in her fiction "rests largely on her treatment of women in modern life, the most thorough and accurate of any in literature. Her achievement is all the more significant in that so few writers have presented women with whom one can identify-complex, intelligent, questioning women who are not content with the status quo, who rebel against the established order."[4] Though Lessing began her career in the 1950s, writing realistic fiction focusing on themes of racial injustice and colonialism, she went on to compose fiction that anticipated many major feminist concerns of the late 1960s and 1970s. Her strong willed independent heroines often suffer emotional crises in male-dominated societies and must struggle with dominant socio-political constructs to reach higher levels of identity and liberation. The consistent themes of her fiction are feminism, the battle of the sexes, individuals in the search of violence and also the need for individuals to confront their assumptions about life in order to challenge preconceived belief system acquire self-awareness.

Lessing's feminine manifesto, *The Golden Notebook* (1962) was hailed as a landmark by the Women's Movement. Written in form of diaries, *The Golden Notebook* is "best known as 'the Bible of the Women's Movement,' a proto feminist novel."[5] *The Golden Notebook* raised the consciousness of a generation of women readers and played a major part in the second wave of feminism. As Joyce Carol Oates states confidently that the novel "has radically changed the consciousness of many young women."[6]

However, the most fascinating factor of Lessing is her refusal to be categorized. For instance, though *The Golden Notebook* is rightly celebrated for its engagement with feminism, Lessing doesn't see it as a "treatise on feminine stereotypes of the 60s."[7] As she says, that she wrote *The Golden Notebook,* "from the view point of a woman because I am one. I tried to write a book that was a kind of a map of the human mind. We tend to label and pigeon hole things.... If men write books...nobody dreams of saying that they are...antiwoman. But if woman writes about the despair of human relationships, she is regarded as a kind of Mrs. Pankhurst, the Fourth."[8] Wanting to "tell a story which neither political positions nor sociological analyses were capable of exhausting,"[9] Lessing wrote a new preface for *The Golden Notebook* in 1971, explaining that it was not intended as a 'trumpet for Women's Liberation.' Instead, she identified the central theme as 'breakdown,' which is a way of 'self healing.' Scott is quick to perceive that "Lessing does deliberately invoke Woolf in *The Golden Notebook* by naming her woman artist, Anna Wulf.... By absorbing Woolf into her own work, for example through her fictive self Anna in *The Golden Notebook*, Lessing is confirming to some extent Woolf's belief that," "we think back through our mothers if we are women."[10]

Many critics have drawn on the similarity between Virginia Woolf and Doris Lessing. Lynda Scott too focusses on their common distrust and unreliability of memory and "use of 'self representational' or 'autobiographical' text as the therapeutic means of self-discovery...both write multipersonal and dialogical self...so that they may avoid the presentation of single or unified truth which they believe would be subjective, nostalgic and distorted due to memory."[11]

The Golden Notebook deals with a novelist Anna Freedom Wulf, who keeps four notebooks while working on her fictional novel, entitled, 'Free Woman' narrated from different perspectives, each notebook incorporates aspects of Wulf's latest novel in narratives that assume multiple levels of significance. The title refers to Anna's attempt to integrate her fragmented experiences in order to achieve wholeness through art. Struggling with crisis in her personal and political life, Anna in the end gives the 'golden notebook' to her American lover, the conventional narrative ends prosaically with Anna's declaration that she is about to join the Labour Party. Thus, a befitting example of a metafiction, where Lessing has ironically titled her novel within *The Golden Notebook,* "Free Woman," and demonstrated how Anna and Molly, although in one sense free of traditional conventions are actually bound with their lovers and children. *The Golden Notebook* can be compared to Gide's, *The Counterfeiters*—the quest to capture the self, the journey through madness, and the visions of violence are common in both the books.

In her article, 'Flipping through her golden notebook,' Lessing confesses, "I had no idea I was writing a feminist book.... But something said doesn't have the effect of something written. People behaved as if I had done something amazing, yet I just wrote down what women were saying."[12] Whether it should be read a treatise on feminism or not is debatable, but what is not debatable is the praise accorded to the novel, as Irving Howe remarked, "It is the most absorbing and exciting piece of new fiction I have read in a decade."[13]

Her first novel, *The Grass is Singing* (1950) was one of the first books to confront the use of apartheid. Deriving its title from T.S. Eliot's *The Waste Land,* it introduces two of recurrent themes of Lessing's fiction—the causes and effects of racism and the myriad ways that history and politics can determine the course of a person's life. The novel is a painful picture of a woman's failure, in which the drama and conflict are mostly internal. The story set in South Africa, is about sexual and racial tension between a disillusioned South African farmer's wife, Mary Turner, and a black servant named Moses. The novel describes the white couple's isolated life on a Rhodesian farm and the wife's reaction to the social and political condition. The novel is a notable analysis of the colonial experience and tells the story of a lonely and desiccated Rhodesian white woman, Mary Turner, who marries a white farmer working on a small farm in Rhodesia, Dick Turner. Brutalised and emotionally vacant, Mary is a misfit for the hardship ridden life at the farm. She gets involved in an ultimately destructive sexual relationship with one of the Black Rhodesian farm workers, Moses; who eventually kills her. The story opens with the announcement of a white woman's murder and closes with the act of murder itself. In between we see Mary's growing relationship with Moses, a relationship which had to discontinue due to the burning issue of apartheid. Thus, *The Grass is Singing* is a bleak and terrifying analysis of a failed marriage, the fear of black power as well as of the question of a woman's loneliness, abnormal consciousness and fragmentation. Lessing's concern with women's liberation is evident here as it is in her subsequent novels too. Her heroines emerge not merely as vehicles for social criticism or as trumpets for some causes. They are ultimately not Lessing's contribution to any cause but they remain the fully realized works of fiction —Lessing's contribution not to any cause but to literature.

Her next important literary effort is the five volume series, *Children of Violence*, a major achievement by a writer, whom London Times called, "not only the best woman novelist we have, but one of the most serious and intelligent honest writers of the whole post-war generation."[14] When *Martha Quest*, the first of the series was published, C.P. Snow remarked—"She is one of the most powerfully equipped young novelists now writing."[15] Lessing's growing reputation was secured with the acclaimed *Children of Violence* series, a 'bildungsroman' where she traces the intellectual development of Martha Quest, a fictional heroine who resembles Lessing in a number of ways. Like Lessing, Martha "is a child of violence," born at the end of the First World War, brought up in the bleak post war era of struggle and who has to face the tragedies of the Second World War. In the course of the series, Martha progresses from personal, self-centered concerns to a larger awareness of others and the world around her, she pursues various beliefs to gain psychic wholeness. Thus, the new volumes follow *Martha Quest* through the 1940s—through the war, a grotesque second marriage, the embracing of Communism, the decision to leave Africa for a new life in England. The novels in this series are rather semi-autobiographical telling the story of Martha Quest, a girl growing up in Africa who marries young despite her desire to avoid the life her mother had led. Due to estranged relationship with her mother, Martha turns rebellious, enters matrimony twice against the wishes of her parents, indulges in a divorce and (like Lessing herself) gets involved in the cause for the Blacks.

The second book in the series, *A Proper Marriage* (1954) describes the unhappiness of marriage and Martha's eventual rejection of it. *A Proper Marriage* and *A Ripple From the Storm* recount Martha's two unsuccessful marriages to politically oriented men and her involvement in left-wing, anti-apartheid and communist activities. It carries on the story Lessing began so promisingly in *Martha Quest*. *Martha Quest* showed Martha then in her mid-teens, leave the South African farm on which she was brought up to seek the excitement she craved in 'the big city.' Although disillusioned she feels drawn towards the hectic life of the big city and ends up marrying. *A Proper Marriage* shows how Martha's rebellious temperament reacted to her new life and her growing discontentment with marriage, the arrival of her baby which poses a threat to her freedom, the outbreak of the war and her husband's departure with the army.

The sequel, *A Ripple from the Storm* (1958) explores Marxism and Martha's growing political awareness and displays

Martha's involvement in left-wing, anti-apartheid Communist activities, and her failure to satisfy social and political needs.

Landlocked (1965), the fourth novel in Lessing's *Children of Violence*, series reflects Lessing's emerging interest in telepathy, extrasensory perception and Sufism—the mystical branch of Islam. It is the product of Lessing's growing interest in Sufi mysticism which was responsible for her undeterred quest for cosmic harmony, which stood endangered in the growing global violence. Through *Landlocked*, Lessing warns us against the imminent Third World War and its disastrous aftermath and sermonizes in favour of harmony, universal fraternity and peace. It brings the series into the 1940s and completes Martha's estrangement from collective politics and from Africa. The novel follows Martha as she travels to England where she experiences an apocalyptic vision.

The most important work of Lessing after *The Golden Notebook*, *The Four Gated City* (1969) provides a befitting climax to *The Children of Violence* series. Post-war London is the setting for this novel, in which the mature Martha has abandoned her political activism for introspection. The series ends with an apocalyptic vision of the future. The previous four novels were set in Africa and looked back to the past, to our heritage which shaped our present, in this novel she takes Martha Quest to London and the world—into the present and the future. The novel covers the social history of the 20th century—the Cold War, the Aldermaston marches against nuclear proliferation which is Lessing's prophecy about destruction of Mankind, the deepening of poverty, social anarchy and Swinging London. Through a fantasy, Lessing visualizes a new generation of children born on an uncontaminated island that are not only physically healthy but mentally superior too—the island being a replica of the mythical four-gated city, the 'New Jerusalem.' This final volume follows Martha's involvement with the major social forces of post-war Britain and then chillingly takes the story into the future and Third World War. Lessing portrays a modern society that cannot see what is under its nose but she never forgets the characters and their story. Thus, this five volume epic traces the development of Lessing from social realism to science fiction and presents Martha Quest as the "prototypical questing protagonist of contemporary women's fiction."[16] As Gayle Greene remarks, "Both Lessing and Martha seek 'something new' against the 'nightmare repetition' which is the burden of history; something oppositional to the culture that has formed them."[17]

Briefing for a Descent into Hell (1971) is what Lessing called "inner space fiction," which records the breakdown of Charles Watkins, the first male protagonist who is found wandering on the streets of London with no memory of 'normal' life. The novel is a major step forward in the study of abnormal psychology, which records the pressures of social conformity on the individual, leading to what Joyce Carol Oates calls, the "broken-down psyche."[18] The central character, Charles Watkins lives in a perpetual chaotic state of self division in himself undertaking a series of symbolic journeys in a state of amnesia. The novel charts the mysterious journey of Professor Charles Watkins as he is shipwrecked on an unknown shore, witnesses war and ritual, taken away on the back of a great White Bird and is swept away on a cosmic journey. Found wandering at night on London's embankment, Charles is admitted as John Doe by the police into the Central Intake Hospital of London. Taken to the hospital and heavily sedated, he tells the doctors of his incredible fantastical voyage, adrift on the ocean, landing on unknown shores, flying on the back of a huge white bird. When identified as Charles Watkins, a Cambridge Classic Professor, he is visited by family, friends, each revealing clues to the nature of his breakdown. As the doctors try to cure him, Watkins begins a fierce battle to hold on to his magnificent inner world, as it gradually acquires a greater reality than the everyday outer world. Following R.D. Laing, Lessing explores the possibility that only mad are sane and also fashions the language of madness from the idioms of science fiction experienced through ESP. The novel links her early works exploring the nature of subjectivity to her later experiments with science fiction.

Named as one of 1973s outstanding books, her next novel, *The Summer before Dark* (1973) confirmed that "Doris Lessing is a plain speaking, somewhat awkward but immensely attractive master of modern fiction."[19] One of Lessing's most perfectly crafted novels, it tells the moving story of a woman's coming to terms with aging. The novel focusses on Kate, a middle aged London woman who feels unwanted by her grown up children and her husband who is preoccupied with his business concerns. In order to rediscover a sense of identity, she goes in for a small job, gets involved with a younger man and when disillusioned by the affair shares quarters with a young woman. Each experience helps her understand herself better and enables her to face the dreadful consequences of independence. The two women work upon each other; Kate's dream is completed, she returns to her husband as a woman who acts for her own reason not merely to please others. The novel hints at semi-autobiographical touches which are evident in Kate's assertion of the domineering mother who played a destructive role—Lessing too had a very dominating mother.

Kate, the central character achieves a kind of enlightenment through what doctors would describe as a breakdown. Psychoanalysis and psychotherapy emerge as dialogical processes probing an individual's past; his memories, and so do Lessing's sub representational texts which present the author in various guises, and provide opportunities "to reach the past, analyse past experiences and reinvent them again, while living in the present."[20]

The Memoirs of a Survivor (1975) is a sub representational text of Lessing which marks a transition from her earlier preoccupation with psychological inner space to her space fiction series. Set in the nearest future at "a time for savagery and anarchy." It is the memoirs of a nameless woman who has survived a nameless war that has left the cities of England empty shells, with the conclaves of people living barricaded in their apartments, while the gangs of youth roam the streets and the polluted air is purified by hand driven machines. The narrator tells a story blending the dreamy, prophetic timeless moments with a chilling realistic account of 'ordinary' life in a ravaged London apartment. Her memoirs end with the realization that the darkest times were over and 'something new' would be built.

The novel demonstrates Lessing's persistent interest in familial groups as alternatives to nuclear family. The novel however, doesn't elaborate, which global crisis brought about such anarchic conditions. Here, the degradation of atmosphere, the collapse of law order and material infrastructure led to the breaking of stable, biologically related families.

In the late 1970s and early 1980s, Lessing turned exclusively to writing fantasy and science fiction in the *Canopus in Argos: Archives* series developing ideas which she had touched on towards the end of *Children of Violence* and *Briefing for a Descent into Hell*. The series is composed of five volumes in which Lessing creates a fantasy world that allows her to diagnose the malaise of our society, to observe phenomena which cause disharmony. "It is neither science fiction nor free wheeling fantasy," says Robert Taubman, "but has something in common with the myth making in Rousseau or William Morris that offers visions of hope or disaster for mankind."[21]

After dealing with themes like racialism, generation gap, woman's liberation and sexual maladjustments, Lessing's first experiments with the visionary mode started with *The Four Gated City*, followed by somewhat similar experiments in *Briefing for a Descent into Hell* and *Memoirs of a survivor*. Lessing's themes in her later novels are rather unconventional like nuclear holocaust, societal degeneration, cosmic consciousness and inner stellar harmony, and show Lessing's progress from the realistic to the fantastic. As she says—"what is happening in this world is so fantastic that it needs fantasy—a rebirth of imagination.... It was inevitable that with the development of science would come a new literature." She even traces the element of fantasy in realistic fiction,—"There have been dreams and fantastic ventures even in realistic fiction, as in *Jane Eyre*.... In Thomas Mann's *The Magic Mountain*, the hero has dreams and even tries to pull back his brother from the other side of the grave...."[22] She further says, "I think that one writer can contain two worlds—the realistic and the fantastic."[23] Not simply science fiction, Lessing's novels too, are related to fantasy fiction.

Canopus in Argos: Archives, a series of fantastical novels set in space, continues Lessing's interest in Sufism, stressing the theme of cosmic evolution which aimed at raising mankind to a higher level of existence, and the interconnectedness between ones own fate and well-being to that of others. When in 1979, with the publication of *Shikasta,* Lessing launched her "space fiction" series, her readers were perplexed, disgruntled and unhappy at seeing their advocate of social concern, turn into "a cosmic visionary."[24] Likewise Margaret Atwood's novels too, had explored science fiction themes but her fiction was quickly claimed to be "speculative fiction" by the publishers.

Shikasta recapitulates the Biblical History from Genesis to the "Century of Destruction" and visualizes a golden future where the new world is founded on the principles of harmony with Cosmos. Canopus is a galactic empire whose dispassionate agents oversees a good scheme for cosmic welfare, concentrating on a rather troublesome, Earth like planet named Shikista. It is a compilation of reports, historical documents, letters and psychiatric diagnoses is used to unfold the story of an alien envoy, Johor's three visits to Shikista (Earth), the last taking place in the final phase just following the Third World War. Johor is an emissary from the galactic Empire of Canopus, sent to Shikista to report on the colony. Johor had been used to life where beings lived in harmony and hence is appalled by the destructiveness and dogma of the Earth. He is sent to educate those who have survived the Third World War.

With *The Marriages between Zones Three, Four and Five* (1980) Lessing enters the territory of legend, of myth, dealing with the story of the lovely Queen of Zone Three and her forced marriage to Ben Ata, the soldier King of Zone Four and later the marriage of Ben Ata to Vahshi, the ruler of Zone Five. Here we have Zones instead of cities. Fantasy is given much freer play in this novel—the unexpected, the discoveries of an imagination surrendering itself to visual inventions adds to the charm of the novel. Thus the novel locates its legendary action in the fabulous zones and concentrates on the relation between the sexes.

The Sirian Experiments (1981) recounts the colonial experiments practiced upon *Shikista,* leading its people into their twentieth century of Destruction. It describes the stages of human history, from the view point of a female Sirian colonial administrator who deals mainly with a series of exotic earlier periods, in contrast to Johor, the narrator of *Shikista* who speaks at great length of the twentieth century. Ambien II the narrator of The *Sirian Experiments* offers more novelistic interests than her counterpart in *Shikista* because Johor has the Canopean disadvantage of virtual moral perfection. Ambien II is by turns rash, foolish, headstrong, imperceptive but finally brave enough and persistent enough to learn the truth. The novel deals with the theme of involvement of the super aliens in human affairs. Both *Shikista* and *The Marriages between Zones Three, Four* and *Five* relate the same story, but the narrators change. Human affairs are governed by the super aliens who are termed "Canopean Super Agents" in *The Sirian Experiments* and The Providers in *The Marriages of Zones Three, Four* and *Five.*

The Making of the Representative for Planet 8 (1982) evidences Lessing's interest in dystopian themes in its story of a slowly freezing planet whose inhabitants expire while awaiting a promised transport to a warmer environment. Perhaps the Antarctic expeditions of Robert Falcon Scott profoundly motivated Lessing's *The Sirian Experiments* and *The Making of a Representative* and provided her with an understanding of the landscape of paralysing ice and snow but by offering her insights into the social processes of the Edwardian era to which Scott belonged—an era of national pride and imperial longings. It tells of Johor's journeys to the planet and the ordeal that he and Doeg, the narrator of the novel, along with other representatives, encounter when the planet begins to freeze to death. The earlier novels had depicted how Johor had saved Shikista from extinction arising due to the meanness of the inhabitants. He had taught them the finer values of life but Planet 8 threatened by the coming of an ice age, poses a greater challenge for him. Johor assist them to confront this calamity bravely even though the entire Planet 8 is submerged under ice and only fifty chosen representative survive who are transported to Canopus and await the end of the Cataclysm.

Like the earlier four novels of this series, *The Sentimental Agents* (1983) occurs in a galaxy where the struggle between good and evil takes place written in the tradition of Voltaire and Swift, this novel shows Lessing's use of socio political satire more than her deft employment of science fiction. It is an indictment of the misuse of powers of speech by man and his self flattering sentiments about emotion. The book brings us to the Volyen Empire where Incent, a Canopean agent who was deputed to convert the Volyens a moral way of life but he succumbs to a "stubborn condition of "Undulant Rhetoric" after years of sporadic attacks of simple Rhetoric. Agent Klorathy is sent to Volyen to redeem the Volyen Empire. He is rejected in the start but is called for help in face of sudden invasion from Planet Sirius. Sirius conquers Volyen and turns it into a prosperous state thus symbolizes the victory of good over evil. Though many critics have not thought highly of her decision to leave the traditional concerns for the cold and unemotional regions of outer space abandoning realism which had made her earlier works so valuable, Jeanette King argues that, "even in her most experimental fantasies Lessing has consistently explored the relationship between the individual psyche and the political, sexual and religious ideologies that structure it.... For if Lessing's work has a single message... only by distancing ourselves from our own most deeply held assumptions and beliefs can we ensure individual or social growth."[25]

After completing five books in her science fiction sequence, *Canopus in Argos: Archives* in 1983, Lessing startled the public by turning away from the Antarctic cold of her planetary realms to novels of post-war London. With *The Good Terrorist* (1985) Doris Lessing has returned to Earth, after years of voyaging in space in her *Canopus in Argos: Archives* series. It is the story of Alice Mellings, aged thirty-six, a college graduate with a degree in politics and economics, and is the daughter of upper middle class parents in Hampstead. Her extreme liberal idealism leads her to organize a group of would be revolutionaries who commit an act of terrorism. Though a brilliant organizer otherwise, Alice who knows how to cope with almost anything, except the vacuum in his life. A vivid portrayal of communal life, *The Good Terrorist* focusses on a common character type marks her return to realism. The novel shows how personal loyalties, naivety and a sense of grievance, can be manipulated to a point where violence seems reasonable.

The Fifth Child (1988) marks Lessing's return from her excursions into space to the flawed crumbling social fabric again. A moral fable, it is the story of a British couple, Harriet and David who react to the hedonism and excesses of the 1960s by setting themselves in a large house and embarking on an enthusiastic programme of child bearing and domestic bliss. But the family idyll is disrupted with the birth of fifth child, a monster child who wreaks havoc in his family and society. Its sequel *Ben in the World* (2000) follows Ben as he enters adulthood and is let loose upon the wide world.

Also responsible for her autobiography, *Under My Skin* (1994) Lessing believes however what Suzanne Nalbantion asserts: "The autobiographical act is an enactment of certain drama of an already completed self."[26]

Her recent fiction includes *The Sweetest Dream* (2001) which tells the story of a family beginning in 1960s, and following through in the 20th century. It examines the consequences of the war through the relationship of Frances Lennox the "earth mother" of the 1960s and a group of children of war who she keeps at her home. The novel then explores the major issues of the late 20th century life—anorexia, AIDS and the psychological damage of war. Despite the disillusionment individual acts of goodness create hope in this dark world. The message is of promoting all round welfare by humanist efforts and in *The Grandmothers,* Lessing continues to probe the human condition.

Lessing's twenty-first novel, *General Dann and Mara's Daughter, Griot and the Snow Dog* (2005) is an extension of her earlier considerations of the manipulations of knowledge and power in the context of macro climatic image as in *The Making of a Representative.* It is set during an ice age some 15000 years in the future, and takes place on the continent of

Ifrik, one of the few habitable regions on the earth. The book refers to the past and to how the world got to be the way it had become—chiefly because of an asteroid that hit the Mediterranean.

Her most recent novel, *The Cleft* (2007) is strikingly different from the other novels of Lessing. Instead of the wide landscapes of politics and family in which individual characters and settings are depicted, this novel makes its track through the earliest world of women, the clefts as creatures of the sea and the coming of men, the monsters in their lives. In her latest novel, *The Cleft* (2007), Lessing is retelling the oldest story the beginning of the human race. Inspired by a scientific article which suggested that the original human stock was female and males only a genetic aberration, Lessing has upset the Biblical story about Creation. A mythological fantasy by a feminist author, *The Cleft* provocatively asserts that the primal humans are female psychic beings fused with the natural environment, the sea and the rocky terrain. A tale about an ancient community of women living in Edenic wilderness, Lessing explores a world occupied solely by women who have no knowledge, and ultimately no need for men. Through the cycles of moon they control childbirth. Babies are born but only female. Males do not exist, as their biological functioning is not required for reproduction.

The tale is told by an old Roman senator and historian who reconstructs the story through a pile of ancient documents he is studying. Trying to make sense of times ancient to him and what he finds about the roots of relationship between women and men seem to be eternal truths. Throughout his telling he digresses his anecdotes from his life now and before. The world of the Cleft's, strong and fearless in an untouched wilderness is set in turmoil with the birth of a new child, a boy. Born in this all female enclave, the males are considered to be monsters and are left on the "killing rock" to be eaten by the eagles who without the knowledge of the women; carry the boys to another place and a men's colony is formed. The novel traces the Clefts as creatures of sea, and the coming of men, the monsters and squirts, into their lives and the consequent struggles as the females learn to adjust to a changed world and the men fight to prove their place in it. With the birth of the monsters, the Clefts feel distressed and the monsters begin to flourish and in an attempt to rid themselves of the monsters they resort to cruelty; an established social system thus begins to break down. The story takes us on a journey through time spanning generations, to descending of these mythic women who ultimately form relationships with men—men and women discover each other, the women lose their ability to conceive without men, and the two sexes, struggle to find a way to live harmoniously together.

Thus, Lessing, one of the most significant writers of the post World War II generation, displayed various interests and issues of the twentieth century ranging from racism, communism and feminism to psychology and mysticism and in every possible post-modernist fictional form, be it magic realism, metafiction, surrealism, fantasy, space fiction. A writer of epic scope and startling surprises, Doris Lessing is above all "the archaeologist of human relations,"[27] deeply concerned with the human condition, and hungry to explore new dimensions to redefine relationships. Her novels expose a world out of control and attempt to teach us how to better manage our world and find a way through the ravages of the twentieth century to a condition beyond the one of personal unhappiness that plagues so many human relationships. Though writing out her own intense experience she also writes out of the spirit of the times with great sensitivity. A quote by Lessing herself best sums up the genius of this matriarch of British literature: *Some people obtain fame, others deserve it*[28] said Lessing.

NOTES AND REFERENCES

1. Leonard, John: *The New York Times.*
2. Lessing, Doris in a 1957 essay, "The Small Personal Voice."
3. Singleton, Mary Ann in The City and the Veld, The Fiction of Doris Lessing, 1977.
4. Brooks, Ellen. W: Comments on Doris Lessing.
5. Williams, Linda R: The Twentieth Century (London: Bloomsbury Publication, 1994), p. 11.

6. Oates, Joyce Carol: "One keeps going" (1972) Doris Lessing: Conversation, ed. Earl. G. Ingersoll (Princeton: Ontario Review Press, 1994), p. 37.
7. Montremy, Jean Maurice-de: "A Writer, is not a Professor" (1990) Doris Lessing: Conversation, ed. Earl. G. Ingersoll (Princeton: Ontario Review Press, 1994), p. 193.
8. Mitgang, Herbert: Mrs. Lessing addresses some of life's puzzles, April 22, 1984.
9. Montremy, Jean Maurice-de: "A Writer, is not a Professor" (1990) Doris Lessing: Conversation, ed. Earl. G. Ingersoll (Princeton: Ontario Review Press, 1994), p. 193.
10. Rubenstein, Roberta: "Fixing the Past: Yearning and Nostalgia in Woolf and Lessing," "Woolf and Lessing: Breaking the mould, eds. Ruth Saxton and Jean Tobin (New York: St. Martins Press, 1994), p. 16.
11. Scott, Lynda: in her article 'Similarities between Virginia Woolf and Doris Lessing.
12. Lessing, Doris in an article 'Flipping through her golden notebook'—In an interview with John Freeman—Sunday, Jan 15, 2006.
13. Howe, Irving's comment about *The Golden Notebook*.
14. *London Times*.
15. Snow, C.P. in *The Sunday Times*.
16. Greene, Gayle: Doris Lessing's Landlocked: "A New Kind of Knowledge." Contemporary Literature, Vol. 28, No. 1 (Spring 1987).
17. *Ibid.*
18. Oates, Joyce Carol on Lessing.
19. Sale, Roger in a review dated October 13, 1974.
20. Scott, Lynda: Writing the Self: Selected works of Doris Lessing.
21. Taubman, Robert on Lessing.
22. Mitgang, Herbert: Mrs. Lessing addresses some of life's puzzles, April 22, 1984.
23. *Ibid.*
24. Hazelton, Lesley in an article entitled, "Feminism, Communism and Space Fiction."
25. King, Jeanette on Lessing.
26. Aesthetic Autobiography (London: MacMillan, 1994), p. 38.
27. Howe, Irving on Lessing.
28. Lessing, Doris quote.

Toni Morrison's Love—'An Epic of Enslavement and Liberation'

> "The black woman is one of America's greatest heroes.... Not enough credit has been given to the black woman who has been oppressed beyond recognition."
>
> —*Alice Walker*

"Everything I've ever done in the writing world has been to expand articulation, rather than to close it"[1] says Toni Morrison and, "to put forth an argument for extending the study of American literature...."[2] remains her prime concern. One of the forbears of post-modernism in African American literature, Toni Morrison broke through the barriers for women and blacks, when the Swedish Academy awarded Toni Morrison, the Noble Prize for literature in 1993. The remarkable feat left her "outrageously happy"[3] as she herself remakes—"Winning as an American is very special but winning as a black American is a knockout"[4] Writers like Toni Morrison, Alice Walker, Zora Neale Hurston and Terry McMillan often represent "black literature" to contemporary audiences. Morrison creates a new fiction by her accounts of the black experiences and the celebration of black community in clear and human terms. Her novels have made black history contemporary and brought black literary experience into the American mainstream. The problem of black invisibility and namelessness, the black strivings caused by the terrifying African encounter with the absurd in America are effectively recorded in Morrison's fiction. Her novels reveal the attempts of the black people to sustain their mental sanity and spiritual health, social life and political strife, in the midst of a slave holding and dominating white civilization. With both a Pulitzer and a Nobel Prize to her credit, no American writer is more distinguished than Toni Morrison and no one tells the story the way she does. Her fiction achieves its distinctive style by fusing the universal themes in the particularity of the African American experience, the use of folklore, magical realism and the African American women's narratives with her most lyrical and distinct prose style. Her unique narrative style keeps varying in each novel and even though its roots stem from Faulkner and American writers from farther south, its lasting impression is one of sympathy and humanity. Like Faulkner, her main concern is to define the beauty and brutality of human condition and evoke the pathos and tragedy of human life.

Morrison writes out of a consciousness of living in a "wholly racialized world."[5] Her fiction ponders over the effects that living in a racialized society has had on American writing in nineteenth and twentieth centuries. As she says, "I am always annoyed about why black people have to bear the brunt of everybody else's contempt. If we are not totally understanding and smiling, suddenly we are demons."[6] A determined monoculturist, Toni Morrison is concerned to give written form to the texture of African American life from the last days of slavery to a nation reshaped by the civil rights movement. Morrison's novels depict the trauma of the black community who migrated towards north to escape the problems of southern racism but there too they were subjected to an existence of mistrust and alienation. Hence, her fiction beautifully evokes the legacies of displacement and slavery bequeathed to African American communities. While giving a lecture at Princeton, Morrison was asked by a student, "Who she wrote for?" She swiftly replied, "I want to write for people like me, which is to say black people, curious people demanding people—people who can't be faked, people who don't need to be patronized, people who have very, very high criteria."[7] Through her fiction, Morrison has explored the experiences and roles of black women in a racist and male dominated society—"Tell us what it is to be a woman so that we may know what it is to have no home in this place. To be set adrift from the one you knew. What it is to live at the edge of town that cannot bear your company."[8] All of Morrison's novels, from her first novel, *The Bluest Eye* to *Love,* explore both the need for and the impossibility of real community and the bonds that both unite and divide African American women. In this context, Maya Angelou's remarks are quite revealing—"If growing up is painful for the growing Southern Black girl, being aware of her displacement is the rust on the razor that threatens the throat. It is an unnecessary insult."[9] Linda Brent too feels that, " slavery is terrible for men but is far more terrible for women."[10]

From her first novel, *The Bluest Eye* (1970) through *Beloved* and *Jazz*, Toni Morrison cast an unblinking eye on slavery and its legacies while also offering hope particularly in the strength of bonds among women. Her first novel, *The Bluest Eye* tells of "a little black girl who wanted to rise up out of the pit of her blackness and see the world with blue eyes"[11] (p. 138). It reveals the tragic effect of racial prejudice on the black girl, Pecola Breedlove, yearning to assert her individuality in a community which fails to recognise her identity. The shattering effect of racism on the black girls is pertinent in Morrison's fiction. As Shelby Steel puts it "to be black was to be a victim, therefore not a victim was not to be a black."[12] The novel presents the psychological and social effects of a black girl trying to live according to the white standard. In order to get rid of her unworthiness, she prays each night with a haunting passion for the blue eyed beauty of Shirley Temple—so that she will also be beautiful, so that people will look at her so that her world will be different. Her next novel *Sula* tells of a women who refuses to confirm to community mores. The novel depicted two black women friends—Sula and Nel—both black, both smart, both poor, raised in a small Ohio town. The novel follows the life of Sula, of free spirit, who is considered a threat against the community. She defines herself outside of the sex, class, race definition of the society. Her third novel *Story of Solomon* was hailed by critics as a major literary achievement. It was based on an African American folktale about slaves who can fly back to Africa when they choose. Morrison fictionalises this folktale through the character of Solomon who is the great grandfather of Milkman Dead. It tells a story of a character named Milkman Dead, who in search for his families' lost fortune discovers instead his family history. The novel is at once a romance of self-discovery, a retelling of the black experience in America that uncovers the inalienable poetry of that experience and a family saga a luminous in its depth and universality. In her next novel *Tar Baby,* Morrison attempts to heal the traditional rift in American fiction between representational realism and the symbolic mythological dreamscape. The novel is suffused with her tense and passionate enquiry, revealing a whole spectrum of emotions underlying the relationship between black men and women, white men and women and black and white people. *Tar Baby* takes place at the Caribbean Mansion of a white millionaire Valerian Street and focuses on the themes of racial identity, sexuality, class and family dynamics. Her fifth novel *Beloved* was inspired by the true story of a black American slave woman, Margaret Garner who escaped with her husband Robert from a Kentucky plantation and sought refuge in Ohio. Morrison's most successful novel which received the Pulitzer Prize *Beloved,* is the story of Sethe, a mother who kills her daughter Beloved rather than have her grow up as a slave. The book explores the theme of the black American's return to slavery—the novel's complex interweaving of past and present produce a compelling portrait of a black families struggle with devastating and inescapable effects of slavery. In this context, Calvin Hernton's remark seems quite revealing—"The sexual atrocities that the Negro woman has suffered in U.S., South and North and what these atrocities have done to her personality as a female creature is a tale bloodier and brutal than most of us can imagine."[13] Once again Toni Morrison has given us a novel of daring, fascination and power. *Jazz* is a land mark on the American literary landscape—A profound love story of haunting passion, bittersweet lyricism and refined sensuality of its powerful style. It uses an innovative narrative technique to echo the improvisational character of the eponymous musical form. Focusing on the story of an aging couple and the loss of love they experience, *Jazz* is a rich combination of history, legend, reminiscence and a mysterious voice whose identity is a matter of each reader's imagination a voice which captures the black urban life in the most human terms. *Paradise* her seventh novel, focuses on an all black town called Ruby in Oklahoma and a violent attack that a group of men make on a small all female community at the edge of the town. A tour de force of storytelling power, "the book coalesced around the idea of where Paradise is, who belongs in it."[14] Weaving together folklore and history, memory and myth, Morrison beautifully renders a meditation on race, religion and gender.

Talking of her latest novel *Love*, Bread Hoopen says, "Love is a preformed novel. As a vivid painter of human emotions, Morrison is without peer, her impressions indeed in an exquisitely metaphoric but comfortably open style."[15] Like her other novels —*Paradise, Jazz, Beloved, Sula* her eighth novel *Love*, too bears a one word title. In all her novels, Toni Morrison says that she is "answering a question," here in *Love* too, she is doing the same—"I was interested in the way in which sexual love and other kinds of love lend themselves to betrayal."[16] A multilayered, multithemed, multigenerational novel, *Love* is a complicated story, where the various forms of love are catalogued in a concatenation of elegant structure. The story centres on Morrison's great theme, the intimate relationships that women have and how they can be damaged by the random cruelties of fate and time. Told as a series of flashbacks, Morrison follows the development of her characters and reveals the traits of their personality gradually as the story unfolds. The story spans the twentieth century, from the proud black communities of the segregated South, to the much less glamorous modern black communities and in doing so it examines the effects of integration on ordinary black people.

The narrative terrain covered by Morrison is the African American experience as seen through the microcosm of a family history, and it is a history with many claimants, including shadows and ghosts from the past. However, a new territory is explored here which is concerned with issues of race, but is not predominated by them. More than race, it is a story of class, friendship, envy, obsession and, most important, the machinations of love. It is also, unlike her overly ambitious last novel, *Paradise*, a perfectly compacted and utterly efficient narrative. No less a literary critic than Morrison herself has pronounced her new novel, *Love*, to be "perfect" and continues her project of exploring African-American history and culture.

A tale of childhood confusion and miscommunication *Love* takes place in a place called Silk, in a house at, Monarch Street. A successful black entrepreneur, Bill Cosey, runs a popular beach resort on the East Coast, most likely North or South Carolina. The son of a snitch, Bill Cosey inherits his affluence from his father a courthouse informer and lover of money. Prodigal, sentimental charming and morally unquestionable at the age of fifty two, Cosey was a wealthy and powerful man whose acts of love and violence, generosity and cruelty, structure the novel. A gregarious personality, he had a natural talent for attracting the wealthiest clientele and the jazziest musicians to his hotel—"Mr. Cosey was a smart man. He helped more coloured people here than forty years of government programs"[17] (p. 9) says the narrator in *Love*. The resort serves as an elegant world unknown to many in the pre civil rights era with Bill serving as its personal zeitgeist, attracting famous entertainers, black politicians and lots of women. He has a dangerous and destructive tendency of being surrounded for more than half a century with "needy wild women," who jostle for his affections and whose enmity perseveres through several decades of retributions and counter accusations. Cosey's resort was a place where people planned to act against injustice and racial discrimination and found time to discuss issues like death in cities and murder in the Mississippi.

As the novel opens, all the women, who are obsessed with Cosey, along with two of the men, explore and explain their relationship with him. Cosey is a father, a lover, a husband, a guardian, a friend and above all like all the other characters he is shrouded in mystery from the very beginning. Cosey's son, Billy Boy marries May, "a sweet tempered daughter of a preacher, was bred to hard work and duty, and took the business like bee to pollen" (p. 103). Cosey's second wife, Heed is just eleven years old and is quite close to Christine, Cosey's granddaughter. As inseparable as 'two peas in a pod,' the narrator too tells that Heed "belonged to Christine and Christine belonged to her" (p. 105). However, Heed's marriage to Cosey turns them into declared enemies. Heed sees the image of a 'father figure' and 'sugar daddy' in the person of Cosey who pampers her thoroughly after marriage and the eleven year old Heed "could hardly wait to get back and tell Christine all about it. Hurt by her reception, she kept her stories to herself" (p. 129). Heed even offers to share her wedding ring with Christine but gets reprimanded by May. Christine however detests Heed and full of 'hate and bitterness' she remarks, "One day we built castles on the beach: next day he sat her in his lap. One day we were playing house under a quilt: next day he slept in his bed" (pp. 131-32). Having fought for her and defied her mother to protect her, to give her clothes and having "shared the same stomach ache laughter, a secret language, and knew as they slept together that one's dreaming was the same as the other one's" (p. 132), Christine's sense of betrayal is not without reason. Heed's marriage changed Christine's life and turned her into a lifeless stone" (p. 132). Heed's hatred for Christine makes her 'dangerous' and she becomes responsible for the fire in Christine's room.

The women who inhabit Cosey's world are Heed, his second wife was eleven at the time of her marriage and now is a recluse determined to keep the family's legacy; Christine his granddaughter, who was Heed's best friend until she married Cosey; Cosey's mentally retarded daughter in law, May, who is jealous of Heed and does everything possible to distance her daughter, Christine from her; Celestial, his pleasure woman, the only one who asks to be his equal and who was able to inspire his romantic love; Junior Vivianne, a young women who has applied for a job in the Cosey House in 1, Monarch Street and is hired by Heed, Cosey's widow as a companion and also to assist her in her wicked plan and last but not the least is the voice of the hotel's former cook whose presence may be ghostly but she is the voice of the narrative, who has seen all of these relationships develop, fall apart. She weaves her judgment of Cosey's women and through her series of recollections at the same time disclosing her own infatuation with Bill Cosey. The relationship of this ladies man with women who surround him are the guiding elements of Morrison's novel, while during his life these women vied for his attention, after his death, their rivalries grew stronger. Even Junior, who has never seen him or known him, worships his memory and idealizes him as a 'perfect man.'

When the story opens we find that Bill Cosey has been dead for twenty-five years, but is still a very real presence to the women who shared his life. As in *Beloved*, where a dead baby's ghost at the centre of the novel, here in *Love*, the murdered dead, Bill Cosey is at the centre of the novel. Years after Cosey's death, the women are still obsessed with him, suggesting that death does not stop love: "Those you have loved deeply and who have died live on in you, not just as memories but as real presences."[18] Further, Brenda Marie Osbey contends that "[e]ven when people are dead, we maintain relations with them." She goes on to assert that, at times, we are able to love better, more freely and openly, our dead than our living.[19] Of course, how we mourn, commune with, and love our dead is tricky business in Morrison's work, for the balance between remembering and disremembering the past is a fragile one.

Heed the Night, the child bride of Bill Cosey, and Christine Cosey, his granddaughter, were best friends as children and are now bitter enemies occupying the family home on Monarch Street, a house haunted with the spectral presence of Bill Cosey, who is "everywhere [a]nd nowhere" (p. 189). Likewise, Cosey occupies a similar position in the novel, as it begins twenty-five years after his death, yet each chapter references only him: "Portrait," "Friend," "Stranger," "Benefactor," "Lover," "Husband," "Guardian," "Father," and "Phantom." These descriptions reveals that he is no longer alive, yet the seven names bracketed by these two ossified descriptors suggest Cosey's continuation of the identifying roles of father, husband, and so on. The presence of both being and nonbeing forces the question of whether one ceases being a lover or a friend in death. According to hooks, "[l]ove is the only force that allows us to hold one another close beyond the grave."[20] Indeed, death has done very little to stop the Cosey women from having intimate relations with this powerful patriarch. He overshadows their lives, their home, and their relationship with one another.

Cosey's strong presence is matched only by the compelling figure of L, whose animated and opinionated voice, which punctuates the novel with candour and insight, overshadows the reality that she, like Cosey, is dead, a phantom who haunts "Up Beach" (73). Just as the word "love" is almost never uttered in this novel, L's full name is withheld, as is her voice in the community. From the outset, L claims, "My nature is a quiet one, anyway. As a child I was considered respectful; as a young woman I was called discreet. Later on I was thought to have the wisdom maturity brings. Nowadays silence is looked on as odd and most of my race has forgotten the beauty of meaning much by saying little" (3). While her voice is critical to the narrative, the community knows her primarily through action, not proclamation. L is reminiscent of the narrator of *Jazz,* for both are straightforward, opinionated, and knowledgeable about their communities.

A novel about the past, *Love* begins closer to the present with Junior, long a resident of juvenile correctional halls, applying for a job which was advertised in the Harbour Journal which said—"Companion, secretary sought by mature, professional lady-light but highly confidential work, apply to Mrs. H. Cosey. 1, Monarch Street, Silk" (p. 20). Next, we are introduced to the Cosey household where two warring woman live—Heed, Cosey's second wife and Christine, his granddaughter. "Each woman lived in a spotlight separated...or connected...by the darkness between them"[21] Heed, the beneficiary of her husband's contested will, lives a lonely life in house's richly appointed upper floors and Christine lives in the small basement apartment near the kitchen. Heed wants her to forge a will but Junior's mind is on Roman Gibbons, the teenage grandson of Sandler—Cosey's fishing friend and his wife Vida Gibbons; out of the chaos, Junior creates redemption and healing. Confined to the same house, they stay away from each other, erupting into violent arguments occasionally. Heed can relate to Junior and finds similarities between themselves—"That's what it is, what made me take her on. We're both out here alone" (p. 127).

It is while the women are living together that each hatches a plan for claiming Cosey's inheritance—Christine hires a lawyer, and the semi-illiterate Heed, whose "grasp of handwriting skills was limited," pays an assistant, Junior, to forge a second will, printed on another of L's menus stored in Cosey's Resort and Hotel. This will was to identify herself, without question, as the sweet Cosey child. It is fitting that Heed's trip to this memorial site would end with her death, a noteworthy confluence of handwriting, love, and death. This time, it is Christine and Heed, former best friends, who must confront the ghosts of their pasts, their love and its continuation after death.

The pre-eminent manifestation of love, or its absence, in Morrison's latest novel, is Cosey's composition of his last will and testament. Cosey's will, at the centre of the legal and personal battle between Christine and Heed, leaves all his possessions to his "sweet Cosey child." Each woman believes the reference is to herself: Christine is, after all, the remaining blood relative to Bill Cosey, and Heed, who called her husband "Papa," claims that the term is her husband's endearment. Here, the will, scribbled on L's menu, is an example of the word made material, as it inaugurates action, the transference of property and goods. Beyond receiving Cosey's wealth, each woman vies to hold the position of Bill Cosey's sweet child: "The process of will making operated in a context in which the transfer of property was interpreted as a communicative event: the giving of gifts made statements about past, present, and future relationships and was, therefore, implicated in the reproduction of relationships beyond the grave."[22] If wills, then, not only comment on previous relationships but bespeak further connections, it is not surprising that the women's competition for Cosey's affection is fierce. Thus, as Cosey apparently left no will, the two women have been locked in a war of attrition that seems to have no end. That all changes one day with the arrival of a cunning girl named Junior, who has answered a help wanted advertisement, surreptitiously placed in a newspaper by Heed. Junior begins an intense affair with Romen, a neighbour boy who has been doing chores around the Cosey house, and she realizes that Heed plans to enlist her help in thwarting Christine's plans to get a lawyer to secure her inheritance. The two old foes' confrontation will force them both to reappraise the past: their own tangled relationship, as well as the roles that Cosey and Christine's paranoid mother, May (who was married to Cosey's son), played in igniting and fuelling their feud.

Though the subplot concerns itself with the ambiguous circumstances of Cosey's death, his secret affair with Celestial, and his will, we gradually come to understand that the deepest love story in *Love* is between Christine and Heed, who met as little girls on the beach, and formed a pre-sexual bond cruelly destroyed when Cosey decided to take the 11-year-old Heed as his child bride. More or less sold to the old man by her shiftless parents, the illiterate Heed learns to be a lady and to fight with Christine for primacy in the Cosey family; as adults their childhood roles are reversed, with Heed the heiress and Christine her servant. Their relationship is almost gothic in its ferocity and passion, as if they were African-American female versions of Cathy and Heathcliff.

In this way, the conclusion of the novel echoes Morrison's *Sula*, her most sustained exploration of the profundity of female companionship. Heed and Christine's intimacy mirrors Nel and Sula's. The girls' opposite complexions—"their faces, as different as honey from soot, looked identical" (p. 34)—are recalled in Sula as Nel is the colour of "wet sandpaper" whereas Sula is "heavy brown"[23] (Sula, p. 52). And like Nel and Sula, whose "friendship was as intense as it was sudden" (Sula, p. 53), so too do Christine and Heed fall quickly in love as children, as the narrator of *Love* reveals: "It's like that when children fall for one another. On the spot, without introduction.... If such children find each other before they know their own sex, or which one of them is starving, which well fed; before they know colour from no colour, kin from stranger, then they have found a mix of surrender and mutiny they can never live without. Heed and Christine found such a one. Most people have never felt a passion that strong, that early" (p. 199).

While the love of and for a dead man haunts the novel, it is the depth of female friendship that substantiates love. The old women come to realize that they should have disallowed Cosey's destruction of their friendship: "We could have been living our lives hand in hand instead of looking for Big Daddy everywhere" (p. 189). This reinforces hands as the pre-eminent site of intimacy, which is highlighted in Christine and Heed's post-mortem embrace: "Both look asleep but only one is breathing. One is lying on her back, left arm akimbo; the other has wrapped the right arm of the dead one around her own neck and is snoring into the other's shoulder" (p. 195).

As time goes on, it becomes clear that Junior was hired for more confidential work. Junior is transformed by the love of Romen—a true and upright soul and gives her the love she so desperately desires. Romen's grandparents Sandler and Vida Gibbons are responsible for his decency, which is evidenced throughout the novel especially in the gang rape scene in the beginning, where he saves the girl. In the end Romen and his actions become an example of the goodness that can evolve when people take the time to express themselves carefully and lovingly. After years of seething resentment the Cosey conflicts are resolved with the help of Romen Gibbons, the errand boy and outsider Junior, the truth is brought to life.

The brevity of wit in Cosey's dialogue, the eruptions of hatred that Christine and Heed have for each other, the elaborate affair between Junior and Romen, the painful yet beautiful ending where both Christine and Heed depict what they have done in their lives, reveals Morrison's sheer brilliance and places her as the clearest heir to Zora Neale Hurston in so much that she finds the universal in the vernacular, myth, ritual, ceremony and interrelationship dynamics of African American life. Literary critics over the years have praised Morrison's lyrical descriptive style. In announcing the award the Nobel selection committee praised her lavishly—"She delves into the language itself, a language she wants to liberate from the fetters of race. And she addresses us with the lustre of poetry."[24] Her fellow author Maya Angelou too says—"If

I were to describe her writing, I would say that she has the insight of a shaman and the lyricism of a great poet.... She has the courage to concentrate and say what she saw, and it is said lyrically."[25]

An "ever moving tribute to the past, all the while making evident, the realities of the present,"[26] *Love* abounds in characters which are full of life and emotions. Symbolising what Joyce once called "the nightmare of history,"[27] Morrison effectively weaves together the sea's dynamic with nature and human nature, the lost black paradise of the old Cosey hotel, inhabited by the two warring women, Christine, Heed and their blinding hatred for one another. Thus, Morrison successfully creates a threadbare family saga to cover large ideas about race and gender and with *Love* she adds yet another brilliant classic to her collection.

When Diane McKinney Whetstone, author of the nationally acclaimed *Tumbling*, interviewed Morrison, she learned that Morrison deliberately deleted the word love from the manuscript of her latest novel, *Love*. In the final version the word appears only a few times—"I was blown away by her ability to express love, that most powerful human emotion throughout the expanse of a novel without using the actual word."[28] *Love* is an audacious exploration into the various aspects of love, its appetite, its rich characters, striking scenes and a profound understanding of how alive past can be. "A gorgeous deployment of enigmatic flashbacks.... Love is an elegantly shaped epic of infatuation, enslavement and liberation: a rich and heartening return of Nobel worthy form."[29]

Thus, the terra firma of her works chiefly brings out the universal concerns of humanity and rests chiefly on the question of relevance of human existence. Her novels are not merely novels of protest but, "conscious as she is of the dilemmas of black people, her novels reflect the tension between protest and transcendence; between suffering and strength and between collective and individual identity."[30]

NOTES AND REFERENCES

1. Morrison, Toni: In an interview with Don Swaim, 1987.
2. Morrison, Toni: Playing in the Dark: Whiteness and the Literary Imagination, 1992.
3. Morrison, Toni: In an afternoon writing class at Princeton University.
4. *Los Angeles Times*, October 8th, 1993.
5. *Ibid.*
6. Morrison, Toni: Playing in the Dark: Whiteness and the literary Imagination, 1992.
7. Morrison, Toni: Quotes; Brainy Media.Com.
8. Morrison, Toni: While giving a lecture at Princeton University.
9. Morrison, Toni: Nobel Lecture, 1993.
10. Angelou, Maya: I knew why the caged bird sings. U.S.A: Random, 1969.
11. Brent, Linda: Incidents in the life of a slave girl "In the classic slave Narratives." Ed. Henry Louis Gates, Jr, New York: American Library, 1987.
12. Morrison, Toni: The Bluest Eye, New York: Knopf, 1969.
13. Steel, Shelby: Quoted in Sumana, K. The Novels of Toni Morrison: A Study in Race, Gender and Class, 57, New Delhi: Prestige, 1998.
14. Hernton, Calvin: Sex and Racism in America, p. 123, New York: Grove, 1965.
15. Morrison, Toni: In an Interview in *The New York Times*, Jan. 8th, 1998.
16. Morrison, Toni: In an Interview with Diane McKinney—Whetstone, October, 2003.
17. Morrison, Toni: Love (p. 20), Vintage International Random House, New York, 2003.
18. Quoted in Hooks, Bell: All about love: New Visions. New York: Morrow, 2000 p. 189.
19. Osbey, Brenda Marie: An interview with Brenda Marie Osbey. Interview with John Lowe. The future of Southern Letters. Ed. Jefferson Humphries and John Lowe. New York: Oxford University Press, 1996, p. 105.
20. Hooks, Bell: All about love: New Visions. New York: Morrow, 2000, p. 202.
21. Morrison, Toni: Quoted in review of Love by Barbara Lipkien Gershenbaum.
22. Hallam, Elizabeth and Jenny Hockey: Death Memory and Material Culture. New York: Oxford University Press, 2001, p. 164.
23. Morrison, Toni: Sula, New York: Knopf, 1973, p. 34.
24. Nobel Selection Committee while announcing Morrison's Nobel Prize in 2003.

25. Angelou, Maya: In *Los Angeles Times*, October 8th 1993.
26. In a review of Love by Katie Fraser.
27. Joyce, James: Quoted in a review of Love by Robert Lashby, 2006.
28. Diane McKinney Whetstone: In an interview with Toni Morrison.
29. Quoted in Kirkus (starred review).
30. Das, Shruti: "A Critique of Toni Morrison's Feminism," Feminist English Literature, ed. Manmohan K. Bhatnagar. New Delhi: Atlantic Publishers and Distributors (P.) Ltd., 1999.

The Theme of Self-Definition in Margaret Laurence's 'Manawaka Women'

> "I do not wish them to have power over men, but over themselves."
>
> —*Mary Wollstonecraft*

"Margaret Laurence" says. J.M. Kertzer, "has become through her own efforts and the commentary of critics one of the most important and most Canadian of novelists."[1] One of Canada's finest female authors, she has emerged as a predominant shaper of post-war Canadian literature. Still, an essential figure in Canadian literature after twenty years of her death, her reputation rests chiefly on her Manawaka fiction which established her as one of Canada's literary giants. Though not steeped in the feminist movement of 1970s as Betty Friedan or Virginia Woolf, Laurence's Manawaka series creates women characters who speak to all women and portray the cycle of life for women. Her novels portray strong women striving for self realization while immersed in the daily struggle to make a living in a male dominated world.

In the film of the National Film Board, talking of what she can do as a writer; Laurence says that in all her writing, a very strong kind of celebration of life itself comes through and on another occasion she insists: "If freedom is, in part, the ability to act out of one's self-definition, uncompelled by fear or by the authority of others, it is also a celebration of life and of the mystery at life's core."[2] Despite the accusations made against Laurence's works by the censors, her works are moral in the deepest sense, because they seek to clarify and proclaim and enhance life, not to obscure and demean and destroy it. Her protagonists elucidate the fact that self-definition, after all, can be established in relation to others. And that requires affirming the irreplaceable uniqueness of each individual at the same time with common humanity. In other words, survival with some human dignity is possible only when the reality of others is respected. In her works, her native prairie experience is populated by racially and culturally different people—multiple layers consisted not only of Scots, Irish, English and French, but of Indians, Métis, Ukrainians, Germans and Jews. They do not mix easily and there are covert or sometimes overt discriminations between them. Describing the growth of her female protagonists against such a multi-racial, multi-cultural back ground, Laurence seems to maintain that in order to acquire self-definition to become an independent person spiritually, as well as externally, they have to understand the validity of others.

Throughout her life, Margaret Laurence had been lionized by the public and revered by many as one of the greatest novelists of post-war Canadian literature, setting the pace for other women like Margaret Atwood and Alice Munro. Munro's short stories focus on women who are trying to make sense of their public and private lives and dramatize the conflicts women face when they have made choices based on one set of social and moral values, and later find that the world has changed and that they are asked to reassess their lives and perhaps, wisely or not, to choose again. Atwood's feminist fiction *The Edible Woman*, *Life Before Man* and *Bodily Harm* also amplifies themes of sexual oppression, in an urban context. *The Handmaid's Tale* conjectures about the terrible consequences for women forced into reproductive servitude in a dictatorship of the near future. Laurence's women characters derive their universal and enduring power in their quest for identity. In Laurence's novels, the quest of identity can be seen to progress from the problems of persona in *The Stone Angel* and *A Jest of God*, through acceptance of animus figure in *The Fire Dwellers* to the completed individuation of Morag Gunn in *The Diviners*, running parallel to the Jungian theory. While the earlier women, Hagar, Rachel and Stacey represent only aspects of Jung's concept of personality, Morag the protagonist of the last novel goes through a process of development corresponding to Jung's most penetrating intuitions.

It is interesting to note that Laurence like her Japanese contemporary, Minako Oba, was acutely conscious of their generation, and concerned with their ancestry, with the world to come. According to Laurence, 'the possession of a history, after all, is like the recognition of another person's common humanity.'[3] Consequently, they make use of history, or history in its guise as myth or legend, and of fairy tales or nursery rhymes as shared experiences. On the other hand, their concerns are materialized in the characters and their relationships—particularly those between woman and man as sexual beings, or mother and daughter in terms of femininity and maternality. The theme of incest is often included in Oba, and even Laurence tackles it in one of her short stories, *A Queen of Thebes*, leaving a frightening and yet impressive vision behind. In both authors, several of the same characters appear in different works, in which the protagonist changes and so does the author's focus, which seems to suggest the interrelatedness of human existence. Plants, trees, or birds and animals are frequently and vividly used in their metaphors or similes. Oba at times goes close to animism, in which Laurence had a great interest when she was in Africa. Thus the comparable aspects of Laurence and Oba can be indicated one after another.

Laurence's work is for the most part lodged in Manitoba, in an invented small town—the author calls Manawaka. "Laurence" says Morley "has turned the Manitoba town of her youth into a metaphor of universal human experience." The Manawaka cycle—a series of five books is concerned with the intertwined lives of four generations of prairie women. It includes *The Stone Angel* (1964), *A Jest of God* (1966), *The Fire Dwellers* (1969), *A Bird in the House* (1970), and *The Diviners* (1974). Each of these books is narrated by a strong women growing up in a town and struggling with physical and emotional isolation.

Her chief concern, the development of woman characters is explored in such novels as *This Side Jordan* (1960), *The Stone Angel* (1964), *A Jest of God* (1966), *The Fire Dwellers* (1969),

The Diviners (1974) and *Heart of a Stranger* (1977). Due to the success of her Manawaka fiction, *The Stone Angel* is often mistaken as her first novel, the debut actually being *This Side Jordan*. Thus, Margaret Laurence's first novel, *This Side Jordan*, recreates that colour-drenched world: a place where men and women struggle with self-betrayal, self-discovery, and the dawning of political pride. It explores the personal journey of Nathaniel Amegbe, a young African schoolteacher who is anxious to be part of a new Africa and leave his tribal past behind. Nathaniel's story of personal freedom mirrors Laurence's experience of Africa during Ghana's move towards independence. In all his contradictions, Nathaniel embodies Africa's struggle to enter the modern world. It throbs with a palpable sense of the urgency of its time, the era of independence in 1950s West Africa. *This Side Jordan* transcends the traditional limits of the first novel. Its powerful and compassionate characterizations and its themes of exile and community anticipate the five later novels that make up Laurence's acclaimed Manawaka series. A major work of lasting significance, *This Side Jordan* creates echoes in the mind of the reader as resonant as the drums of Ghana.

Margaret Laurence's, *The Stone Angel* is one of the most acclaimed Canadian novels of all times. It was a landmark event for Canadian Literature and the keystone of Laurence's career. It set the town, Manawaka, firmly in Canada's imaginative landscape and pointed the way for the works to follow. Unreconciled to old age and approaching death, relentlessly critical, unable to reach out to others, Hagar Shipley is the ninety year old narrator of the novel. Irascible, uncharitable, and impatient with the faults of others, she fears that she is about to lose her independence by being placed in a nursing home by her son Marvin and his wife, Doris. Although tough-minded, she is physically frail, often in pain, forgetful, and confused. She speaks impulsively and sometimes regrets her harsh words even as she speaks them. She often surprises herself by crying without warning. She prizes the ability to speak correctly, criticizing and correcting those who do not. As a tall, black-haired, beautiful young woman she had pride and wilfulness. She married beneath her, to the coarse Bram Shipley, in defiance of her father's wishes. After twenty-four years of marriage, during which she gives birth to two sons, Marvin and John, she once again asserts her independence by leaving her husband and taking a job in another town as a housekeeper. Although she dotes on her younger son, John, Hagar's negative attitude towards others eventually alienates him, and he returns to live with his father. Even as a ninety year old, Hagar retains her independence of spirit, fleeing her home and taking refuge in an abandoned building near the sea. But at the end of the novel she realizes that it is her pride that has stopped her from achieving happiness or peace of mind. *The Stone Angel* tells the story of Hagar's last journey towards recognition of love and freedom and reveals that through her journey she will eventually give up the excessive pride that she had demonstrated throughout the novel. John Moss believes that, "Hagar's pride repeatedly imprisoned her within the confines of thwarted affections and misdirected emotion."[4] Her pride serves her best on her dying days when—"she will not submit to frailty and deferential concern. She rages against the dying of the light with the same wrong headed spleen that she had always displayed...in the counterpoint present her...pride is heroic."[5] "The pride she felt in her youth is present also when she's grown up. She is frustrated at both, her lack of co-ordination and her arthritis which causes her to fall. Her reaction is as follows: I perceive the tears my own they must be, although they have sprung so unbidden I feel they are like the incontinent wetness of the infirm. Trickling they taunt down my face. They are no tears of mine. I dismiss them, blaspheme against them—let them be gone."[6]

A wanderer in exile, Hagar is cut off from the experience of connection to God and others. Hence she wants to break out of her alienation and return to true human community. Her redemptive journey culminates in two incidents. Firstly, when Sandra, a sixteen year old who shares Hagar's hospital room needs a bed pan in the middle of the apologizes for his impatience towards her, Hagar tells him what he wants to hear that he has always been good to her. It is a highly acclaimed story of an independent woman striving to sustain herself on her own terms. "What gives Margaret Laurence's vision, the resonant dimensions of universal truth is the interlacing of the destructive and constructive effects of recalcitrant pride."[7] It helped her cope with the many difficulties of her life. The novel is an unforgettable tale about a proud and courageous woman, Hagar, who is determined to leave the world dependent on no one. Hagar does not want anyone to feel pity for her, mourn her or worry about her journey. Hagar accomplishes her goal, even though in the process she has to shatter her illusion and accept the harsh facts about life and reality. In the final scene, the reader obtains the message that Hagar has reached her independence when she holds the glass of water. As a result she can leave the world peacefully knowing that in the end she succeeded in freeing herself of any help. Hagar bravely survived her last moments with her heart and the reward of satisfaction. Hagar Shipley can be considered a tragic hero because through her struggles she managed to retain her spirit and free will, which she exhibited throughout the novel. We can relate to Hagar's struggle through her journey, sympathizing with her, feeling her pain and keeping a part of her with them. In Hagar, Laurence has created the most unforgettable female character in all Canadian fiction. "Laurence's triumph is in her evocation of Hagar at ninety.... We sympathize with her in her resistance to being moved to a nursing home, in her preposterous flight, in her impatience in the hospital. Battered, depleted, suffering, she rages with her last breath against the dying of the light. *The Stone Angel* is a fine novel, admirably written and sustained by unfailing insight."[8]

Laurence's *A Jest of God* narrates the awakening of Rachel Cameron, a thirty-four year old elementary schoolteacher in the small prairie town of Manawaka, Manitoba, Canada. Read usually as a novel in the realist tradition, *A Jest of God* epitomises Margaret Laurence's focus on characters whose stories are usually never told. The protagonist, Rachel, is a spinster schoolteacher in small town Manitoba. She is stifled both by her closed community and by internalising their pettiness. Rachel's inner-dialogue sets the claustrophobic atmosphere, while also being funny, frustrating and moving. Laurence's portrait of an ordinary woman coming to terms with herself and with surroundings is flawless and highly readable. In this celebrated novel, Margaret Laurence writes with grace, power, and deep compassion about Rachel Cameron, a woman struggling to come to terms with love, with death, with herself and her world. *A Jest of God* is, in Atwood's words, "an almost perfect book...plain, self-contained, elegant in form, holding within it the essentials of life."[9] It is the story of a woman, who through the ordeal of one summer in Manawaka in 1960's finds a fragile but sustaining self hood. She has come into middle age with little romantic experience. For years, she dreamt of leaving her small town and domineering mother but duty and caution kept her at home. Trapped in a milieu of deceit and pettiness—her own and that of others, Rachel longs for love, and contact with another human being who share her rebellious spirit. Through her summer affair with Nick Kazlik, a schoolmate from earlier years, she learns at last to reach out to another person and expresses her desires to be independent from her mother and have an adult relationship with another human being. In *A Jest of God* the relationship between Rachel and her mother is strained due to unspoken expectations that each had of the other—the largest weapon which spearheaded the communication war between the two was the generation gap. At thirty-four, she confronts passion and death, finally and realizes that she cannot continue to sacrifice love and freedom but needs both to survive. Rachel passage through self-discovery is exciting, sad, funny and true. Joan J. Hall finds that, "*A Jest of God* has extraordinary clarity, beautiful detail as well as the emotional impact of honest confession."[10] Marilyn Gardner says—"Laurence's rendition is close to faultless...reaffirming her ability to draw, without pathos life-sized woman...skilfully wrought and eloquently told."[11]

In *The Fire Dwellers*, Margaret Laurence has given us yet another unforgettable heroine—smart, witty but overwhelmed by the responsibilities of raising four children and trying to love her overworked husband. Convinced that life has more to offer than the tedious routine of her days, Stacey MacAindra yearns to recover some of the passion of her early romance. "Stacey's state of mind is revealed in a swift flowing stream of dialogue, reaction, reproach and nostalgia...." In the telling of her life, Stacey rediscovers for us all the richness of the commonplace, the pain and beauty in being alive, and the secret music that dances in everyone's soul. Despite the lack of a strictly theological framework for Stacey's self-examination, the narrative dramatises a spiritual exercise of laying open the memory in order to awaken self-perception. The novel is structured by a series of narratees, including Stacey herself, several character-narratees, and the super addressee God, who serve as confessors to move the protagonist from isolation to engagement and self-perception in a gendered confession. An analysis of the narratees reveals Laurence's use of the confessional genre in a polyphonic novel to explore female subjectivity and to construct a narrative of female self-transformation. Stacey MacAindra of *The Fire Dwellers* is Rachel Cameron's sister. She burns to burst through the shadows of her existence to a richer life, to recover the passion, she can only dimly remember from her past. It is an extraordinary novel of a beleaguered wife, mother of four children and married to a struggling salesman who is hard working but uncommunicative. She has a spinster sister and an abiding conviction that life has more to offer than the tedious routine of her days. Stacey thinks of herself as commonplace and ordinary, but Laurence's great achievement is to reveal to us her qualities of love, fortitude and vitality.

In *A Bird in the House*, the maturing of Vanessa MacLeod, the heroine is based on Laurence's own experiences. It is a series of eight inter connected short stories narrated by Vanessa MacLeod, as she matures from a child at age ten into a young woman at age twenty. Wise for her years, Vanessa reveals much about the adult world in which she lives. "A Bird in the House," says Kent Thompson, "achieves the breadth of scope which we usually associate with the novel (and thereby is as psychologically valid as a good novel), and at the same time uses the techniques of the short story form to reveal the different aspects of the young Vanessa."[12] Pittsburgh Post Gazette reveals, "Not since... To kill a mocking bird, has there been a novel like this. It should not be missed by anyone who has a child or was a child."[13] The theme of entrapment is evident in Margaret Laurence's *A Bird in the House*; all the characters in the novel are entrapped. These characters deal with the sense of confinement and the need for escape. Vanessa, Ewen and Aunt Edna all reach personal freedom, however only to a small extent because they are left with the pain of their memories and regrets. Vanessa reaches personal freedom to a small extent. The stories in *A Bird in the House* show the pains that Vanessa goes through while growing up. Vanessa travels on a journey form ignorance to knowledge. This journey is her comprehension of why things happen, and how the past, present and future are tied together. Vanessa realizes that the past affects the present which affects the future. While growing up Vanessa is faced with having to live with the dominance of Grandfather Conner. Grandfather Conner represents a dominant patriarchal figure that rules the family. He always had a strong control over the people that lived with him. He was a perfectionist and was very proud of what he had accomplished and at no cost would he let his reputation be scarred. After her father's death Vanessa moved into the Brick House with Grandfather Conner, this is when she noticed the trapped conditions that aunt Edna was living in and her mother was going to have to live in again. Vanessa always tried to free herself of the things that went on around her by writing exaggerated adventure stories. When Vanessa wrote, it was her chance to get away from the things that made her feel trapped. Vanessa is freed of Grandfather Conner's tyranny when he dies, at least one thinks so. The painful memories that she has of him will remind her everyday that she is not free of his oppression. In addition, Vanessa was unable to achieve personal freedom because of the pain that her regrets brought her. It is evident in the story "Horses of the Night" that Vanessa does not open up to Chris because she is worried about the age difference between them; "[Chris] was twenty-one. The distance between [them] was still too great. For years [she] had wanted to be older so [she] might talk with him, but now [she] felt unready."[14] This holds her back from getting close to him and understanding him better. Vanessa later realizes that when she went camping with

Chris he had wanted to open up to her, because he trusted her. When Chris is admitted into a mental hospital Vanessa concludes that if she had let Chris talk to her, he would not have ended up in a mental institution. This regret that Vanessa feels keeps her from reaching personal freedom.

The Diviners, the story of writer Morag Gunn, is true in its spirit to Laurence's own maturing and is the climatic work of the Manawaka cycle. A complex and profound novel, it brings the Scottish pioneers and the Métis out casts of Manawaka together and culminates in the joining of past and the present and the affirming of the future in the person of Pique, the daughter of Morag and Jules Tonnerre. Morag Gunn, a fiercely independent writer has a difficult relationship with her daughter Pique and her First Nations lover Jules Tonnerre, and her struggle to maintain her independence. For Morag Gunn, growing up in a small Canadian prairie town is toughening process—putting distance between herself and a world that wanted no part of her. Morag's quest for selfhood begins early and abruptly as a result of the accident of her parents death, which leaves her under the guardianship of Christie Logan, the Manawaka garbage collector, and his wife, Prin. Growing up with a local trash collector, Morag is an outsider who sees the towns people all the more clearly for her alienation from them. Escaping to the city Morag seeks salvation in a conventional and ultimately stifling marriage. Eventually, she finds herself a writer and the single mother of a daughter, the product of a relationship with a Métis she has known since childhood, Jules Tonnerre. As is common in Laurence's fiction, this novel delves into such themes as the alienation of the individual within a community, sexual awakening and the false expectations sexual stereotyping encourages. Austen's aware of the Métis and Native culture Laurence is unafraid to depict the marginalised groups in her work.

It is really the story of the past and the present, and the part they play in women's lives. Morag is quite cognizant of her own life, of her daughter's life, and the forces that pry them apart. However, Morag is also quite cognizant of the past, and the effect the past has had on her as a writer, and as a woman. That is one reason she hangs on to the photographs of her past so tightly, and one reason that she often writes about the past, and reflects on how women lived in years gone by. She thinks: "Women working like horses. Also pregnant most of the time. Baking bread in brick ovens, with a loaf in their own ovens. Looking after broods of chickens and kids. Terrible. Appalling."[15] Her tenacious exploration into the past—'the meaning of the ancestors, both the long ago ones and those in remembered history,'[16] have returned to her origin to know the place of her own belonging for the first time. Once Morag thought to herself—"A popular misconception is that we cannot change the past—everyone is constantly changing their own past, recalling it, revising it. What really happened? A meaningless question. But I can keep trying to answer, knowing there is no answer."[17] By recalling and revising it she has tried to reconstruct her past with the help of imagination and has managed to free herself from its bondage, establishing a different relation to it. Laurence's novels seek to clarify and proclaim and enhance life, not to obscure and demean and destroy it, primarily because they are moral in the deepest sense. Laurence's fiction portrays God having the qualities of mercy, grace, suffering, pity, joy, humour, truth, fear, strangeness and disarray. Whenever someone referred to her as a religious writer, however, Laurence felt "a little confused," as if she had been "both complimented and insulted at the same time."[18]

The novel, *The Diviners* presents an increasingly common social phenomenon: the woman who chooses not to be constrained by the tradition that expects a woman to enact a home-centered role of wife and mother. Instead, Morag has found within herself the strength to unite the diverse aspects of the feminine which society has so long kept apart. Again and again she is forced to test her strength against the world, and finally achieves the life she had determined would be hers. In Morag Gunn Laurence has created a figure whose experience emerges as that of all disposed a person in search of their birth right, and one who survives as an inspirational symbol of courage and endurance.

The characters in her novels struggle to understand themselves in relation to God. Throughout *The Fire-Dwellers* Stacey carries on a conversation with God in her head. "At the Day of Judgment, God will say Stacey MacAindra, what have you done with your life? And I'll say, Well, let's see, Sir, I think I loved my kids. And he'll say, Are you certain about that? And I'll say, God I'm not certain about anything any more. So He'll say, To hell with you then. We're all positive thinkers up here. Then again, may He wouldn't. Maybe He'd say, don't worry, Stacey, I'm not all that certain, either. Sometimes I wonder if I even exist. And I'd say, I know what you mean, Lord. I have the same trouble with myself."[19] In *A Bird in the House* her grandmother tells narrator Vanessa MacLeod that "God loves order."[20] After doing some hard observing, Vanessa concludes that "Whatever God might love in this world, it was certainly not order."[21]

"One of the Canada's best loved writers,"[22] Laurence more than any other writer of her time, seemed to enjoy her life by writing these remarkable novels. Throughout her writing career, she brought her readers to Manawaka, recreating the world in which her heroines, Hagar, Stacey and Rachel grew up in. Through these novels, Margaret showed how the apparition of power by women could be conducted according to principles of self-interest.

NOTES AND REFERENCES

1. Kertzer, J.M.: *Margaret Laurence and Her Works*. ECW Press, Toronto, Ontario.
2. Laurence, Margaret remarked in the film of National Film Board.
3. Laurence, Margaret: *Heart of a Stranger*, p. 28.
4. Moss, John: Quoted in *Pride and Journey* by Michelle Dauma and Stephen Weiler.
5. *Ibid.*
6. Laurence, Margaret: *The Stone Angel*, p. 33.
7. Moss, John: Quoted in *Pride and Journey* by Michelle Dauma and Stephen Weiler.
8. Granville Hicks remarks in Saturday Review.
9. Atwood, Margaret: From the *After Word*.
10. Hall, Joan J, comments in Saturday Review.

11. Gardner, Marilyn in Christian Science Monitor.
12. Thompson, Kent: *The Fiddlehead.*
13. Pittsburgh *Post-Gazette.*
14. Laurence, Margaret: *A Bird in the House,* p. 140.
15. Laurence, Margaret: *The Diviners.*
16. Laurence, Margaret: *Heart of a Stranger*, p. 237.
17. Laurence, Margaret: *The Diviners*, p. 70.
18. Moss, John: In an article entitled *Margaret Laurence.*
19. Laurence, Margaret: *The Fire Dwellers.*
20. Laurence, Margaret: *A Bird in the House.*
21. *Ibid.*
22. King, James: The Life of Margaret Laurence Alfred. A. Knopf publishing. UDA, 1997.

A Post-Colonial Study of 'Racism and the Realm of the Other' in Nadine Gordimer's Fiction

6

"The reason racism is a feminist issue is easily explained by the inherent definition of feminism. Feminism is the political theory and practice to free all women: women of color, working-class women, poor women, physically challenged women, lesbians, old women as well as white economically privileged heterosexual women. Anything less than this is not feminism, but merely female self-aggrandizement."

—*Barbara Smith*, 1979

"Where once, the transmission of national traditions was the main theme of a world literature, perhaps we can now suggest that transitional histories of migrants, the colonised or political refugees—these border and frontier conditions may be the terrains of world literature."[1]

For Nadine Gordimer, the 1991 Nobel Prize winning South African writer, the major theme was exile and alienation. One of apartheid's fiercest critics, Nadine Gordimer has long been considered as a pre-eminent interpreter of South Africa and also its conscience. Her life is a vivid portrait of apartheid in human terms. Firmly grounded in physical and psychological detail, memorably evoking the texture of daily life for South Africans of every stripe, her works have earned worldwide acclaim. "Gordimer...cannot only capture but express in the lives of human beings these moments which are so fleeting, so impalpable as well as so common. They are overlooked by all but a very rare artist."[2] Having grown up in a post-colonial South Africa and lived through the various stages of its apartheid regime, Gordimer's stories reflect her affection for her homeland and people and a love of its epic, haunting landscapes and potent past. A fervent campaigner against racism, Gordimer emerges as a champion of tolerance, free speech and understanding revealing the ravaging consequences of apartheid on the life of the South Africans. It was out of her commitment to black liberation and for the sake of black South African writers, who were silenced and for whom she wanted to speak, that Gordimer stayed back in South Africa and endured the black decades, unlike so many who had opted to move abroad. Her conviction and self belief in refusing to become an exile despite the banning of three of her works by the South African regime is laudable. With her restless energy and prodigious discipline, Gordimer is able to enter into the existence of others, whether they be black or white, men or women.

Always questioning power relations and truth, Gordimer tells stories of ordinary people, revealing moral ambiguities and choices. Gordimer's stories concern the constant tension between personal isolation and the commitment to social justice, the numbness caused by the reluctance to accept racial segregation, the powerlessness to alter it and the abrogation of exile. Her work "reflects the psychic vibrations within that country, the road from passivity and blindness to resistance and struggle, the forbidden friendships, the censored soul and the underground networks."[3] Gordimer was often militantly critical of South African life and tendered little moral hope for whites who lived under apartheid. Apartheid was the dominant theme, she chose to write about and in her works articulated key issues for White South Africans, empathizing with the disenfranchised blacks and presenting to the world the true face of racism in all its human complexities. Though most of her works deal with the moral and psychological tensions of her racially divided home country, her strong political and moral views are interwoven with a keen sense of how South Africans both white and black function in their everyday life.

Her fiction establishes her as one of the most eminent modern women writers, although she has resisted being classed as a feminist, insisting that she is simply, "a writer who happens to be a women."[4] Gordimer had often been criticised for dismissing feminism in its early days, now, a few decades later, she acknowledges the increasing diversity in feminism in the recent years. "It's interesting I can't see any vestiges now of that trivial feminism that I was talking so disparagingly in the early times."[5] Gordimer had never shirked the difficult issues raised by the legacy of white European domination in South Africa. Her works document what the radical form of "othering" did to people and their cultures. To Gordimer, understanding racism was something, universal, if one were human, one should be able to comprehend the horrors of racism even if one hasn't experienced it first hand. As she says in an interview, "For me being Jewish is like being black: you simply are. To want to deny it is disgusting. It's a denial of humanity."[6]

Gordimer's first novel, *The Lying Days* derives its title from a poem by W.B. Yeats—"The Coming of Wisdom with Time" (1990):

> "Though leaves are many, the root is one through all the lying days of my youth I swayed my leaves and flowers in the sun Now I may wither into the truth."[7]

The lines suggest the many branching paths that the female protagonist Helen Shaw follows, while remaining tied to one. As a bildungsroman, the novel traces the development of a young girl, Helen Shaw, towards maturity, who grows up and discovers sexuality and at the same time recognizes the racism of her society. The novel describes the interaction between the personal and the public, for it is both a bildungsroman as well as a topical novel dealing with apartheid stricken South Africa.

Though she says that she "shall never write an autobiography" and that she is "much too jealous of my (her) privacy for that,"[8] her autobiography seems already to have been composed in her novels and short story collections. *The Lying Days* was based largely on the writer's own life and depicted a white girl, Helen and her growing disaffection towards the narrow mindlessness of a small town life. *The Lying Days* is set in Transvaal, an East Rand mining town outside

Johannesburg, the place where Nadine Gordimer was born. When Helen's mother disapproves of Helen's friendship with Mary, a black student at a university, she leaves her parent's home. Her adolescent feelings well up from her inmost self and propel her beyond the narrow life of her parents. In her pursuit of identity, she becomes involved with Paul Clark, a welfare officer. However, a tiff with Paul forces her to quit her job at African Welfare Agency. When Helen feels that it was difficult for her to be totally committed to the struggle for freedom of the blacks, she decides to leave South Africa. However, just as she is about to leave she decides to return to South Africa. Her acceptance of her identity as a South African, makes her declare—"I am not running away form now because I know. I'm coming back here."[9]

Her second novel *A World of Strangers* (1958) shows the first fruitful but often frightening encounters between white and black people in the heady days of Sophia town. It presents the dilemmas of well meaning liberalism. In *A World of Strangers*, Gordimer, the keen reporter of the minutiae of daily life in 1950's South Africa juxtaposes the lavish excesses of white South African life with the chaotic lives of the South African blacks. It is through the eyes of her reluctant protagonist, Toby a young English businessman, an outsider that Gordimer exposes the hypocrisy of both African societies. He knows little about apartheid and so at first sees no contradiction in developing a relationship with an elite upper class white woman and with a woman dedicated to fighting apartheid but as he makes friends with one of the black South Africans, the truth of oppression begins to dawn on him. Toby Hood however, recognizes the injustices but accepts them nevertheless. He is conscious of the unreality of the society life but like a tourist he chooses not to involve himself deeply in the reality.

Occasion for Loving (1963) is a story of an illicit love affair between a black man and a white woman which ends on a bitter note. The white girl Ann Davis is married to a gentle Jew called Boaz Davis, a committed scholar who has travelled widely in search of African music. A black talented painter Gideon Shibalo gets involved with Ann Davis, and Boaz the cuckold remains on the side of South African black majority. *Occasion for Loving* concerns itself with theme of South Africa's cruel racial law—the theme Gordimer was preoccupied with—"A line in the statute book has more authority than the claims of one man's love or another's. All claims of natural feeling are overridden alike by a line in a statute book, that takes no account of humanness, that recognizes neither, love nor respect, nor jealousy nor rivalry, nor compassion nor hate nor any human attitude where there are black and white together."[10]

For Salman Rushdie, replacing literary values by political once was something to beware of—it was simply the murder of thought. Gordimer too, strongly felt politics was corruption and writing, an art, which should be kept away from the narrowness and limitations of politics. Thus, to Gordimer, writing was not a political act and she herself says that she was not a political person. Even though, Gordimer makes no claims of being politically motivated, yet every interviewer and critic seems to consider the influence of politics in her writing. "...her writings document the impact of politics on personal lives and what an increasingly radical white South African woman felt during the rise and fall of apartheid."[11] Her fiction is interesting politically, where she acknowledges the need to defend her right to write about black characters and ensures that their voices be heard.

The Late Bourgeois World (1966) was motivated by the actual political events of the 1960's like the African Resistance Movement. The heroine, Elizabeth Van Den Sandt of The Late Bourgeois World opts for involvement and commitment instead of detachment and towards the end of the novel she dedicates herself to a revolutionary cause. She agrees to help Luke Fokase, the black revolutionary by agreeing to transfer funds from London to a local bank account for the liberation movement. The novel reflects Nelson Mandela's decision to switch from passive resistance to sabotage.

In 1971, Gordimer published *A Guest of Honour*, a huge novel about the birth pangs of the new Africa. Here the individual history and great ideological perspectives are woven into a chronicle whose protagonists embody the social political and moral problems arising when victorious liberation front splits up into factions. Idealism and goodwill are replaced by a new brutality and corruption. "A Henry Jamesian enterprise, where society and marriage, politics and landscapes, mix without obscuring the pattern,"[12] the novel is about James Bray, an English colonial administrator who was expelled from a central African nation for siding with its black nationalist leaders and is invited back ten years later to join in the country's independence celebrations. A magnificent literary feat, *A Guest of Honour* was highly recommended by Gordimer herself, "I'd like people to read a rather...ignored novel of mine, called A Guest of Honour.... It's not set in South Africa, but in an imaginary African country. In terms of some of the post-colonial situation...*A Guest of Honour* has been in a sense prophetic."[13]

The Conservationist (1974) which won the Booker Prize for 1974 is a magnificent novel. Like Faulkner's, *The Sound and the Fury*, *The Conservationist* deals with the theme of sterility of white community and racial stratification. A kind of sequel to the first classic of South African literature—*The Story of an American Farm* (1883) by Olive Schreiner, the book depicts South Africa from both sides, the blacks and the whites in a very realistic way. Written and set in the 1970's, Gordimer's novel is a subtle and sensitive protest against the apartheid social system, then prevalent in South Africa.

It is the story of Mehring, the Afrikaner anti-hero, whose farm is as barren as his life. Gordimer observes South Africa's decay through interior monologues, reflections, fragments of conversations of Mehring with the distant son, lovers, acquaints and the workers of his farm, revealing the emptiness and solitariness of his life. *The Conservationist* can be read as the story of failed domesticity which mirrors national failure of South Africa. Mehring is not a male chauvinist. He is tolerant but not a liberal, who likes to be seen as a country gentleman but sexually he is seen as a colonialist, picking up a coloured girl and taking her to a mine property. Using Zulu creation myths, Gordimer presents South Africa differently and her powerful landscapes and descriptions and presented with great precision and an unerring eye for minutest detail. Using Mehring's character Gordimer gave us a portrait of a South Africa divided by the Apartheid where social status is linked with the colour of the skin and at the same time gave us an idea of the idiosyncrasy of all the characters mentioned in the story, the Boers, Indians and Blacks who interact and live together but are separated by the racial laws of South Africa. It remains without doubt, Gordimer's densest and most poetical novel as she herself says, "The Conservationist, it's my most lyrical novel."[14]

Burger's Daughter (1979) remains Gordimer's "coded homage,"[15] to Bram Fischer, the communist lawyer who was sentenced to life in prison. Written during the aftermath of Soweto uprising the novel has as its backdrop, the disturbing and distressing events of Sharpeville, Soweto and Black consciousness. It is the story of the life of a child of a revolutionary activist, a story in which the daughter Rosa Burger analyses her relationship to her father, Lionel Burger, a martyr of the anti-apartheid movement. Rosa Burger undergoes series of experiences before becoming a committed revolutionary, making her realize rather early in life that—"We belonged to other people. I must have accepted that...."[16] However, Rosa rejects the ideals of her father and decides not to deny her own individuality for political needs. A series of incidents took place which influenced her decision to leave South Africa. Firstly, people's dying faith in her father's vision, secondly the casual attitude of people at the death of an African and lastly the sight of a black man violently whipping a donkey thus giving vent to his own frustration. She identifies the scene with the suffering of this own country and feels that she no longer knows, "how to live in Lionel's country,"[17] hence she decides to escape to Europe to get out of the stifling atmosphere of South Africa. However, she can't keep away from the political situation for long and joins the French branch of the Anti Apartheid Movement. Slowly, she gets involved in underground work and is detained in Terrorist Act and finally lands up in solitary confinement like her father. The novel remains a commentary on "the infinite variety and gradation of suffering by lash, by fear, by hunger, by solitary confinement—the camps, concentration, labour, resettlement...."[18] Thus, "In this brilliantly realized work Gordimer unfolds a riveting history of South Africa and a penetrating portrait of a courageous woman."[19]

Perhaps Gordimer's most powerful novel *July's People* (1981) projects into the future the final collapse of white supremacy and what that might mean for white and black people on an intimate level. It "offers an unforgettable look into the terrifying, tacit understandings and misunderstandings between blacks and whites in South Africa."[20] It is a futuristic novel about a white family fleeing from war torn Johannesburg into a country where they seek refuge with their African servant in his village. July's people are Maureen and Bamford Smales—he is an architect, she a housewife with three children, a nice suburban house and the servant July. July had been working for them since the past fifteen years. He hides his master's family to protect them from catastrophe. Here, Gordimer portrays a future bloody South African revolution which happily never took place.

A Sport of Nature (1987) tells of Hillela Kgomani, who rebels against colour discrimination and marries a black South African revolutionary, Whaila. After Whaila's assassination, Hillela whole heartedly engages herself in the task of liberating her own people and rises from insignificance to unprecedented political power. It is like a Cinderella tale summing up Africa's post-colonial history, the heroine runs off from an idyllic childhood into the mess of the world's variety and from a rebellious little white nobody she becomes the intelligent sensual heroine who emerges in the end as an honoured guest of her own country.

My Son's Story (1990) is about Hannah, the committed activist, who is not only a participant of the liberation movement but also a motivating factor. For Hannah, "the people in the battle are her only family, her life, the happiness she understands."[21] She even foregoes her relationship with Sonny, a coloured school teacher her lover who shares with her, tenderness for the depressed blacks. Through Hannah, Gordimer has shown hope for white South Africans who want to be a part of the struggle. Here Gordimer describes both the unexpected moment when the revolutionary spark ignites and the daily routine when internal dissension rocks the upper reaches of the anti apartheid movement. The novels central character, Sonny is trapped between being a teacher and a politician, a father and a husband. He is caught in a transition, about to enter a political collective struggle, he is caught between one state and another to come through him and others. Gordimer enters into a dialogue with the future, a dialogue with the absent forces that are to rule our lives in years ahead.

None to Accompany Me is a lyrical explanation of radical social change as a possibility of changing oneself. It takes place in a tumultuous South Africa in the final throes of apartheid. The upheaval is reflected in the life of Vera Stark, a white civil rights lawyer who sheds the trappings of her married life in her pursuit for space in existence. Vera is one of Gordimer's most complex and intriguing creations—pragmatist and sensualist, wife and mother, lover, and political activist. *None to Accompany Me* is a "radical and complex novel...Gordimer demonstrates again that when her imagination transforms experience, the result is a literature for the world."[22] It advocates a kind of radical feminism and poses questions related to the status of women in modern African society. Vera Stark, a lawyer representing black struggle, rebels against the male dominated society and emerges as a privileged woman who has attained economic and social autonomy in her profession as a lawyer. However, in her quest for selfhood, she ends up as a loser in her personal life. Her daughter Annie feels she had always been available to so many other people and her son fails to establish any psychological synergy with his mother, who didn't know how "to show her son how moved she was by the pleasure of having him home from the boarding school."[23] Unmoved by this rejection though, Vera transforms herself into a self isolated person and accepts the realities dispassionately. Gordimer stands midway between the radical feminism of Mary Wollstonecraft and Beauvoir's vindication of the rights of the women focusing on women's liberty within socio-ethical structure of society. Agreeing partially to both Wollstonecraft and Beauvoir, Gordimer's female protagonists are rebels, liberated souls who find their own ways of satisfying themselves in every respect, yet living a part of society.

The House Gun (1998) explores the violence ridden post apartheid society through a murder trial. A morally complex and moving story from the liberated South Africa the book is about a highly educated black man on whom two intelligent well read parents, depend for survival and sanity of their souls. Their architect son Duncan has killed his friend Carl Jesperson, out of jealousy. Natalie, the mistress, who is the reason behind the murder is self destructive and rebels against personal dependence. The novel remains a fable of violence and new forms of liberation, evoking reflections on the rise of violence in the world. Gordimer's first novel to become a feature film, *The House Gun* exhibits a firm but casual brilliance.

The Pick Up (2001) continues to deal with the issues of race and class, the connection between the private and the political and shift from the local and national to the global. From a simple scenario of girl meets boy, Gordimer's *The Pick Up* evolves into an exploration of freedom, responsibility, love and identity. The racial opposition between the 'Black and White' has been replaced by a cultural opposition between 'East and West.' The author picks up the theme of Arabic Islamic culture —a theme which came quite naturally to Gordimer, who represents many a times, the 'commonwealth literature' or 'New Literatures in English' from an unspecified Arab country. The story begins when her car breaks down and she starts a love affair with Abdu, the mechanic at her garage. Abdu's actual name is Ibrahim, an illegal immigrant, who has no problems with capitalist fetishes and has great admiration for Julie's father's car and the jet set world of Julie's father. When his identity is revealed, he cannot avert his expulsion. Despite Abdu's initial resistance, Julie decides to accompany him to his home. Both Julie and Abdu are radically dissimilar—for Julie, the outcast Abdu, without family and friends in a foreign country reminds her of her own independence, while Abdu regards this 'independence' as a deficiency and wonders why should Julie shy away from contact with her parents. The second part of the novel is set in a small Arabian town, probably in

Northern Africa, whereas Abdu starts applying for immigration into the western states, Julie gets integrated into Abdu's family and perfectly fulfils the role of social harmonizer combining beautifully, her communal integration with a strong sense of self-determination. At the same time, Julie alienates herself from Abdu and finally when Abdu gains a permit to immigrate into the United States, Julie, in another last minute decision refuses to come along. Identity happens to one of the central themes of *The Pick Up*. For Abdu, identity is a sort of luxury only the privileged can afford. Unwilling to accept the role that his family and tradition ascribe to him, he makes himself a no body in his own culture. He stoically accepts the traditional duties in his family without completely identifying with it.

Julie finds her own identity through radical difference from the bourgeois world of her parents, making herself a 'home' in the social network of liberal friends at EL-AY cafe. Through her contacts with the Oriental women, she positions herself within their culture and alienates herself from Abdu when he tries to define himself through his distance to that culture. Her attempts at self definition are triggered by her encounters with the desert, the ultimate sublime and she creates a room of her own at the border of the civilized world. Fascinated by the sight of a rice plantation in the middle of the dessert, she translates her dream accordingly and decides to cultivate the land. Thus, Abdu's prospects in the states seem anything but promising and Julie's dream of a rice plantation in the desert is based on a camouflage enterprise for an arms struggling business. The novel isn't merely a standby in race and class but also discourse on gender. The book's very beginning describes a situation of sexual discrimination, where a woman causes a traffic jam when her car breaks down. However, as far as the relation between Abdu and Julie is concerned we find a reversal of power relations because it is Julie, who picks up Abdu, invites him for a cup of coffee and initiates their first sexual contact. Later also, the more Abdu and Julie come under the influence of the Arabic-Islamic world the more they adapt a patriarchal view. Abdu willingly accepts the new gender relation and Julie too, surprisingly complies with his family wishes, out of respect for foreign culture. Thus, "her latest fiction shows a welcome readiness to pursue new awareness and a new sense of the world."[24] We can easily conclude that even at the age of seventy-eight, she is still flexible enough to look for new frontiers.

Gordimer's latest novel *Get a Life* (2005) is a challenging novel that explores the themes of conservation and survival, death and compromise, while dealing with the various issues of contemporary South Africa like illness, fidelity, career choices, the family and the environment. Though rooted deeply in Gordimer's native Johannesburg, the novel reaches out to universal issues of conservation. Paul Bannerman, a thirty something ecologist is passionate about his work with his multiracial wilderness team. But when he is diagnosed with thyroid cancer, he has to be physically isolated due to radiation treatment, that he has been prescribed. Following this treatment he stays with his parents Adrian and Lyndsay and his wife Berenice who holds an executive position at an advertising agency and the toddler son Nicholas visits him but are advised to avoid contact with Paul while he is radioactive. Suddenly the white conservationist is reduced to being a "leper" and even after he recovers, he is still an 'untouchable'. Though Paul loves his wife, he also realizes that her advertising projects are a looming disaster, strongly conveying the message of conservation. The novel deftly exposes the complacency of politically aware, upper-middle class whites in post apartheid South Africa.

Thus, Gordimer's fictional oeuvre establishes her, like her fellow Nobel laureates, Gunter Grass and Alexander Solzhenitsyn, as a towering figure of world literature and the moral conscience of her nation. Her persistent concern with the 'realm of the other' is evident in all her works and has lent her an iconic status in South Africa. A tireless examiner of moral and psychological truth, Gordimer as a spokesperson for a crusade against racism, effectively presents in each successive novel from *The Lying Days* to *Get a life*, the complexities of 'the Other.'

NOTES AND REFERENCES

1. Bhabha, Homi K: The Location of Culture. London: Routledge, 1994, rep, 2000, 12.
2. Quoted in *New York Times* Book Review.
3. Quoted in an article by Per Wastberg, 'Nadine Gordimer and the South African Experience,' 26 April 2001.
4. Driver, Dorothy: "Nadine Gordimer: The Politicalization of Women," English in Africa, Vol. 10, No. 2, October 1983.
5. Lazar, Karen: An interview with Nadine Gordimer.
6. *Ibid.*
7. Yeats, W.B.: The Coming of Wisdom with Time, 1910.
8. Gordimer, Nadine in conversion with Dwight Garner.
9. Gordimer, Nadine: The Lying Days, Simon and Schuster, 1953, p. 340.
10. Gordimer, Nadine: Occasion for Loving. London: Cape, 1963.
11. Bazin, Nancy Topping in an interview with Nadine Gordimer.
12. Quoted in an article by Per Wastberg, 'Nadine Gordimer and the South African Experience,' 26 April 2001.
13. Gordimer, Nadine in an interview dated 1st May 1995 from her home in Johannesburg.
14. *Ibid.*
15. Gordimer, Nadine while talking of Burger's Daughter.
16. Gordimer, Nadine: Burger's Daughter, Viking Press, 1979, p. 84.
17. *Ibid.*, p. 80.
18. *Ibid.*, p. 208.
19. Quoted in *New York Times* Book Review.
20. Quoted in Newsweek.
21. Gordimer, Nadine: My Son's Story. London: Bloomsbury, 1990, p. 67.
22. Quoted in San Francisco Chronicle.
23. Gordimer, Nadine: None to Accompany Me. London: Penguin Books, 1995, p. 14.
24. Coetzee, J.M. on Gordimer in the New York Review of Books, 23 October, 2003.

Atwood's Fiction: 'A Barometer of Feminist Thought'

"One is not born, but rather becomes, a woman."

—*Simone de Beauvoir*

A prolific, controversial and innovative writer, Margaret Atwood has emerged as one of the most eminent contemporary figures in Canadian literature. After the recent passing of Canadian greats like Robertson Davies and Timothy Findley, Atwood along with Alice Munro was the first to elevate Canadian literature to the world stage and through her profuse writings, critiques and activism, has ultimately contributed to the growth of women's writing and to the established legitimacy of Canadian literature.

She has "questioned stereotypes of nationality and gender, exposing cultural fictions and the artificial limits they impose on our understanding of us and other human beings."[1] Atwood has been variously assessed as "a feminist writer, for her incisive commentaries on sex roles, a religious writer, for her visions of spiritual ecstasy, a gothic writer, for her images of grotesque misfits and surreal disorientations of the psyche, a writer of Canadian wilderness; a nationalist writer and a regionalist."[2] Despite the fact that she mostly writes about women, from a female perspective and with a noticeable feminist slant, her writing transcends the boundaries of what is often described as 'female fiction'. In all her works, she focusses on Canadian national identity—on Canadian relationship with United States and Europe, human rights issues, the Canadian wilderness and women's exploitation as well as her relation to the world and individuals around them. Atwood's novels are filled with characters who are all seeking something; whether for answers, equilibrium, freedom, revenge, understanding, or fulfilment. The plots are complex, at times very dark, but always filled with passion and drive and the stories range from childhood cruelty to grownup inhumanity of people towards each other; from the search of a father, to the search for answers in a post-apocalyptic wasteland. The locales stretch from nineteenth century Toronto to the Caribbean islands, to dystopian future landscapes.

In Atwood's fiction, "there is no essentialist definition of 'woman' of 'feminism' of even 'Canadian', but instead representations of the endless complexity and quirkiness of human behaviour which exceeds ideological labels and the explanatory power of theory."[3] Though, there is no definition of feminism in Atwood's fiction, her work has been regarded as a barometer of feminist thought. Her protagonists are often a kind of 'every woman' characters or the weaker members of society. Through female protagonists and narrators who often journey from victimization to self-actualization, Atwood explores women's issues using elements of science fiction, historical fact, fairy tale, and dystopian vision. Atwood's novels feature female protagonists who are characteristic of Atwood: they are, as Judy Klemesrud reported in *The New York Times*, "intelligent, self-absorbed modern women searching for identity," who "hunt, split logs, make campfires and become successful in their careers, while men often cook and take care of their households."[4] In Atwood's plots, the lives of these women are shattered by overwhelming threats: cancer, divorce, violence—and those that persist quietly, naggingly—solitude, loneliness and desperation.

Atwood's fiction is one of the most deep rooted critiques of the Canadian society in relation to the values represented by the Canadian dream. As the Canadians pride themselves in their superiority in human values and adherence to old world civilization values, they had refused to go with United States at the time of American War of Independence and had escaped the efforts of second sin, of materialism and cutthroat rivalry which characterised the American dream. Atwood's concern was to free the Canadian psyche from English and American imperialism and to liberate women from their perception of themselves as victims of masculine privilege.

Atwood's early feminist treatise, *The Edible Woman* (1969) was both funny and terrifying story about a young woman who works for a consumer company. The novel chronicles the fantastic and dramatic ego disintegration of Marian McAlpin, who seems at first to be a perfectly conventional young woman, with friends, a successful and attractive man in her life, and a reasonably good job working for a market research company. Everything in her life seems to fly out of control with her engagement, just as Marian seems ready to fulfil "every woman's" dream of trading in her troublesome job for marriage and a new life at home with children. It has clear themes relating to gender. In the novel, Atwood expresses the role that men and women play, while showing that women can rise above their role and be themselves, instead of taking on the role that society has prescribed for them. Atwood communicates this theme by having a strong female and male character, each representing their gender. The character representing the male gender is Marian's fiancé Peter. Like Marian, Peter's role has also been created out of what society communicates to him. Marian refers to this at one point when speaking of the places Peter has wanted to make love, saying "Peter's abstractions on these occasions gave me the feeling that he liked doing them because he had read about them somewhere."[5] This shows that Peter's ideas on gender have come from society itself. His ideas on the male are that the female is there to meet the male's needs. He represents the typical male attitude and the role that society prescribes for men.

Besides, the theme of commodity production, its advertisements and the permeation of the society by the consumerist values is ubiquitous in Atwood's writings. The novel critiques not only capitalism but also the dehumanizing effect of technology on man. Through the protagonist, Marian McAlpin, Atwood shows that in the modern technologically advanced consumerist society, human beings are reduced to commodities. Marian is a young unmarried consumer research analyst who works for Seymour Surveys whose job is to turn "the convoluted and overly—subtle prose of the psychologists into simple questions which can be understood by the people who ask them as well as people who answer them."[6] An account of Marian's job with Seymour Surveys further highlights the way in which human appetites are manipulated in a technologically advanced consumerist society. In this technologically advanced consumerist society human beings have become somewhat similar to commodities which are packed and presented for consumption. As Marian herself comes to agree that Peter is "nicely packaged" (162), and she feels "proud ownership" when she looks at him. After her engagement Marian notes that Peter "sounded as though he'd just bought a shiny new car. I gave him a tender chrome plated smile, that is, I meant the smile to express tenderness, but my mouth felt stiff and bright and somehow expensive" (194). In such a society, to decide to get married is also to decide to enter into a major commercial contact. In fact Marian thinks of marriage as "contracting out." She even fondly imagines Peter buying a marriage manual. "If you got something new you went out and bought a book that told you how to work it" (206). She knows that Peter thinks of her as an object to be "displayed" (194) to his friends and that, were he jealous, it would be only because he thinks "someone had been infringing on his private property rights." But she herself is not immune to this kind of thinking—as she watches Lucy flirting with Peter, she thinks Lucy should know better, for "Peter was off the market" (264). Seymour Surveys is preoccupied, like most commercial enterprises, with problems of packaging, and the application of the phrase "nicely packaged" to Peter is both complicating and disturbing. Marian feels herself to be a commodity nicely packed in plastic for making it presentable. She, therefore, presents, Peter a cake made in the shape of a woman and tells him: "You've been trying to destroy me, haven't you.... You've been trying to assimilate me. But I've made you a substitute, something you'll like much better. This is what you really wanted along, isn't it? I'll get you a fork" (301).

The Edible Woman is about women and their relationships to men, to society, and to food and eating. It is through food and eating that Atwood discusses a young woman's rebellion against a modern, male-dominated world. The female protagonist, Marian McAlpin, struggles between the role that society has imposed upon her and her personal definition of self; and food becomes the symbol of that struggle and her eventual rebellion. At the end of *The Edible Woman*, Marian partially reconstructs that new persona, or concept of self, through a renewed relationship to food. This novel, in a sense presages Margaret Atwood's attitude towards problems like colonialism, feminism and the so-called Canadian dream which corresponds to the American dream in the US culture. Margaret Atwood has repeatedly stated in her non-fictional writing that the relation of America towards Canada is analogous to that of man towards woman in a male dominated society.

Surfacing (1972) demonstrates the complex question of identity for an English-speaking Canadian female. Identity, for the protagonist has become problematic because of her role as a victim of colonial forces. She has been colonised by men in the patriarchal society in which she grew up, by Americans and their cultural imperialism, or neo-colonialism as it has come to be known as, and the Euro-centric legacy that remains in her country although the physical presence of English and French rulers have gone. This collective colonial experience of the protagonist, and the analogous nature of imperial and feminist discourses, is succinctly described by Coral Ann Howells, quoted by Eleanora Rao in 'Strategies for Identity': "Women's experience of the power politics of gender and their problematic relation to patriarchal traditions of authority have affinities with the Canadian attitudes to the cultural imperialism of the United States as well as its ambivalence towards its European inheritors."[7]

It is a novel which follows the female protagonist's awakening from a personal, sexual, and national alienation to an integrated sense of identity. It also concerns itself with the cause of woman, presenting an ecofeministic commitment and careful analysis of its return to the natural world. It is the story not of an individual but of a race, of man's predicament in the problem ridden modern world, where man has alienated not only from others but also from himself. *Surfacing* is built around a complex of metaphors, a dead frog, an aborted foetus, lost father, all of them associated in a young women's mind following a climatic descent into water, which is also descent in her subconscious. The associations lead her into madness, as she searches for her identity as a woman, daughter and mate. The novel shifts from the urban to the wild where the protagonist searches for her missing father. Passing through the madness and finally freeing herself through grief over and acceptance of her father's death, the protagonist realizes herself.

Margaret Laurence has said about *Surfacing* that the novel had many themes but most important among them was the ecological, which she found expressed in Atwood's search for the meaning of a human life shadowed always by morality: "The themes are many, and the nature of reality is one of the most interesting. Some of the themes concern our most burning contemporary issues-the role of women, the facts of urban life, and most of all, the wounding and perhaps killing of our only home-Earth."[8] Atwood sees the whole earth threatened by the urge to exploit its resources rather than to cultivate its potentialities with ecological awareness. She in her first novel, *The Edible Woman* gave a vision of the society in which man had converted the whole of his environment into a 'commodity market' so much so that even man himself had become a commodity fit to be consumed. In *Surfacing* Atwood goes further to identify the forces which have brought about this degradation in environment.

The novel begins like a detective story. The unnamed narrator/protagonist comes back from Toronto after nine years' absence to Northern Quebec where she had lived as a child. She has been told that her father, an eccentric botanist, living alone on a lake island, has vanished without trace, and though she has not been in touch with him for many years, she feels bound to go on an attempt to find what has happened to him. While going to her childhood place along with her friend Joe and another couple David and Anna, she finds that Canada is being victimised by Americans and Americanism. She also notices that nature is a victim of civilization and is being contaminated and spoiled. She can see the signs of the disease called Americanism as soon as she takes the road to Quebec. She is of the view that the Americans are keen to exploit and victimise Canadians and their land psychologically as well as geographically. She wishes that there is a need for the revival of Canada. The Canadian people have to check this victimisation otherwise they will find no place in history.

Surfacing is a short, sharp exploration of how past and present intersect—endlessly, damagingly—when a young woman returns home to the remote north of Quebec to search for her missing father. Alongside evocative glimpses of life on the edge of the wilderness and a masterclass in characterisation, Atwood uses the tale to examine the pitfalls of memory, the effects of modernity, the gulf between rural and urban life, and the legacy of the 1960s sexual revolution. Convinced her father has drowned in one of the area's many lakes and frustrated at having found nothing after days of looking, she dives in. 'It was below me, drifting towards me from the furthest level where there was no life, a dark oval trailing limbs. It was blurred but it had eyes, they were open, it was something I knew about, a dead thing, it was dead.' She recovers the past that has been submerged for years, recalling her abortion and affair with a married man. She undergoes an extraordinary and almost mystical metamorphosis. The natural world exerts its hold over her and she enters a barely sane state in which she rejects the trappings of civilisation and declares, in a sentence destined to become one of defining logos of the feminist movement of the 1970s, 'This above all, to refuse to be a victim.'

The Handmaids Tale (1985) is partly an extrapolation of Rachel Carson's *Silent Spring*, attempting to imagine what kind of values might evolve if environmental pollution, rendered most of the human race sterile. It is also a product of debates within the feminist movement in 1970's and early 1980's. Atwood has been very much a part of that movement, but she has never been a mere mouth piece for any group, always insisting on her individual perspectives. She has developed an individual Atwoodian voice that has consistently tested the limits of theory and ideological limitations. Atwood extrapolates outrageously from this point, as is typical of dystopian writers: it is highly unlikely that the puritanical religious right would ever adopt the sexual practices depicted in this novel; but she is trying to argue that patriarchal traditions which value women only as fertility objects can be as demeaning as modern customs which value them as sex objects. She makes clear that this is a reductio ad absurdum, a theoretical exercise designed to stimulate thought about social issues 'rather than a realistic portrait of a probable future by comparing herself to Jonathan Swift., who in *A Modest Proposal* highlighted the hardheartedness of the English in allowing the Irish masses to starve by satirically proposing that they should be encouraged to eat their own children.

The Handmaids Tale was a dystopia, influenced by Orwell's classic 1984. The story is set in the near future U.S.A. in the Republic of Gilead, a state ruled by religious fundamentalism. Birth rates are down in the post-nuclear age of Gilead, so Handmaids—women who are fertile—are designated as sexual slaves to produce offspring for childless couples considered morally fit to raise children. Women in Gilead are not allowed to read, hold jobs, or have money. Narrated by a young Handmaid named Offred—or Of Fred, the man to whom she belongs—the novel is considered a powerful dystopian vision of anti-feminist totalitarianism. The new world of *The Handmaid's Tale* is a woman's world, even though governed, seemingly, and policed by men. Its ethos is entirely domestic, its female population is divided into classes based on household functions, each class clad in a separate colour that instantly identifies the wearer—dull green for the Marthas (house workers); blue for the Wives; red, blue and green stripes for the Econowives (working class); red for the Handmaids (whose function is to bear children to the head of the household, like Bilhah.

In this novel, all the freedom women have gained are revoked and language is forbidden to all but the male elite. The heroine, Offred, is valued for her ovaries, because she is one of the few women whose reproductive systems have survived the chemical pollution and radiation from power plants. The book was filmed and in the film the protagonist becomes an active revolutionary who finally cuts the throat of her owner. However, in Atwood's book, the events are seen through the eyes of the main character whose weapon is irony and keen observation. The tale is interspersed with flashbacks to her earlier life, when she had a husband, Luke, a five year old daughter and was allowed to read. Here, Atwood examines some of the traditional attitudes that are embedded in the thinking of the religious right and which she finds particularly threatening. Atwood's strong point is satire, often hilarious, often very pointed. Humour is scanty in this novel, but it is a satire nonetheless. Most of Atwood's fiction and poetry concerns women's issues on some level, but her novel The Handmaid's Tale has generated the most feminist commentary.

Cat's Eye (1989) is a gripping and haunting book of Atwood making huge demands on one's empathy, compassion and patience for the main character. It exhibits great moments of beauty but also real encounters with evil, apathy, and terror. Atwood's tales resonate with deeply real and intimate characters, and in *Cat's Eye* too, she gets inside the skin of a teenage girl, not only scorned, but tortured by her peers. *Cat's Eye* told of a painter, who explores her childhood memories. Males have plenty of outlets for the aggression that all humans feel at times, but women are allowed no similar outlets for aggression, even if they are stressed. Hence, women take out their aggression on each other, rather than joining together according to Atwood in *Cat's Eye*. For instance, the torture that Cordelia inflicts on Elaine is the torture that her father had inflicted on her. In this novel, Margaret Atwood tells the story of Elaine Risley, an avant garde painter who finds herself reflecting on her tumultuous childhood when she returns to her home town of Toronto for a retrospective art exhibit. The story is told in flashbacks, as the story of her current life as painter, on her second marriage, is told in between the story of her childhood. Two plots run parallel to each other, until the very end when both the past and her present collide. In *Cat's Eye*, the childhood antagonist is Cordelia, the ruthless ringleader of Elaine's small group of friends who Elaine fears but is unable to escape. Cordelia's treatment goes beyond simple playground bullying, but is rather a cunning and manipulative psychological abuse that begins to take its toll on the young Elaine. As she grows up in a state of perpetual anxiety and self depreciation, she eventually comes to confront her relationship with Cordelia. In the process, however, Elaine loses a part of herself to that very same domineering behaviour. As the power dynamics between Elaine & Cordelia shift as they stumble towards adulthood, it becomes clear that though the new Elaine is stronger on the surface; she is perpetually unable to escape the old fears and vulnerabilities of the past. As the older Elaine grapples with the clinging threads of her past, she is forced to come to terms with her identity as woman, a daughter, and an artist. Considered by many an allegorical exploration of the realities confronting individuals at the approach of the twenty-first century, this work reveals the implications of evil and redemption in both a personal and social context. In *Cat's Eye*, as in all her works, Atwood forgoes specific political or moral ideologies, concentrating instead on the emotional and psychological complexities that confront individuals in conflict with society.

Alias Grace (1996) represents Atwood's first venture into historical fiction. It contains a character called Grace Marks, who is based in a real person of the nineteenth century who wasn't only convicted in connection with a double murder, but who was thought, for a couple of years at least, to be mad. Atwood's portrayal of Grace Marks in her novel, owes much to Shakespeare's plays, the madness of writers of the Romantic period like Wordsworth and Sir Walter Scott, the operatic traditions of the nineteenth century, all the way to the real-life Susanna Moodie's view of the real-life Grace Marks in the Toronto Lunatic Asylum in 1851. One of the most notorious women in Canada, Grace was imprisoned in 1843, at the age of sixteen, for almost thirty years as an accomplice to the murder of her employer, Thomas Kinnear and his mistress, the housekeeper Nancy. Her guilt was never incontrovertibly established, but she raised the interest of journalists and researches. Before she was arrested, she had escaped with another servant, James Mc Dermott to the United States. Atwood first found her story from *Life in the Clearings* by Susanna Moodie.

Moodie's treatment of Grace Marks' story reflects her absorption of contemporary ideas. The motive for Grace Marks' double murder according to Moodie was Grace's obsessive passion for her employer, the gentleman Thomas Kinnear, and her jealousy for Kinnear's housekeeper and mistress, Nancy Montgomery. Grace is the sullen temptress and the co-murderer is the manservant James Mc Dermott who is driven by his own lust for Grace. In exchange for sexual favours, James kills Nancy. Later he kills Kinnear as well and threatens to kill Grace too if she interferes. In real life, however Grace and James were convicted and condemned to death. Atwood thus faced a lot of problems because of the sheer number of accounts about Grace Marks—a celebrated figure in her own time because of the hint of transgression and aberration and sex and plain craziness that hung around her. Since Atwood wanted to represent all points of view she devised certain guidelines for herself. In a speech given at Stratford festival in September 1997, she says—"every major element in the book had to be suggested by something in the writing about Grace and her times, however dubious such writing might be; but in the gaps left unfilled, I was free to invent. Since there were a lot of gaps, there is a lot of invention."[9]

In her next novel *The Blind Assassin* (2000) Margaret Atwood has again used the formula of multiple layers of signification to reflect her social image of Canada at the end of the twentieth century. The main story of the novel however is the story of Chase family and it starts like a detective fiction. The narrator Iris Griffen, is an irascible octogenarian in the present day, with little to do to pass the time but reminisce about her youth and her family, now in decline but once wealthy industrialists who dominated their small Canadian hometown. Most prominent in her thoughts is her younger sister Laura Chase, now renowned as the author of the classic novel *The Blind Assassin*, which Iris arranged to have published posthumously after Laura drove off a bridge in 1945. The first words of the novel are—"Ten days after the war ended my sister Laura drove a car off a bridge."[10] There were two witnesses: a retired lawyer and a bank teller who had claimed to have seen the whole thing. "They said that Laura had turned the car sharply and deliberately" (3). The problem is presented in a form of a who done it. The story that comes out in snatches is the story of two families—the Chase family and the Griffen family. The protagonist is the daughter of Captain Normal Chase whose father had started the first button factory in the town called Post Ticonderoga. Captain Chase had been wounded in the First World War and became a hero. After coming back he inherited the business of his father and expanded it during the period of affluence in the twenties. He became the most respectable citizen of the town and lived in a substantial mansion in the town with his two daughters Iris and Laura. Then came the depression with its strikes and lockouts and labour disturbances. Captain Chase was a benevolent man and tried to save his enterprises and help his workers. However, the inevitable hand of forces beyond his control made his position untenable. He was forced to ally with Richard Griffen, a big capitalist and greater entrepreneur who in fact took over his factories and merged them in his own business. One of the results of this financial arrangement was the marriage of Iris to Richard Griffen who she did not love. The whole transactions appear like the sale of wives and children by the aristocrats of Zycronites to save themselves from becoming bankrupt.

The novel within the novel is the story of Iris Chase Griffen who develops love for Alex Thomas who though he belonged to a non-descript family remembering that of the working class had developed expertise in certain cultural accomplishment like poetry, etc. He, therefore, by his merit enters the membership of the superior class. Consequently Laura, the younger sister had developed platonic idealistic love for this working class hero. The story of the love triangle between Iris, Laura and Alex Thomas is very much like an ordinary detective fiction. However, it also becomes a prototype of the forces underlying the social establishment in the twentieth century.

Life Before Man (1979), a bleak exploration of contemporary sexual machinations, ends on an enigmatic note that is both distressing and strangely hopeful. In the novel Atwood attempts an archaeology of the propulsion to love, excavating a parochial world of despairing confusion, self-centred motive and romantic backstabbing, that is all too recognizable. *Life Before Man* presented a harsh view of human life in which marriage is a vanishing way of life. Elizabeth and Nate are a married couple foundering to preserve their decaying marriage until the suicide of Chris, Elizabeth's lover, illuminates the futility of their efforts. Nate rushes to the arms of Lesje, Elizabeth's timid co-worker at the Natural History Museum's Palaeontology department, in retaliation, while Elizabeth fights to regain a modicum of control over both her husband and her crumbling self-esteem. Their adolescent daughters, wrenched by the upset of the divorce, become pawns in Nate, Elizabeth, and Lesje's ensuing struggle to redraw family and battle lines. Atwood draws wry and witty parallels between the lives of her characters and those of the dinosaurs that Elizabeth and Lesje seek to immortalize in their museum exhibits. She reveals the strata of humour and pathos that make-up modern familial and romantic love, all the while reminding us of the constant threat of imminent extinction.

Atwood's latest novel, *Oryx and Crake* (2003), short-listed for the 2003 Man Booker Prize for Fiction, is a cautionary tale set in a future in which genetic science, climate change and social inequality have laid waste to civilization. Featuring a male protagonist for the very first time, the novel is once more a puzzle in which the reader spends a great deal of time unsure of what is happening. *Oryx and Crake* was a love triangle set in the near future world, where human beings have all but destroyed the planet. This dystopian fiction expatiates on the searing issues within the environment and bio-technology and rivets on an endless transformation of our sense perceptions. Some reviewers called it science fiction but Atwood herself considered it speculative fiction. In an article, Margaret Atwood has herself differentiated between these two terms. "If you're writing about the future and you aren't doing forecast journalism, you'll probably be writing something people will call either science fiction or speculative fiction. I like to make a distinction between science fiction proper and speculative fiction. For me, the science fiction label belongs on books with things in them we can't yet do, such as going through a wormhole in space to another universe; and speculative fiction means a work that employs the means already to hand, such as DNA identification and credit cards, and that takes place on Planet Earth. But the terms are fluid. Some use speculative fiction as an umbrella covering science fiction and all its hyphenated forms—science fiction fantasy, and so forth—and others choose the reverse.... I have written two works of speculative fiction: *The Handmaid's Tale* and *Oryx and Crake*."[11]

In both these works Atwood has evoked a nightmarish world that is reminiscent of Dante's vision of hell. It is mournful, bleak and infernal and in typical Atwood style, it is interspersed with macabre humour. In *Oryx and Crake* Atwood's pilgrim in hell is Snowman, the only human to have survived a biological viral cataclysm. The story opens with Snowman (who was formerly known as Jimmy) having been forced to become arboreal by circumstances. He lives in trees and in shelters of junk, roaming the beaches and picnic grounds of Former Park—where fungi sprout from rotting picnic tables—scavenging for food. His only companions are some humanoids, the crakers. These are gentle and beautiful creations of Jimmy's old, half-mad scientist friend Crake (who was earlier Glenn)—"each one naked, each one perfect, each one a different skin colour chocolate, rose, tea, butter, cream, honey—but each with green eyes. Crake's aesthetic."[12] Freed from their experimental lab the crakers also live near the beach. They eat nothing but grass, leaves and roots; their emotions have been efficiently programmed. Anything deemed inessential, from facial hair to sexual lust has been done away with. To them, the man they know as Snowman is a demigod or a prophet. Unable to bear the harsh sunlight covers himself in a ghostly bed sheet and a grotesque one eyed broken sunglass. For the crakers, the real gods are Crake, whom they have never seen, and his girlfriend Oryx, whom they have. The crakers listen to Snowman telling his stories about Oryx and Crake and, along with the reader, await their return. Thus, is born, a religious myth.

Thus, although Atwood's work deals with murder, emotional cruelty and religious totalitarianism she is never crass, sensational or transparently provocative. Like Graham Greene, she writes intelligent and beautifully crafted books that are also compulsively readable. Her work is profoundly human, and although she is often seen as a feminist writer, Atwood like Greene is a humanist. She places her characters in complex, challenging situations, which allow her to ruminate on the way we live and act towards one another. Moving with deft ease from the particular to the universal, Atwood creates female protagonists who are forced to remake themselves, to achieve a courage and self-reliance in their attitudes and relationships with others and the world around them. Although, she writes of pain and suffering and the essential cruelty at the heart of human behaviour, her ever present sense of the absurd rescues her from an overt and distressing bleakness.

With her work published in fifteen countries, Margaret Atwood has achieved an international reputation. She has truly furthered Canada as a nation, postmodernist thinking, and feminist achievements and has undoubtedly assisted in supporting the development of an imaginative literary future. She transcends traditional genre, gender and national labels and she continuously "surprises her readers with ongoing experimentalism and radical challenges to contemporary social myths and fashionable ideologies."[13] An icon in Canada, Atwood remains "one of the leading literary luminaries, a national heroine of the arts, the rara avis of Canadian letters"[14] and "one of the most intelligent and talented writers to set herself the task of deciphering life in the twenty-first century."[15]

NOTES AND REFERENCES

1. Howells Anne, Coral: Modern Novelist: Margaret Atwood. New York: St. Martin's Press, 1996, p. 2.
2. Rosenberg, Jerome: Margaret Atwood. Boston: Twayne Publishers, 1984, p. 15.
3. Howells Anne, Coral: Modern Novelist: Margaret Atwood. New York: St. Martin's Press, 1996, p. 19.

4. Klemesrud, Judy reported in *The New York Times.*
5. Atwood, Margaret: *The Edible Woman*, p. 56.
6. Laurence, Margaret: "Quarry," Critical Essays on Margaret Atwood. Ed. Judith McCombs (Boston: Hall, 1988), p. 47.
7. Rao, Eleonora: 'Strategies for Identity: The Fiction of Margaret Atwood.' New York: Peter Lang Publishing, 1993, p. xxiv.
8. Howells Anne, Coral: Modern Novelist: Margaret Atwood. New York: St. Martin's Press, 1996, p. 161.
9. Atwood, Margaret: In a speech given at Stratford festival in September 1997.
10. Atwood, Margaret: The Blind Assassin (London: Virago Press, 2001), p. 3. The page references within the text are to this edition.
11. Atwood, Margaret: 'Why we need SF.' *The Hindustan Times*, June 24, 2005.
12. Atwood, Margaret: Oryx and Crake, Virago Press, 2004, p. 8.
13. Howell's Anne, Coral: Modern Novelist: Margaret Atwood. New York: St. Martin's Press, 1996, p. 161.
14. Lipinski, Ann Marie in the Chicago Tribune.
15. The Vogue Magazine.

'In Search of an Authentic Moment': An Ecofeministic Reading of Inez Baranay's *Neem Dreams*

8

> "The goal of ecofeminist environmental ethics is to develop theories and practices concerning humans and the natural environment that are not male-biased and that provide a guide to action in the prefeminist present."
>
> —*Karen Warren*: Ecofeminist Philosophy, 2000

Throughout the course of the last century, Australian literature has undergone some momentous changes, but none as great as the changes that have resulted from growing multiculturalism over just the last decades. There are some important titles which argue not only the existence of a contemporary multicultural literature, but that the emergence of this new literature has caused us to re-read the older literature in order to reassess past assumptions concerning a homogenous Australian identity. Asserting a multicultural identity calls for a consciousness of the multiple identities that together make national cultural ethos, a resistance to invisibility and silencing by hegemonic powers. But more important, it calls for openness, tolerance and cosmopolitanism, a readiness to engage with other spheres of life. "Multiculturism" says. Parekh is, "best understood neither as a political doctrine with a programmatic content nor as a philosophical school with a distinct theory of man's place in the world but as a perspective or a way of viewing human life."[1]

Though more of a fringe writer, Inez Baranay is Australian and Australian literature in English is here to stay. It has come of age in patterns similar to Indian writing in English. Born in Italy of Hungarian parents, Inez Baranay has never been troubled by any racial memories, though she has experienced the trauma of being 'the other' in Australia, the 'otherness' being thrust upon her by the white Australian natives. Quite at ease with this displacement, stemming from her very birth, Inez is as much concerned with diverse issues relating to nature cure; multiculturism and transculturism; assimilation and appropriation; tradition and modernity as with the quest for self-expression.

Baranay had being toying with the idea of writing a novel in India for quite sometime. It was in 1993, at Cairns, that she came across neem products, and at the same time there arose the controversy about neem tree patents which provided Inez with a trope for her novel set in India. From *A Passage to India*, the 'books about India' have been more accurately books about the representation of India. In *Neem Dreams* Baranay too 'weaves a new romance about India, its people and places'. Forster's novel opens with—"the toddy palms and neem trees and mangoes and pepul that were hidden behind the bazaars now become visible and in their turn hide the bazaars."[2] In her article Aspects of Two Novels: E.M. Forster's *A Passage to India* and *Neem Dreams*, talking of the influence of *A Passage to India* on her novel *Neem Dreams*, Baranay says—"What becomes visible: what becomes hidden: this might be seen as a theme of both *A Passage to India* and *Neem Dreams*."[3] With an amazing perception of India, Baranay's eye for detail is remarkable—nothing escapes her keen observation—from power politics to population control, from religious sentiments to communal violence Baranay keeps shifting from Sydney to Darwin, to New York to India's metros. Though the narratives focus keeps shifting, the novel centres on the neem project.

As she says—"The neem is a miracle tree...it dates back to dreamtime. I chose it as the leitmotif of my novel as it is a symbol for India."[4] Set in Southern India in 1995, the four characters in *Neem Dreams*, find their lives intertwined with the fate of India's mystic and pharmaceutical neem tree and East converges with the West as the author explores the endangering effects of globalization on a time honoured culture. An Australian,

Indian, British and American, all struggle to make the best use of the miraculous neem tree but instead encounter corporate greed, environmental disaster and political villainy in Baranay's *Neem Dreams*. *Neem Dreams* is "about cultural exchange, it's about how politics and myths, as well as personal products are made, it's about how globalization works to perpetuate the powerlessness of the powerless."[5] Thus, *Neem Dreams* is an amalgamation of various multiculturist issues concerning feminism, local politics, national politics, gay issues, globalization and environmental issues. Using the stream of consciousness technique, Baranay reveals the thought processes of her various characters from different cultures.

Set in Sydney in the late 70's, Inez Baranay's witty, satirical first novel—*Between Careers* (1989) takes a close look at the moral values of both the ancient profession and of more conventional ways of living. The novel takes us into the life of a classy call girl and looks at how sex functions in contemporary society. Her next novel, *The Saddest Pleasure* (1989) has three parts—the first part is travel writing, the "saddest pleasure," of the title, the second part of the book is "stories about self and sex, the third part is a novella in three parts—fragrant with eastern experience, bitter edged with a relentless contemplated life. *Pagan* (1990) offers a highly intelligent analysis of the themes of Australia's twentieth century cultural history. Baranay skilfully brings the full weight of historical perspective to her account of the 1950's antipodean happenings. On the simplest level *Pagan* fictionally recreates the life of Rosaleen Norton who attracted the attention of the media during the 1950's. *The Edge of Bali* (1992) is made up of three related short stories about three unrelated tourists—Nelson, Marla and Tyler. All three are searching all unsure of whether they should be in Bali or where they'll go next. It is full of contemporary dilemmas and deals with the phenomenon of tourism. *Rascal Rain* (1994) is a valuable sociological document on the appalling mistreatment of women and offers a graphic look at the beauty and splendour of the country and amid the savagery, a story of warm relationship of black and white alike. *Sheila Power* (1997) tells of a heroine who is a very rich film producer and a prominent identity who is about to start work on what will be the crowning achievement of her spectacular career.

In the contemporary explosion of diversity in the world, Baranay voices her various dilemmas and concerns and carries on a "conversation of respect with another culture"[6]—She says, 'It is a positive aspect of globalization that we live in hybrid cultures'. Baranay has travelled to India many times since 1980 and recently her later trips to India have included a period as writer in-residence at the University of Madras and a Literature Residency granted by Asia link Baranay is not Indian but has visited the country nine times, immersing herself in the culture so completely that when *Neem Dreams* was published in India, the novel received widespread critical acclaim for its pitch-perfect portrayal. *Neem Dreams* is a dazzling portrait of a complicated country and a thought-provoking look at the price of globalization. Baranay uncannily conjures splashes of Indian reactions, attitudes or relationships with as much authenticity as she does the American, Australian and British ethos. Coming as she does from Hungarian stock, Australia was not always the country of her mind. She discovers her identity in her sojourns in distant lands, as back home her name was always scrutinized for its non-Anglo Celtic sounds. Lack of tradition at home took her to ancient cultures in Europe and Asia. Almost all her fiction includes a travel writer following the use of a journalistic style as spiritual pastiche. Her passages to Indonesia, to Papua New Guinea and to India all evoke an intense sense of place. As she herself remarked that, 'As an Australian, a Westerner, choosing Indian settings and themes (feeling, of course, that they chose me), and as a writer who has found her material outside of Australia before, I was familiar with the troubles that arise out of issues of representation and identity.'

Baranay's *Neem Dreams* breaks new grounds in its attempt to capture the spirit of India through one of her most sacred objects, the neem. She explores the attractions and frustrations of the different perspectives her men and women present to each other against the contemporary material of neem, its patenting and marketing, globalization, victimization and unfair trade practices. Her pro-Indian voice sees in globalization and the transnational capitalism, a threat to the very subsistence base of indigenous cultivators. Having risen above her feminine voice and foreign perspective, she strikes a neutral unbiased language as far as basic values and issues are concerned. Baranay brings a different order of scholarship to her exploration of the landscape of cultural resilience in *Neem Dreams*, where she consigns her protagonists to anchor in India, as the subject is the valuable neem that is nurtured and used by Indians. In an interview with Kausalya Santhanam, she reveals how the idea of neem as the leit motif of the novel came to her—"It came as an organizing principle. I had heard of neem in Queensland where I live and which is hit and dry like Chennai; there is an NGO called Neem Peace that promotes the use of neem. The name appeared to me as the perfect image"[7] (Santhanam, 2003: 4).

Baranay wishes to create a new surface-discourse, to weave a new romance about India—its people and places. India in *Neem Dreams* is not just an exotic backdrop; it becomes the battleground of a new, global Mahabharata of the human race—a war fought largely by committed ecofeminists, concerned with the future of Mother Earth and of the whole human race. *Neem Dreams* reworks "the myth of the neem into the ethos of a post-colonial India—an India in which her culture and tradition is forced to come to term with her progressive 'present', a dreaming that reaches out to India warning her of multinational designs, of her own conniving politicians and of her headlong rush towards globalization."[8] It's a novel about globalization, capital rapacity, environmental annihilation and political villainy.

Baranay explores the attractions and frustrations of the different perspectives her men and women present to each other against the contemporary material of neem, its patenting and marketing, globalization, victimization and unfair trade practices. An Australian, Indian, British and American all struggle to make the best use of India's medicinal neem tree, but instead encounter corporate greed, environmental disaster and political villainy in Inez Baranay's *Neem Dreams*. They meet through travel, sex, death, shopping, gaydar, rumour and the sudden affinities of strangers. Baranay's pro-Indian voice sees in globalization and the trans-national capitalism a threat to the very subsistence base of indigenous cultivators. On being asked if she felt strongly about globalization and patents, she says—"Globalization is the predominant symbol of our times. In my previous book, *Bali's Edge*, I had touched on ecology. But it is specifically introduced in *Neem Dreams*. In the mid-1990s, when I began writing the novel, there was a controversy over the patent issue and the appropriation of traditional knowledge systems. I thought it was an ideal way of exploring the other themes in the novel" (Santhanam, 2003: 4).

In a fictional world that moves from Sydney to South India, her characters overcome personal loss in their quest for a deeper meaning in life, Their personal quests are related to the "miracle tree" of neem as they move towards a realisation that encompasses the self and the politics of international trade relations. Using the neem tree as a central trope, "an organizing principle," Inez Baranay weaves into her fiction ecofeministic concerns with a global system that is at once capitalist and exploitative, patriarchal and imperialistic. As Maria Miles and Vandana Shiva explain: "This system emerged, is built upon and maintains itself through the colonisation of women, of 'foreign' peoples and their lands and of nature, which it is gradually destroying [...]. Everywhere women were the first to protest against environmental destruction [...]. Science and technology were not gender neutral, and in common with many other women, we began to set: that the relationship of exploitative dominance between man and nature (shaped by [...] modern science since the 16th century) and the exploitative and oppressive relationship between men and women that prevails in most patriarchal societies, even modern industrial ones, were closely connected"[9] (Miles et al. 2-3).

Coming from the land of dreaming, Inez presents a composite set of personae—Andy, Pandora, Jade and Patrick in the novel, on a probing mission to India. All the characters have descended on Indian soil, armed with their separate mission but it is the exotica of the East that welds together and transforms them into believers of the proprieties of Neem Tree. *Neem Dreams* brings together people in an international post modern terrain where all cultures meet in the shade of the neem tree. The novel is full of Utopian as well as dystopian representations of the multicultural. Baranay's characters portrayed with uncompromising frankness, strive to find meaning and purpose for their lives in the shade of the neem tree which in the novel, symbolizes the innate strength of the Orient-India. The meeting of all these characters with varying professional backgrounds and personal traumas take place under the canopy of the healing Neem Tree.

The novels' four central characters—Pandora, Meenakshi, Andy and Jade come together as a result of capricious twists of fate: an article in a magazine, a chance encounter at a cafe, and finally a community project in a village centred on a factory producing neem products. The neem tree is a symbol of spirit of multiculturism—empathetic, inclusive and ultimately healing. It spans cultures, draws people and their destinies towards itself. From ancient to modern India—to the west—neem begins to drive market forces. Four individuals spurred on by neem dreams meet up with each other in India. For, Pandora, an ecofeminist from Sydney, India holds a promise of a sustainable grassroots project related to the neem seeds and promoted by an Indian woman, Meenakshi, educated in America and back in India by choice. Pandora leaves Sydney with its typical western metropolitan chaos along with her merry past—the sick father, the separation of her parents, and the subsequent mental breakdown of her brother—and arrives to India to provide news coverage for a scientific magazine. After meeting Meenakshi, the person, who conceived the project. Pandora is impressed and is so inspired by the innate strengths of the rural Indians that she becomes greatly involved in the project and almost succeeds in realizing her dream of an ideal village product involving neem cultivation. Jade, another Australian finds an outlet for her artistic sensibility in procuring Indian artefacts for a New York retailer who has come to procure authentic skincare potions made from neem—neem gel, neem lotion, neem bath beads, etc.... Jade with her upbeat manner is determined to make the best of her stay in India. Her attempt to strike a deal with Meenakshi's factory does not materialize because the neem project was yet to be completed. Andy, the promising English lawyer, in search of a cure for his satanic virus contacted possibly out of dark gay experiences. What apparently seemed to be incurable in his native Europe seems to have a hope, a remedy in India. Having come to India to scatter the ashes of his partner Patrick, in the holy Ganges, he seems to get spiritual comfort in India which had eluded him so far in his own home. Witnessing the people washing in the river along with corpses and ashes in sacred Varanasi, he marvels at the Indian immunity and there in he sees his hope of recovery and salvation—perhaps, he can find a new cure for his condition in the leaves of the neem. Author and coordinator of the neem project is Meenakshi, a young Indian woman, well travelled and educated abroad, recently married to an idealistic young man who has taken over his family's small neem factory, which becomes the centre of both hindutva fundamentalist agitation and the plans of the transnational cooperation that has the most neem patents. Meenakshi struggles to keep alive both her marriage and the neem project against the odds of a burdened past, male chauvinism, and political corruption. Constantly haunted by her experience in America of being jilted by a white man who is 'a serial dumper of younger women of what they call other races,' she seeks to find meaning in being a successful entrepreneur and in successfully fulfilling the neem project. Meenakshi's Indian husband is understanding and helpful, but she confronts opposition in the person of Dinesh, the incarnation of wily politician and generic greed. The neem project promised to give each of the four what they had been looking for—Meenakshi needed something worth while, something more than her marriage to sustain here, Pandora longed to be "an instrument of justice and revenge," Andy needed a miracle cure and Jade wanted source skin care products for an exclusive New York store.

Their personal quests are related to the miracle tree of neem as they move towards a realisation that encompasses the self and the politics of international trade relations. In a recent interview in the Hindu, Baranay recalls that when she began the novel in the mid-1990, "there was a controversy over the patent issue and the appropriation of traditional knowledge systems; I thought it was an ideal way of exploring the other themes in the novel" (Santhanam, 2003: 4). Thus, *Neem Dreams* is an inventive mixture of feminism, gay issues, local politics, Indian history, national politics, global economic situation and environmental issues. "It is as much a tirade against MNCs and First world myopia as it is against Hindutva, sexism and Indian masculinity.... There is outrage in every page, enough to ignite the passion of the droopiest of lyrics, and a palpable sense of mourning for lost traditions and ancient wisdom. It is fiercely philosophical, written in paragraphs of poetic prose...the book is about life, journeys and that intoxicating affinity of spirit we sometimes find in total strangers."[10]

Meenakshi tries to educate and empower the local women sangams through a village project that enables these women to gather and store quality neem seeds through simple training and the use of indigenous materials like gunny sacks to protect the fruit as it falls. However, it is not the women at the sangams who rebel against the manufacture of neem products for pest control, fertilizers, medicines and cosmetics but the tea drinking men at the Jolly Tea House who first voice their protest against the misuse of their miracle tree. They are aware of the biopiracy of MNCs such as W R Kind (with its connotations that may imply Wreck India) and its local dealings with Asogram, an Indian agrochemical company. People in villages rely on their age-old uses of neem that has always been freely available, but so-called development will ensure an end to this. The GATT and the WTO do not recognise the rights of these "first scientists," the experiments of the farmers and the housewives, which "took place before the change that brought the need for protocols, claims and attributions, the legalities of copyrights and patents, ownership of knowledge. They took place before the active ingredient of neem, azadarachtin was isolated, identified, named, made the basis of acceptable proofs"[11] (*Neem Dreams*, 70-75). What people once got free they would now have to pay a high price for. Appeals against such patents will prove futile as pointed out by Andy the lawyer. His firm and many others have already worked out strategies against such appeals: They're trying to patent a tree! cry voices crazed with outrage. You believe in ecology, you are on the side of spirituality, you are a champion of tradition (most especially the tradition of others, perhaps with good reason). Your credentials—your credence demand this rottenness is widely realised. Face it, "they" will commit any atrocity for the sake of profit and glory; "they" scorn the integrity and authenticity of age-old practices. Leave the people's tree alone. Let the people show us its correct deployment (pp. 71-72).

It is the growing resentment of the farmers which makes Pandora and Andy realize that whatever they try to do in turn to stop this biopiracy such as her article in Lifesciences or his knowledge of international company law can never have the same effect as that of a people's rising. However, even this mass resentment is ineffectual as wily Indian politicians looking to amass personal wealth divert attention to communal problems, initiated by their controlling interests. Prashant's uncle is the "Sitting Member" who has signed agreements with W R Kind for the mass production and processing of neem seeds. Wanting to ensure an electorate, he jumps on the Hindutva bandwagon, making sure that trusted Muslim factory workers are sacked, knowing fully well that this would spark off communal riots. Prashant has no say in the running of this factory as Dinesh; the Sitting Member's son provides the funds for Meenakshi's neem project.

The outrage of the farmers against the WTO is rather volatile: "We must demand India's withdrawal from this organization. It allows the transnational to dictate the rules of trade. It is undemocratic and accounts to no one. The WTO is our brutal enemy. The WTO will kill us unless we kill it. The WTO is a new form of colonialism" (pp. 242-43).

The struggle for Indian independence has become one of the twentieth centuries most resonant stories, at its centre is the figure of Mahatma Gandhi, one of the countries most outstanding personalities. Despite choosing India as a back drop for his novel *A Passage to India*, Foster does not mention Gandhi as he felt that inclusion of Gandhi might have turned his novel into something else. Baranay's *Neem Dreams,* however, resonates with Gandhi's legacy, with the mid nineteen ninety demonstration against the transnationals explicitly having a historical connection with Gandhian politics of Swadeshi and Swaraj of the independence movement. Jade, gazes at a statue of Gandhi in her intention to find a landmark to locate an air-conditioned coffee shop and observes, 'they mocked him as a half naked fakir, his body is now a sacred text. He ensures the world's headlines cannot resist these brilliantly succinct gestures—a handful of salt gathered from the sea at the end of a long march, the spinning wheel that makes the simple cloth which is all he wears to Buckingham Palace. ...he is the icon of a universal philosopher saint.'

Using the neem branches as a symbol of their protest they demand: "Quit India." The protestors call for a "second freedom movement" (p. 243), another Quit India slogan addressed to W R Kind. What the Charkha was to the Indian Independence Movement—the Swadeshi Movement the neem is to the new swadeshi movement against neocolonialism. "As Gandhiji's spinning wheel once stood for swadeshi, or self-rule—the days the 'British' ruled India, so the neem branch is our symbol of self-sufficiency, indigenous wisdom and self-rule. Swadeshi for our times" (p. 243). The people realize that they cannot trust politicians or political parties and call for direct action. They know that mass production of neem seeds would affect the biodiversity of the region: "Natural habitats are being destroyed. Traditional agriculture and other knowledge systems are being destroyed. Transnational are allowed to patent the fruits of traditional knowledge. Local development is undermined, poor countries penalized, inequality increased, We are all being converted into objects of consumerism" (pp. 243-45). The most alarming fallout of this new biopiracy is that "new classes of poor people" are created by rich countries.

The echoes of the sensitive and the volatile mood resulting as an aftermath of the demolition of the Babri Masjid leads to communal clashes among the workers of Meenakshi's factory.

Faced with the trying consequences of the communal clashes Meenakshi finds solace in ritual. Jade, the Americanized—

Australian, frustrated by her failure to make any business deals for Neem Care, decides to launch her new "Made in India" campaign, complete with advertisement gimmicks, side shows and the "spiritual luxury" of yoga, when she gets back, but her Karma turns her into a legend. Charmed by the miniature clay Ganesh given to her by her hippie friends, she goes in search of the craftsman and is caught up in a frenzied crowd proceeding to see the milk-drinking miracle Ganesh. A stampede, a flash of red and Jade disappears, never to resurface.

The increasing awareness of the rural population about the General Agreement on Tariffs and Trade and the corporate patenting of seeds and plants including the neem tree, Pandora and Andy commit suicide by setting themselves aflame as neem warriors in order to attract the due attention of the world. Their funeral pyre will ensure that the neem tree will continue to be part of life and ritual, that tradition will continue and globalization will ensure that "there's no difference between other people's causes and your own" (p. 275).

Baranay's exploration of the ecofeministic issues describes in her characteristic subtle style, the invisible global politics that have created a whole new value system based on market economy and a consumerist society. Her fiction reunites men and women in the common aim of sustaining life and preserving our Earth Mother. "I do believe that nativity does not define us. As human beings we are capable of understanding each other and literature makes this possible" (Santhanam, 2003: 4). Her passage to India in *Neem Dreams* is an attempt to bring about a symbiosis between nature and society. The book can be read as an ecological statement. In Baranays own words, "the final image is of the tree—everlasting and abiding" (Santhanam, 2003-4). Her neem warriors combat corporate vultures. As a spiritual feminist, she celebrates the sacredness of the life force. She refuses to be a "future-eater," to use another Australian Timothy Flannery's striking title of his book.

Thus, Baranay takes ecofeminism beyond mere academic discourse as she re-imagines the present in the context of the past. Baranay's *Neem Dreams* describes her ecological concerns as well as her multicultural experience. As she herself sums up: "The whole green check-list, this project has got it all-community based economics, sustainable future focus, feminism, personal and global responsibility, and of course grassroots democracy, in a nonrestrictive sense of democracy. Non-violence. Social justice. Whatever they want. Green for days"[12] (Baranay, 132-33).

Baranay's novel can best be summarized thus: "*Neem Dreams* is about Westerners in India, its about cultural exchange, its about how politics and myths, as well as personal product are made, its about how globalisation works to perpetuates the powerlessness about the power less...."[13]

NOTES AND REFERENCES

1. Parekh, Bhikhu: "What is Multiculturalism" http://www.indiaseminar.com/1999/484/484%20parekh.htm 1.
2. Baranay, Inez in an article 'Aspects of Two Novels: E.M. Forster's *A Passage to India* and *Neem Dreams*.'
3. *Ibid.*
4. Baranay, Inez remarks in *The Hindu*: Speaking through her work, dated 2nd November 2003.
5. Baranay, Inez in an article 'Aspects of Two Novels: E.M. Forster's *A Passage to India* and *Neem Dreams*.'
6. Hill, Patrick J.: "Multiculturalism: The Crucial Philosophical and Organizational Issues." Change. July/Aug. 1991, pp. 38-47.
7. Santhanam, Kausalya: "Speaking Through Her Work: An Interview With Inez Baranay." *The Hindu*, Sunday, Nov. 2, 2003: 4. All quotations by Kausalya Santhanam are from this interview.
8. *The Sunday Pioneer*, Book Review section, 14th September 2003.
9. Miles, Maria and Vandana Shiva: Ecofeminism. London: Fernwood Publication, 1993.
10. Devarajan, Padmini: "Unbiased Perspective." *The Hindu*. Sunday, Nov. 2, 2003: 4.
11. Baranay, Inez: *Neem Dreams*. New Delhi: Rupa, 2003, pp. 70-75. All quotations have been taken from this edition.
12. Baranay, Inez: "Indian Specific" Australian Author, 33.2 (August 2001), p. 34.
13. Baranay, Inez in an article 'Aspects of Two Novels: E.M. Forster's *A Passage to India* and *Neem Dreams*.'

'Exploration of Womanhood and the Affirmation of Self' in the Writings of Alice Munro

> Feminism has as its goal to give every woman "the opportunity of becoming the best that her natural faculties make her capable of."
>
> —*Millicent Garrett Fawcett*, 1878

Till the post-war decades, Canadian literature was viewed as an auxiliary to British and American writing—dealing mostly with extremely typical Canadiana such as outdoors, animals or events in Canadian history. For the most of late nineteenth and early twentieth century the prevailing pattern in Canadian fiction was the portrayal and celebration of wilderness—a portrayal that denied the new society's increasingly urban face. The second half of the twentieth century, saw an intermingling of cultures and social transformation as communications improved. It led to the emergence of a distinctively Canadian multiculturalism making way for a literature that challenged and rethought the ways, in which a nation can accommodate that plurality. Out of this has come the major Canadian literary theme: for the survival and search for identity. It is against this backdrop that the women writers in Canada, had been battling to discover identity to advance the survival of individuals. It seems no accident then that woman writers were a major force in Canadian fiction and Alice Munro remains one of its major voices.

Alice Munro is that rare Canadian whose fame abroad matches the admiration she enjoys in Canada. Celebrated for her superb evocation of place, the elegance and naturalness of her style and her ability to reveal seemingly effortlessly, the subtle, shifting emotional lives of her character, in stories that range widely across time and place, Munro has established herself as a major voice among fiction writers. The subject matter of Munro's stories has clearly developed from her own experience. Her stories are not autobiographical, but she does claim an emotional reality for her characters that are drawn from her own life. Her life experiences of depression and idealism of adolescence, of discovering sex, leaving home, falling in love, getting married and having children, getting divorced—all inform the fiction she creates. Munro acknowledges the autobiographical influences on many of her stories which are most often framed as episodic recollections that chronicle the emotional development of adolescent and adult female characters.

Widely regarded as Canada's best writer of short stories, Alice Munro has consistently produced work in which precise social observation and penetrating psychological insight are complemented by an unerring instinct for exactly the right form of expression. Often referred to as a regional writer because her fiction frequently centres on the culture of rural Ontario, Munro credits the short stories writers of the American South particularly Eudora Welty and Flannery O'Connor, with shaping her fictional perspective. Like many of the best short story writers, Munro is fully steeped in localism and vernacular, though her stories are not as violent as Flannery O'Connor's, or as bleak as Raymond Carver's, hers is one that shines a light on unpleasant truths, but ones that reward us with understanding. Munro has an obvious grasp of human relationships and the emphasis is on choice—everybody is free to make choices. Many writers have tried to achieve a distinction by writing about exotic situations but (the Canadian author) Munro has chosen to write about very ordinary events in the lives of very ordinary women. Although Munro's characters are all notable for their ordinariness, in the stories, *The Connection, The Stone in the Field, The Turkey Season* and *Visitors,* this very ordinariness, is so extreme, that it becomes almost exotic, by the standards of most fiction. In Munro's work, the mundane is juxtaposed with the fantastic, and she often relies on paradox and irony to expose meanings that lie below the surface common place occurrences.

Nearly all of Alice Munro's fiction is set in South Western Ontario, but her reputation as a brilliant short story writer goes far beyond the borders of her native Canada. Her accessible moving stories offer immediate pleasures while simultaneously exploring human complexities in what appear to be effortless anecdotal re-creations of everyday life. Her fictional world ranges across the breadth of Canada from Ontario to British Columbia but most readers agree that her Ontario stories, rooted as they are in her own formative past, represent more evocative settings experienced in childhood and recollected by perceptive adult memory. Alice Munro examines the world of small-town or suburban Canada primarily through the framework of the family, and the emotions she explores are potent. Against the threat of routine and confinement, particularly for women and children, Munro posits a hope for escape in nearly everyone of the eight stories in this volume. Repressed memory, the dark past, and neglected desire (sexual or aesthetic) threaten to tear apart the well-woven fabric of unendurable daily life. Strong feelings are often provoked by an exceptional event, one that seems uncharacteristic of the community, and even "exterior". The event, the outside world itself, is seldom understood, but it is disruptive. The stories communicate a sense of considerable amounts of time passing, of the changes that happen to an individual or a family over decades, and the lag of consciousness in catching up with these changes. The strength of her fiction arises partially from its vivid sense of regional focus, most of her stories set in Huron County as well as from her sense of the narrator as the intelligence through which the world is articulated. Her interest in small town setting has been compared to the American writers of the rural south. As in the writing of William Faulkner and Flannery O'Conner, her characters often confront deep rooted customs and traditions. It is a different matter, however, that the reaction of Munro's characters is less intense than their Southern counterparts. Her female characters are more complex than the male characters that capture the essence of Everyman.

That Munro is a feminist is unarguable, but one that fights small battles instead of loud ones. It is in the small moments, artless and unguarded, that one tastes Munro's bitter world, but one that has an after taste that being familiar is ultimately comforting. In general, her short stories are about everyday life and quiet desperate struggles that go on in ordinary lives, and are thematically bound by sense of disappointment. In all these stories we have female protagonists whose lives have not evolved the way they had expected or desired. "The women in Alice Munro's stories, like the men in the fiction of John Updike, find themselves perpetually torn between two poles: between domesticity and independence; between familial roots and freedom; between a yearning for connection and a more solitary sense of themselves as outsiders. In tracing the choices her heroines make and the fallout of their decisions"[1]—says Michiko Kakutani.

Munro's protagonists tend to be women of her own generation who found themselves caught between traditional gender roles and new possibilities in the wake of the "sexual revolution." They battle against their own desire to accept the apparent security of conventional relationships with men. But Munro's stories undermine the apparent security of conventional relationships with men. But Munro's stories undermine the apparent stability of traditional sexual relationships and chart their fragmentation. Her early writing especially is preoccupied with the politics of self-location, as her narrators struggle to make sense of their own lives in the context of their restrictive rural environment. They also seek to understand the relationship between the public sphere and a secret world of desire that threatens to become known and disrupt social order. Her fiction is pervaded by the sense of mysterious metaphysical world lurking just underneath the surface of everyday existence. Munro's concern with women's lives, exploration of geography and identity, and evocation of the mysterious character of everyday life are the other attributes of her writing. Munro's stories insist upon exploring economic and cultural specificity of this milieu; and she has sought to capture the rhythm and idiom of the region. At the same time, Munro's stories evince a deep scepticism about the right to fictionalize. Her writings are marked by a stark refusal of sentimentalism about rural communities; for her home is a "country we did not know we loved."

Her first book *Dance of the Happy Shades* (1968) meditates on themes of strangeness and secrecy in everyday, which would continue to dominate her writing. It won Canada's highest literary prize for fiction, the Governor Generals Award. In this book Munro has depicted the region so successfully that many of her readers know it simply as "Alice Munro's country" she creates a solid habitat for her fiction—south western Ontario a generation or more in the past and is in sympathetic vibration with the farmers and towns people who live there. In the fifteen stories of this collection, Munro conjures ordinary lives with an extraordinary vision, displaying the remarkable talent for which she is now widely celebrated. Set on farms by river marshes, in the lovely towns and new suburbs of western Ontario, these stories emerge from the layers of experience that lie behind even the more everyday events and lives.

Munro's first novel, *Lives of Girls and Women* (1971) explores the growth of her protagonist and narrator, Del Jordan, through childhood and adolescence and into young adulthood, by which time she has become an aspiring novelist. The setting is the fictional town of Jubilee which is modelled on the Wingham of Munro's youth. Munro's own experiences of growing up amidst poverty and squalor of a small town, economic hardships and gradual discovery of sex and love are sensitively presented in the novel—she has used the small-town settings in the same manner as the American regional writers used the rural South.[2] Patricia Beer noted that in some ways, the book resembles a collection of short stories more than a novel: "each chapter is virtually self-contained yet sheds light on all the others. One of the few criticisms that can be made of the book is that it often explains too much."[3] Her fiction resists "authoritarian designs and thereby questions masculine and feminine stereotypes. The feminist quest of Munro's artist protagonist in her fiction assumes the form of questioning society's expectations about the traditional roles of women both in the past and the present. Munro confronts society not merely as a woman but also as a female artist who expresses woman's freedom through the medium of art."[4]

Lives of Girls and Women draws attention to the challenges facing Del as a woman in a patriarchal world. This book can be seen as a feminist rewriting of the bildungsroman. Critics have compared Munro's book to Joyce's *Portrait of the Artist as a Young Man* (1916) for Munro's portrayal of Del as an alienated and misunderstood artist is akin to Joyce's portrait of Stephen Dedalus. Del Jordan is not the first Munro protagonist to have to struggle with poverty and isolation. Like the Jordan girl of "Walker Brothers Cowboy." Del has an ambitious, dissatisfied mother and a gentle detached father, like the narrator of "The Peace of Utrecht." She has prudent aunts like the narrator of "Red Dress—1946," she faces a choice between conventional and unconventional directions for her like and like the protagonist of "Images" she has to confront madness and death. However, she may be said to differ from her predecessors, due to her ability to act firmly, confidently and constructively in order to shape her own future. She pursues and independent course in finding her way out of religious crisis and overcomes sexual temptation. Male figures are given roles of some prominence but only as supporting actors in the drama of Del's life. The characters who linger in the memory as powerfully imagined creation are all women: Del herself, her mother, her mother's boarder Fern, and her aunts.

Del's inner/intellectual life exhibits an emancipated mind. Nonetheless her group behaviour remains conformist and elucidates her diffidence about openly circumventing the existent stereotypes of gender behaviour. Her first awakening of her growing sexuality takes place in the school where the cruel comments of boys strip away freedom to be what one wanted from girls, and reduce them to the level of females.[5] Her exposure to popular romantic fiction and her friendship with Naomi further encourage her curiosity to know and talk about sex, though she cautiously hides it with attempts to come across as a knowledgeable girl. Initially Del is unable to negate the gender stereotypes, and the larger social behaviour governed by it. The social stereotypes of feminine behaviour are critical of girl's initiative. With the onset of adolescence girls become aware not only of their own sexuality, but also of the behaviour socially accepted of them. The social expectations routinely negate their earlier independence and they are unable to comprehend the changed demands. With detailed sketches of Del's and Naomi's early-youth-behaviour, Munro sensitively portrays the subtle process of social conditioning, and the confusion it palpably generates in the psyche of a girl. Del and Naomi use strong abusive language and scornful laughter, hoping and fearing that somebody would hear it in the street (101). Wild laughter and strong language are "the commonest methods of combat used in adolescent struggle."[6] School girls often burst with laughter or make use of strong abusive language while telling one another sentimental or coarse stories or speaking of their flirtations. "To make game of the feminine body, to ridicule men, to laugh at love, together constitute a way of disowning sexuality. There is in these laughs, along with defiance of adults, a method of overcoming one's own embarrassment and constraint; one plays with words and images to kill the dangerous magic (101)."[7]

Del's attraction towards Jerry Storey is a healthy adolescent response to her own sexuality. Her rejection of Naomi's option of putting herself on the road to marriage reasserts her mental independence (161). With Jerry, she is able to share a common intellectual dream of scholarships and bright future. Academically she has a calibre to outshine most of her classmates. Her relationship with Garnet French distracts her and she retreats from achievement related challenges. Del's withdrawal from mental creativity is part of the mythic pattern of feminine development. The growing up process of Del Jordan clearly shows the constricting influence of gender stereotypes on the individual and social cognition of young girls. Munro's novel questions the prevalent gender stereotypes by highlighting their negative role, and seeks to redress the balance by repudiating them unequivocally. It is sometimes remarked, that Munro's fiction is nearer to autobiography than fiction. In defence of *Lives of Girls and Women* which is most frequently identified as being modelled on her life, Munro has asserted it is autobiographical in form but not in fact. The distinction is perhaps not persuasive, but the charge is difficult to evade, for Munro's ear for the local speech has an absolute pitch and her narrators as filters of past and present possess an intelligence that makes one feel that if it is not her life being told, then it is ours. In 1978, Munro became involved in a controversy when a Huron county group tried to keep several books such as *Lives of Girls and Women* and Margaret Laurence's, *The Diviners* out of local high schools. Munro was one of the three members of the Writers Union of Canada who spoke out against censorship in a local forum. Lives won the Canadian Booksellers Association Book Award in 1972, but Munro feels "sometimes I've regretted that I've done Lives; I've wished I'd done it better and I would like in a way to go back and do it over again, but you can't plough that field again.... It's done."[8]

Munro's next short story collection was *Something I've Been Meaning to Tell You* (1974). Out of thirteen stories only six takes place in South western Ontario; the remainder has contemporary urban settings. William French found the book as an evidence of the broadening of Munro's range and as confirmation of the universal quality of her writing. "There's the same interplay of emotions, the same marvellous perceptions that distinguish the earlier stories."[9] In the thirteen stories in her remarkable second collection, Alice Munro demonstrates the precise observation, straight forward prose style, and masterful technique that led to John Updike to compare her to Chekhov. The sisters, mothers and daughters in these stories shimmer with hope and love, anger and reconciliation, as they contend with their histories and their present as well as future. In his review of *Something I've Been Meaning to Tell You*, Kildare Dobbs says—"All the stories are told with the skill which the author has perfected over the years, narrated with meticulous precision in a voice that is unmistakably Ontario in its lack of emphasis, its sly humour and willingness to live with a mystery."[10]

In *Who Do You Think You Are?* (1978) the theme of identity is central to the book. Originally published as in 1978, Alice Munro's fourth book, *Who Do You Think You Are?* was nominated for the Booker Prize and won the author the Governor Generals award for fiction in Canada. It was published in the United States the following year under the title *The Beggar Maid: Stories of Flo and Rose.* Like *Lives of Girls and Women, Who Do You Think You Are*? focuses on moments of confrontation in the protagonist's life. It is a collection of stories, which though interrelated are self contained and reveal the story of the protagonist Rose growing up in a rural south western Ontario. It presents a series of linked stories chronicling the life of a young woman growing up in rural south western Ontario. The novel presents the challenges that are an intrinsic part of everyday life and experiences of every girl in the patriarchal set up is delineated sensitively in this novel. The conflict becomes more poignant when the women have to balance the traditional gender roles with her hopes and aspirations as well as her sexuality. The woman is often beset with doubts and guilt as she faces each new challenge and overcomes hurdles and trudges on to next milestone. She has to face the accusing question—*Who do you think you are*? Rose, the protagonist grows up in impoverished rural, Hanratty, living with her father, stepmother Flo and younger brother. The family relations are fraught with tensions which in a sense is a reflection of the conditions in their society too. As the novel progresses Rose grows into an awareness of class and gender distinctions. Meeting and marring the rich Patrick, the birth of her daughter Anna, the growing friendship with Jocelyn and Clifford, failed marriage and affairs leave her a lonely woman alienated even when she is well known as an actor. Rose's journey is in many ways a reflection of the desire to break away from strict restrictions imposed on her by family expectations and gender discrimination. She is haunted by the question "Who do you think you are?" "This was not the first time in her life Rose had been asked who she thought she was: in fact the question had often struck her as a monotonous going and she paid no attention."[11] From her early years Rose attempts to answer this question fleeing away from her roots, searching for an anchor, finding it and losing it again and again.

Her next collection *The Moons of Jupiter* was published in 1982. The subject of many of these stories is what is generally called romantic love, either love that the characters are doing their best to make work, or love they are recovering from. But there is little romance in the love Munro's women find, and certainly none of the grand passions and infatuations with which fiction so often concerns itself. Instead, Munro's women find comfort in the best love available to them, or are unhappy over the loss of a love that was not all that good to start with. For instance when Wilfred, in *Visitors*, proposed to Mildred, they were both middle-aged and his way of proposing was to say, "Why not end up in Logan? I've got a house there. It's not so big a house, but it will take two."[12] Mildred asked him why he had never been married before. He said he had often been on the go, and besides, it wasn't often you met a good-hearted woman.

Alice Munro writes in an easy conversational voice. Five of the twelve stories in this volume are in first person, two are primarily in present tense, many are in an easy conversational voice she breaks many of the commonly taught rules for writing stories. In many of her stories, not very much happens and sometimes the characters do not change in any clearly noticeable way. In *Labour Day Dinner*, for instance, as George and Roberta and Roberta's teen-age daughters Angela and Eva visit their friends, Valery and her grown children for dinner, we learn a lot about the dynamics of the relationship between George and Roberta, who married only two years ago, and about his relationship with his two stepdaughters, and about how they are all attempting to make this new relationship work. At the end of the story, nothing has really changed, and nothing really happens, until on the very last page they are saved only by a matter of yards from a fatal traffic accident.

In recent works, Munro focuses on travails of middle-age, of women alone and of the elderly—they also focus on women who are trying to make sense of their public and private lives. *The Progress of Love* (1986) continues to feature stories set predominantly in rural south western Ontario and further evinces a preoccupation with region, the untold or untellable, and the lives of women. Like many of Munro's stories it is as much concerned with the past as with the present, the narrator records the progress of love over a wider range of family relationships. The writer and critic Joyce Carol Oates, hailed the collection as "a volume of unflinching audacious honesty, uncompromisingly downright in its dissection of the ways in which we deceive ourselves in the name of love; the bleakness of its vision is enriched by the author's exquisite eye and ear for detail. Life is heartbreak, but it is also uncharted moments of kindness and reconciliation."[13] Another leading American writer, Anne Tyler, applauded Munro as one of the few contemporary short story writers who can "create those full-bodied miniature universes of the old school.... Some of her stories are so ample and fulfilling that they feel like novels. They present whole landscapes and cultures, whole families of characters."[14] Cynthia Ozick, her fellow acclaimed short story writer, placed Munro at par with Chekhov. As Thacker says, "We are drawn to her writing by its verisimilitude, not of mimesis, so called and... 'realism'...but rather the feeling of being itself...of just being a human being."[15] On being asked how the comparison made her feel, Munro says, "I have recently re-read much of Chekhov and it's a humbling experience. I don't even claim Chekhov as an influence because he influenced all of us. Like Shakespeare his writing shed the most perfect light-there's no striving in it, no personality."[16]

Talking of her most recent book, *Friend of My Youth* (1990) Michiko Kakutani says, "It is a collection that attests once again, to Ms. Munro's complete fluency in the short-story form, her emergence as one of the most eloquent and gifted writers of contemporary fiction."[17] He also pinpoints the key elements that make Munro's stories so compelling: "Munro...reveals how character is formed over time, how choices turn into patterns, and how patterns are repeated with infinite variation over the course of a life time. She situates her characters meticulously observed world, catches them in those unguarded moments that reveal their secrets and their fears, and in doing so, gives the reader a privileged glimpse into their hearts."[18] The novelist Bharati Mukherjee was equally impressed by the architectural complexity of the stories—"Each is a marvel of construction", she wrote, "containing within it parallel narratives of enquiry and retrospection...Each...is a mansion of many rooms."[19]

Most of the eight stories in her next collection, *Open Secrets* (1994) take place in Munro's Ontario, The central character in the stories are all women: An emotionally adventurous librarian; a young women kidnapped by Albanian tribesman in the 1920's, a farmer's wife who yearns for gentility, a young born Christian whose love and anger cause her to vandalize a house. Munro explores female themes with great depth though her vision also includes the eternal and social milieu. *Love of a Good Woman* (1998) is marked by an ostensible digressiveness that makes it untidy, resisting conventional patterns of beginning, middle and end, in keeping with Munro's belief of chaos in life. Here Munro gives us accurate and telling images of personal revolt. Her next collection *Hateship, Friendship, Courtship, Loveship, Marriage* (2001) is a conservative collection of nine short stories, again set in the Southern Ontario. Most of these are stories of aging women and men confronting death and late love yet they share a profoundly life affirming message. In the title story an epistolary prank by two teenaged girls leads to a one sided cross country elopement and a happy marriage. Alice Munro's set of short stories, *Runaway* (2004) all concern Canadian women facing pivotal moments in their lives each standing aloof choosing a path, consciously or subconsciously that varies from societies expectation for women. Thus, they explore not only the themes of women's lives, but of their interaction with lovers, husbands, parents and children. *Selected Stories* (1996) is a volume of Munro's short stories, published in her previous eight books.

A gifted chronicler of traditional values of her childhood environment, the pathos of old age, and the frantic search in our time for a varnished sense of wholeness, Munro has not forgotten the writers obligation to give pleasure. Her stories attest to her remarkable powers of observation, her unfailing ear for speech of all kinds and her capacity for the kind of wit which is unsentimental without deserting compassion. Her genius like Chekhov's, is quiet and particularly hard to describe, because it has the simplicity of the naturalism, in that it seems not translated from life but rather, like life itself. Alice Munro continues to write and does not think of retirement as yet. In an interview in *The Atlantic Unbound* Alice Munro said of her writing career—"That's something I think is growing on me as I get older: happy endings."

Occasionally faulted for limiting herself to a narrow thematic range, Munro is nevertheless, widely regarded as a gifted short story writer whose strength lies in her ability to present the texture of everyday life with both compassion and unyielding precision, and in evoking emotions ranging from bitter hatred to love, from bewilderment and resentment to awe, with conversational ease.

NOTES AND REFERENCES

1. Kakutani, Michiko in a review.
2. Meyer, Literature, http://www.bedfordstmartins.com/literature/bedlit/ author depth/munro.htm
3. Beer, Patricia: Times Literary supplement, March 17, 1978.
4. Prabhakar, M: Feminism/Post Modernism: Margaret Atwood's Fiction (New Delhi: Creative Books, 1999).
5. Munro, Alice: *Lives of Girls and Women* (Canada: Signet, 1974), p. 98. All quotations are from this edition.
6. Beauvoir, Simone de: The Second Sex, tr. H. M. Parshley (London: Four Square Books, 1961), p. 83.
7. *Ibid.*
8. Munro, Alice: Interview for Quill and Quire (March 1974).
9. French, William: In his review for the Bronto Globe and Mail, May 25, 1974.
10. Dobbs, Kildare: In his review of "Something I've Been Meaning to tell you" for the Canadian Monthly, Saturday Night (July, 1974).
11. Munro, Alice: *Who Do You Think You Are*? Canada: Penguin, 1978, p. 243.
12. Munro, Alice: Visitors (Quoted in Lee Lady's review of The Moons of Jupiter by Alice Munro).
13. Oates, Joyce Carol in *New York Times* Book Review (September 14, 1986).
14. Tyler, Anne in a two—part article for the New Republic (September 15 & 22, 1986).

15. Thacker, R.: 1998; Review of Some other Reality: Alice Munro's, Something I've Been Meaning to tell you, by Louis K. Mackendrick. *Journal of Canadian Studies*, Summer, 1998.
16. A Conversation with Alice Munro: an interview on the internet site www.randomhouse.com.
17. Kakutani, Michiko in *New York Times* (March 9, 1990).
18. *Ibid.*
19. Mukherjee, Bharati in *New York Times* Book Review (March 18, 1990).

10

'From Comic Eccentricity to Post-colonial despair' in Kiran Desai's *Hullabaloo in the Guava Orchard* and *The Inheritance of Loss*

> "It may be said that writers in my position, exiles or emigrants or expatriates, are haunted by some sense of loss, some urge to reclaim, to look back, even at the risk of being mutated into pillars of salt. But if we do look back, we must also do so in the knowledge—which gives rise to profound uncertainties—that our physical alienation from India almost inevitably means that we will not be capable of reclaiming precisely the thing that was lost; that we will, in short, create fictions, not actual cities, or villages, but invisible ones, imaginary homelands, Indian of the mind."
>
> —*Salman Rushdie*, Imaginary Homelands

Until the 1990's, Kiran Desai was known only as the prominent Indian novelist, Anita Desai's daughter. Anita Desai, teaching Creative writing at Massachusetts Institute of Technology has been thrice short listed for the Booker prize: in 1980 for *Clear Light of the Day*, in 1984 for *In Custody* and in 1999 for *Fasting, Feasting*. Kiran Desai first came to literary attention when in 1997, her excerpts found an honourable mention in Salman Rushdie edited anthology *Mirrorwork: Fifty Years of Indian Writing*. In 1998, came her celebrated debut, *Hullabaloo in the Guava Orchard*, which was published to unanimous acclaim in over twenty-two countries and went on to win the Betty Trask Award, a prize given by the Society of Authors for the best new novels by citizens of the Commonwealth of Nations under the age of thirty-five. In 2006, eight years later, with *The Inheritance of Loss*, Kiran Desai at thirty-five, not only became the youngest ever woman writer to win the prestigious Man Booker Prize, overtaking Arundhati Roy who won the same at the age of thirty-six for *The God of Small Things* in 1997, Desai also achieved a victory which had repeatedly eluded her mother. With this leading literary award to her credit, Desai beat the bookies who put her fifth out of six in the short list—Sarah Waters' *The Night Watch* being their favourite.

From the mother to the daughter we see a literary tradition being built, starting from Anita Desai's psychological explorations in her fiction to Kiran Desai's experiment in the making of a comic fable in *Hullabaloo in the Guava Orchard* and her insightful and often humorous commentary on multiculturism, globalization and post-colonial society in *The Inheritance of Loss*. After being declared a winner Desai was inevitably asked about her mother's influence on her work, to which she said, that she owed a lot to her mother and that her prize winning novel was as much "hers as it is mine." "It feels like a family endeavour."[1] In an interview Kiran Desai talks of her famous mother, as being a major influence on her own writing—"I'm sure she did have a big influence, because all my life I've grown up hearing her talk about writing and literature and books. It was wonderful to have her around when I was writing this book, to talk to her through this whole process."[2]

Often criticised for being her mother's daughter by those who prefer the mother's style and oeuvre, Desai has also been judged in isolation and acclaimed as a two novel old writer who has begun rather well. Kiran Desai may not have the same intensity that her mother weaves in her potent tales but she does not disappoint in producing a supremely funny and engaging novel in her joyous debut, *Hullabaloo in the Guava Orchard* (1998). Talking of *Hullabaloo* Kiran Desai remarks "I think my first book was filled with all that I loved most about India and knew I was in the inevitable process of losing. It was also very much a book that came from the happiness of realizing how much I loved to write."[3]

The publishers of *Hullabaloo* have been comparing the book to Arundhati Roy's *The God of Small Things*. However,

Kiran Desai seems to have less in common with Roy or Salman Rushdie than with the older generation of Indian writers including her mother Anita Desai and R.K. Narayan. As Narayan has done in his well known Malgudi stories, Desai has conjured up a small Indian town poised midway between tradition and modernity and focused on the life of one of the anonymous inhabitants of that town—a dreamy, introspective fellow torn between his familial obligation and his own desire to be alone.

It is a whimsical tale that blends fable-esque magic with satiric comedy. Set in the fictitious village of Shahkot, the tale traces the chaotic progress of the monumentally unmotivated Sampath Chawla from a failed post office clerk to a guava tree inhabiting Guru. In Kiran Desai's Shahkot, it seems that the atmosphere of Narayan's Malgudi has been delicately captured and given a more boisterous build up than Narayan's mildly Chekhovian humour is inclined to do. Kiran Desai, apparently, is fruitfully familiar with Evelyn Waugh's *Decline and Fall* and *A Handful of Dust* moving from a hilarious comedy to a macabre close. Avoiding the outspread tentacles of Arundhati Roy's characters in *The God of Small Things*, Kiran Desai concentrates within the limited boundaries of Shahkot as against Arundhati's trapezing from Kerela to Assam, with scattered relatives in Britain and America as well. The confines of Shahkot get a better and more concentrated build up in the process and acquire a Narayanesque flavour of Malgudi.

In Anita Desai's *Voices in the City*, goddess Kali is presented as the presiding deity of the city of Calcutta. Kiran Desai's Shahkot is a miniature replica, where for once all characters are being assembled in the orchard to enact a crowded drama of action and atmosphere—the Brigadier with his marching orders to the subordinates, Sampath the Godman, surrounded by devotees, Kulfi with her boiling cauldron, the drunken monkeys raiding the orchard, Pinky and her new love, the ice cream vendor and the spy, hoping to detect some flaw in the entire set up. It is a mildly satirical portrait of the Indian cult of god man modelled on Narayan's Swami in *The Guide* or Mauni Baba of Allahabad. Through a series of gossipy asides and subplots, this gentle comic satire offers a thoroughly funny, charming and occasionally touching insight into the absurdities of life in small town India. R.K. Narayan had stated that the incident of the reluctant holy man was based on a real event which he read about in a newspaper. Desai, too, says in an interview, talking of the process for writing this book—"I'd read a story in The Times of India and heard about a character from many people, a man who was a very famous hermit in India who really did climb up a tree, who lived in a tree for many years, until he died."[4]

The novel opens with a picture of overly heated Shahkot: "It was a summer that sent the dizzy pulse of fever into the sky, in which even rules and laws that usually stood straight and purposeful grew limb, like plants exposed to the afternoon sun, and weak"[5] (p. 2). The multitude of humorous inducements to bring about the delayed monsoons in the midst of a terrible drought are supremely amusing, for instance—"Hungarian musician offers to draw rain clouds from Europe to India via the music of his flute" (p. 1). At last the monsoon was in town—"Who knew whether it came because of the giant fan, the wedding of frogs, the Pied Piper, because of mercurial powers or magician's marvels? And in the end, who cared? The rain had come to Shahkot" (p. 99). Sampath's birth auspiciously coincides with the break of the monsoons and the dropping of a crate of Red Cross supplies by a Swedish relief plane as if people in Sweden had remembered to send him a birthday present, and accordingly named him "Sampath" implying good fortune. Sampath had to cope with his strange family—his father, Mr. Chawla, mother Kulfi, Ammaji and Pinky, his sister. Kiran Desai imbues her characters with stunningly realistic attitudes that only an especially perceptive author could perceive in her everyday life. Those zany characters wreak havoc in a village in India. Sampath, the ambitionless son of the middle class family wants to escape the looming responsibilities of his adult life. He decides to climb into a guava tree and live there in peaceful contemplation. The town's people start to revere him as a holy man and seek his counsel for their problems. His enigmatic responses only increase their awe for him. His father reacts by looking at the commercial possibilities of having many pilgrims coming to see Sampath. His mother spends her days searching the country side for rare and unusual food to prepare for him. His sister struggles to maintain her independence but falls hopelessly in love with the Hungry Hop Ice boy. Inept bureaucrats, bungling army officials, a spy for the atheist society, and a herd of monkeys with a taste for liquor add to this hilariously irreverent story.

Desai has done an excellent job delineating her characters —each one of them is colourful and hilarious in their own manner. Pinky, his sister, finds delight in biting the cheeks or tweaking the bottoms of the men she fancies; the mother Kulfi who had enormous cravings for food during the time of pregnancy—"Her stomach grew larger, her dreams of eating more extravagant. The house seemed to shrink" (p. 7). The only stereotypical character in the novel is the father, Mr. Chawla, reminiscent of middle class fathers, he is a government employee who exercises regularly, shows his concern for his children's future, but remains aloof from the extraordinary oddities of life around him.

Twenty years later, we see Sampath, employed in a post office at Shahkot, where he has a wonderful opportunity of surreptitiously reading the various letters providing ample hints of where his or her secrets lay buried. Sampath examined the postcard and letters—"He held them up against the light, the envelopes filled with promise, with the possibility of different worlds. He steamed them open over mugs of tea...and lazily through the rest of the day he perused their contents" (p. 34). It is that knowledge that enables him to acquire the proportions of Mauni Baba. Unlike his father Mr. Chawla, the distinguished pater familius, Sampath, is quite retiring and subdued kind of a character for once, erupting himself of his trousers and underpants and standing in absolute nakedness. The impossibly absent minded Sampath is sacked from his dismal post office job. Horrified at his father's suggestion that he applies for a post at the Utterly Butterly Delicious factory, he feels that everyone was conspiring to build a net about him. He felt terribly sorry for himself—"How he hated his life. It was a never ending flow of misery. It was a prison, he had been born into" (p. 43). "He wanted open spaces" (p. 44), his mother offers him an egg, he says "No, I do not want an egg I want my freedom" (p. 47).

He escapes frantically into a bus, and at a convenient point jumps out of it, and jumps into the guava orchard and quietly perches himself in the fork of the guava tree. He refuses to descend to the ground inspite of the repeated request of Mr. Chawla, until Mr. Chawla is compelled to fix a string cot onto the tree. Mr. Chawla, the sedate head clerk of Reserve Bank of Shahkot is transformed into the manager of the riches that pour at the feet of Swami Baba. From his perch, Sampath becomes comically misconstrued as a great visionary, a religious guru of sorts. He proceeds to find fame, fortune and eventually chaos—in the form of bumbling bureaucrats and a group of unruly, liquor loving monkeys, who only Sampath can tame, by bestowing his wisdom upon the many people who make the pilgrimage to meet the Monkey Baba. The novel acquires the dimensions of the fable, when the drunken monkeys raise a hullabaloo in the guava orchard.

The pastoral idyll is shattered by the riotous tribe of alcoholic monkeys. Depicting the ensuing descent into anarchy, Desai is in her element, cataloguing the various insane schemes proposed to solve the monkey's problem. In a series of rollicking hilarious incidents, she presents the metamorphoses of Sampath into a godman. There is in these scenes a manifestly Dickensian tilt towards the comic, particularly in Ammaji's repeated search for dentures in the company of young Pinky and the misbehaviour of the dentures falling now in the boiling curry and acquiring its special colour and flavour and then while tasting the ice-cream her dentures gets stuck in it a book of rare humour and craft, *Hullabaloo in the Guava Orchard* traces the chaotic process of the monumentally unmotivated Sampath Chawla from failed post office clerk to guava tree inhabiting guru.

Sampath as a godman inevitably draws comparisons with Raju in Narayan's *The Guide*, where Raju after serving time in prison advertantly becomes a spiritual saint for the people of Mangala when he took refuge in an abandoned temple on the outskirts. Where as Sampath's mother Kulfi makes culinary experiments for her son, Raju makes the resolution to chase away food—"Why not give the poor Devil a chance, Raju said to himself, instead of hankering after food..." (p. 213). Sampath undergoes no transformation after becoming the Monkey Baba, on the contrary, we trace a marked transformation of Raju the rogue to a genuine sanyasi—"For the first time, in his life he was making an earnest effort, for the first time he was learning the thrill of full application, outside money and love. He felt suddenly so enthusiastic that it gave him a new strength to go through the ordeal" (p. 213).

Yet, another difference between *The Guide* and *Hullabaloo in the Guava Orchard* is quite noticeable. *The Guide* also begins as a comic look at the life of a rogue but it evolves into something different. In Hullabaloo, on the contrary, "from the very first page it is evident that the novel is going to be supremely funny and engaging an immediately delightful celebration of the Hullabaloo of Indian life."[6] A small brilliant fable, *Hullabaloo in the Guava Orchard* showed off its young author's profound comprehension that every novel, large or small is at heart an intimate thing. Its success depends on its authors' unwavering attention to a group of characters who are the readers' emotional conduit to the books wider drama. It is a well written magically realist vignette on the line between a novel and a novella. Her novels are full of wisdom and subtle parallels. It is both funny and bitterly sad but generally optimistic.

Kiran Desai's delirious tale of love, faith and family relationships is funny, smartly written and reminiscent of other works by Indian authors, writing in English, such as Salman Rushdie's *The Moor's Last Sigh* and Shashi Tharoor's *Show Business*. Though, not as intense as her mother's novels Kiran Desai doesn't disappoint in producing a maddeningly entertaining novel. The *Hullabaloo in the Guava Orchard* reminds one of Shakespeare's *Hamlet*: "Though this be madness, yet there is method in't."[7] The novel derives its strength from the steady fluidity in which the story unfolds itself by use of brilliantly lucid images and a distinct choice of unaffected words and phrases and an eccentric set of characters. In an interview, talking of *Hullabaloo in the Guava Orchard*, Kiran Desai classifies—"It is a comedy and it is satiric in many ways, I think, and its fantastic. It reads very much like a folktale or a fairy tale."[8] Kiran Desai had stated that she wrote the novel, "Very much for myself...but I think anyone with a sense of humour would enjoy it."[9] True enough, through this radiant novel, Desai evokes a bright, buoyant world, which is wryly hilarious and enchanting.

From the sweet natured playfulness of her joyous novel, *Hullabaloo in the Guava Orchard* to the exploration of such complex issues as colonialism, racism, immigration, young love, regret, hope, the role of family, and the myths of both India and America in *The Inheritance of Loss*, Desai makes clear her intentions to expand her reach from the narrow boundaries of her first novel to the global arena where luminaries like Salman Rushdie and Zadie Smith already perform. Unlike her first sprightly novel that ends in a raucous bang of comic eccentricity, the prevailing mood in *The Inheritance of Loss* is one of implacable bitterness and despair. Full of pathos and tenderness the novel presents its characters as ultimately frail human beings struggling in a search for love and happiness.

When talking of the characters in *The Inheritance of Loss*, and of her own life, she says, "The characters of my story are entirely fictional, but these journeys (of her grandparents) as well as my own provided insight into what it means to travel between East and West and it is this I wanted to capture. The fact that I live this particular life is no accident. It was my inheritance."[10] It was this feeling of being caught between two continents that infuses *The Inheritance of Loss*—a story replete with sadness over globalization and with pleasure at the surviving intimacies of Indian village life. Hermione Lee, the head judge for the Booker Prize, describes the book as "a magnificent novel of human breath and wisdom, comic tenderness and powerful political acuteness."[11] John Sutherland, chairman of last year's Man Booker judges said: "Desai's novel registers the multicultural reverberations of the new millennium with the sensitive instrumentality of fiction, as Jhabvala and Rushdie did previous eras.... It is a globalised novel for a globalised world."[12]

Both Rushdie and Rohinton Mistry believe that, with this her second novel, Desai has secured her place with the great contemporary Indian authors exploring life and society in India and elsewhere. Salman Rushdie had earlier described *Hullabaloo in the Guava Orchard* 'as lush and intensely imagined.' Her second novel, *The Inheritance of Loss*, too, has earned his complimentary blurb at the back of the new novel—"Kiran Desai is a terrific writer."[13] Whereas, *Hullabaloo in the Guava Orchard* was a "charming, lyrical, fable about destiny,"[14] a "festival of comic eccentricity, exuding charisma, poetry and joy in language and life,"[15] *The Inheritance of Loss* is a majestic novel, "illuminating the pain of exile, the ambiguities of post-colonialism and the blinding derive for 'better life' when one person's wealth means another's poverty."[16] It zips back and forth between Kalimpong, a tiny Himalayan burg, and the streets of New York City. Its primary setting is India, in this case the remote province of Kalimpong during the mid 1980's.

In this alternatively comical and contemplative novel, Desai effectively illuminates the pain of exile, like lingering effects of post-colonialism, the characters struggling as exiles to maintain their dignity and self-respect in the encroaching morass of Westernization. Dealing with all levels of society and different cultures, Desai reveals life's humour and brutality, its delicate emotions and passionate commitments so convincingly that, her mother's remarks seem to be no exaggeration—"I think Kiran's voice is extremely original, she brings, something totally fresh and new to the writing scene."[17]

Desai takes us to the north eastern Himalayas, where a rising insurgency challenges the old way of life. It's a good tale with a globalization undercurrent connecting India's Nepal border with New York City—"...there was a report of new dissatisfaction in the hills, gathering insurgency, men and guns. It was the Indian—Nepalese this time, fed up with being treated like the minority in a place where they were the majority. They wanted their own country, or at least their own state, in which to manage their own affair"[18] (p. 9). It spans continents, generations, cultures, religions and races. Desai has wonderfully presented the human face of globalization and showed how individuals living in different parts of the planet often intersect in surprising ways. A father's love for his son, that son's ambition to succeed, the bitterness of a lonely man living out his days on the edge of civilization, two sister's yearning for the past, all of these lives are presented by Desai as fully realized and ultimately frail human beings in recognizable search for love and happiness. Although the story has as its backdrop, Kalimpong and the Gorkhaland agitation, it is actually about loss—the loss of identity, nationality and loyalty, and the realization of this loss—the Gorkhaland agitation is merely a catalyst for the loss. The loss in her title is chiefly the loss of faith in India felt among the legions who over stay tourist visas and become illegal immigrants in the U.S.

Writing with wit and perception, Kiran Desai creates an elegant and thoughtful study of families, the losses each member must confront alone, and the lies each tells to make memories of the past more palatable. *The Inheritance of Loss* opens with a teenage Indian girl, an orphan called Sai, living with her Cambridge educated Anglophile grandfather, a retired judge in the town of Kalimpong on the Indian side of Himalayas. For the judge, all opportunity has passed him by. The hopes of his family rested on him, and he succeeded in leaving India for a difficult education in England. His colour, his religion, his language all made him the embodiment of "other" in England, and he began to question his identity and his connection to India while there—"He retreated into a solitude that grew in weight day by day. The solitude became a habit, the habit became the man, and it crushed him into a shadow" (p. 39).

The novel presents the judge, Jemubhai cast away from the colonial times, carrying scathing memories of aborted attempts to acculturate into the metropolitan. The memory of his home sick passage from his hometown to Cambridge stays in his mind, his shame at the pickle and bananas that his mother packed—"He was furious that his had considered the possibility of his humiliation and thereby, he thought, precipitated it. In her attempt to cancel out one humiliation she had only succeeded in adding another. Jemu picked up the package, fled to the deck and threw it over board.... Undignified love, Indian love, stinking, unaesthetic love—the monsters of the ocean could have what she had so bravely packed.... The smell of the dying bananas retreated, oh, but now that just left the stink of fear and loneliness perfectly exposed" (p. 38)—the hungry nights spent as a tenant of Mrs. Rice—"After a spate of nights lying awake listening to the borborygmus of his half-empty stomach, thinking tearfully of his family in Piphit who thought him as worthy of a hot dinner as the queen of England, Jemubhai worked up the courage to ask for a proper evening meal" (p. 39)—and the long hours at the bathroom to scour away the smells that emanate from his body—his Indian roots that he is ashamed of—"To the end of his life, he would...prefer shadow to light, faded days to sunny, for he was suspicious that sunlight might reveal him, in his hideousness, all too clearly" (p. 40)—the colonial society that allows him no entry—he carries memories of experience of alienation and loneliness that he carries back home.

He is one of those 'ridiculous Indians,' 'who could not rid themselves of what they had broken their souls to learn' and those whose Anglophilia can only turn to self-hatred. As a student, isolated in racist England the future judge feels "barely human at all" (p. 40) and leaps "when touched on the arm as if from an unbearable intimacy" (p. 40). Yet, on returning home he vented his anger and frustration on his innocent young wife because of her docility and her silent battle that she puts up by withdrawing into herself. Unloved, uncared and hated she lives a desultory life until the judge sends her back to her parents' home, their child, a daughter is born after the separation about whom the judge never knew. Alone and recluse the judge settles after retirement in Cho Oyu, with a dog Mutt, whom he loves more than any human being and a cook for whom he has no feelings. To this cottage and to partake in the old mans arid life arrives Sai, his orphaned granddaughter born to the judges daughter. After the death of her parents under the wheels of a bus in Moscow, when Sai arrives at Cho Oyu, the judge begins to confront his own sufferings as a victim of racism and colonialism as well as the violence he perpetrated against his wife. The judge, seems to have had his heart frozen long ago when he studied at Cambridge University and learned to despise his fellow Indians. The only creature he truly loves is Mutt, his dog. Living in a large, decaying house, her grandfather considers himself more British than Indian, far superior to hard working but poverty stricken people like his cook, Nandu, whose hopes for a better life for his son are the driving force in his life.

Fortunately for Sai, however, the cook at Cho Oyu cherishes her as if she were his own. His actual child Biju is living in New York, eking out a bare existence waiting tables and sleeping in a basement (Even as his father imagines him to be amassing wealth and prestige). The story of Sai living in Kalimpong, near India's northeast border with Nepal, alternates with that of Biju, Nandu's son, an illegal immigrant trying to find work and a better life in New York. Biju working in a series of decadent jobs epitomizes the plight of the illegal immigrant who has no future in his own country and endures deplorable conditions and semi-servitude working illegally in the U.S. With Biju we experience the world of illegal aliens, the 'shadow class...condemned to movement'—"Biju put a padding of newspapers down his shirt...and sometimes he took the scallion pancakes and inserted them below the paper, inspired by the memory of an uncle who used to go out to the fields in winter with his lunch time parathas down his vest. But even this did not seem to help, and once, on his bicycle, he began to weep from the cold and the weeping unpicked a deeper vein of grief..." (p. 51). He spends much of his time dodging the authorities, moving from one ill-paid job to another. As Desai explores the aspirations of Sai and Biju, the hopes and expectations of their families, she also creates vivid pictures of the friends and relatives who surround them, evoking vibrant images of a broad cross-section of society and revealing the social and political history of India.

Inevitably, however, as Sai has grown older, the cook's love has no longer been enough, and now she turns her attentions to her young tutor, Gyan. Gyan, an ethnic Nepalese, loves Sai in return-until he is swept away by a group of insurgents agitating for freedom from India and decides he needs to despise her and her bourgeois ways. Other finely sketched Kalimpong characters include two elderly Anglophile Indian sisters who sip tea and read Jane Austen, safe within the confines of the estate they call Mon Ami, and a Swiss priest named Father Booty who keeps a dairy and dreams of teaching Indians to make cheese. Sai is young enough to live in the moment, which helps her overlook some of the issues with her boyfriend Gyan. Sai's identity and her relationship with India is very different from Gyan's. Sai belonged to a formerly powerful, educated and western thinking family and Gyan's Nepalese family lives in poverty, struggling to make ends meet while providing him with a good education. When Gyan's friends start to explore, first peacefully and then with violence, the inequalities present in India itself, he is caught up in the furore and clashes with Sai. Both Sai and Gyan lose their innocence and love in the turmoil of unrest. Meanwhile, on opposite sides of globe, Biju and his father lose themselves in the fantasy that is America; the cook hoping for better things for his son while the son, living the gruelling reality of life as a poor and illegal resident, is condemned to menial labour and abject living conditions. Biju longs for home. He is not immune from nostalgia. He can, "feel the pulse of the forest, smell the humid air, the green black lushness; he could imagine all its different textures, the plumage of banana, the stark spear of the cactus, the delicate gesture of ferns" (p. 230).

Longing is perhaps the thing that the characters in this novel do best. They long for home, they long for love, and they long for acceptance—yet rarely are they skilled at locating any of the above. As the insurgency grows in strength, however, all the characters of the novel come to share Sai's suspicion that life is more often defined by loss than by fulfilment. Desai wants us to explore the pain of the immigrant and the unfairness of a world in which, 'one side travels to be a servant, and the other side travels to be treated like a king'. The Epigraph to the novel includes a line from Borges—"My humanity is in feeling we are all voices of the same poverty"—But it isn't only physical poverty that Desai's characters seem to recognise—All of them seem to crave for a sense of belonging. What bind these seemingly disparate characters are a shared historical legacy and a common experience of impotence and humiliation. Desai is sometimes compared to Salman Rushdie, and the energy and fecundity of imagination in her works do make them somewhat similar to his. But the tenderness in her novels is all her own. One can feel the tenderness, when Gyan, the young tutor, says it best, when he glimpses after failing to find a sense of purpose in history and politics that "Happiness has a smaller location" (p. 272).

As events unfold, the novel alternates between Kalimpong and New York. At the same time, it shuttles back and forth between Sai's youth and that of her Anglophile grandfather, Jemu. Through Jemu, a Third World Horatio Alger, we experience the post-colonial era in all the cruelty of its old, ingrained hatreds and prejudices. Through Sai, we experience the precarious present—"What was a country but the idea of it?... How often could you attack it before it crumbled? To undo something took practice; it was a dark art and they were perfecting it" (p. 236). Desai effectively explores in this novel, the post-colonial chaos and despair. Early in the novel, she sets two Anglophilic Indian women to discussing A Bend in the River, V.S. Naipaul's powerfully bleak novel about traditional Africa's encounter with the modern world. Lola, one of the characters thinks Naipaul is "strange. Stuck in the past.... He has not progressed. Colonial neurosis, he's never freed himself from it" (p. 46). Lola goes on to accuse Naipaul of ignoring the fact that there is a "new England," a "completely cosmopolitan society" where "chicken tikka masala has replaced fish and chips as the number one take-out dinner" (p. 46).

A comparative study of Kiran Desai's *The Inheritance of Loss* and Anita Desai's *Fire on the Mountain* brings out some obvious similarities between the mother and the daughter in their respective storylines and choice of characters. Both the novels were written when the authors were between the age period of thirty-five and forty. Both the novels establish the author's position in the realm of serious writing in Indian English literature. In Anita Desai's novel, the story centres around a reclusive old widow and her great granddaughter and

Kiran Desai's book tells the story of a retired judge and his granddaughter. As Hermione Lee too perceives the similarity between the mother and the daughter, "It is clear to those of us who have read Anita Desai that Kiran Desai has learned from her mother's work." and she adds, "Both write not just about India but about Indian communities in the world."

A careful observer of behaviour, with a fine eye for revealing details, Desai brings her narratives and characters to life, illustrating her themes, without making moral judgments about her characters, creating neither saints nor villains, just ordinary people leading the best lives they can, using whatever resources are available. Her characters both the major and the minor ones are very real and compelling. With these characters, Desai explores such complicated issues as colonialism, racism, immigration, young love, regret, hope and the myths of both India and America. Like people from all cultures, they make sacrifices for their children, behave cruelly towards people they love, reject traditional ways of life, rediscover what is important to them and grow and make decisions about their own lives. Dealing with all levels of society and many different cultures, Desai shows life's humour and brutality, its delicate emotions and passionate commitments in *The Inheritance of Loss*. Another remarkable thing is Kiran Desai's eye for detail, as is amply evident from her settings from Kalimpong to New York, from Victorian England to rural Gujarat. It is very rarely that one comes across a book which touches upon big issues, in such a richly felt, detailed yet economic manner. For the grand scope and long journeys of the plot, this book is compact while being infinitely wise.

The first sentence established the landscape as central: "All day the colours had been those of dusk, mist moving like a water creature across the great flanks of mountains possessed of ocean shadows and depths. Briefly visible above the vapour, Kanchenjunga was a far peak whittled out of ice, gathering the last of the light, a plume of snow blown high by the storms at its summit" (p. 1). In the end too, the landscape that has engendered great passion and destruction survives both. Characters, plot, theme—all are subsumed into it. "Sai looked out and saw two figures leaping at each other as the gate swung open. The five peaks of Kanchenjunga turned golden with the kind of luminous light that made you feel, if briefly, that truth was apparent. All you needed to do was to reach out and pluck it" (p. 324).

Juggling between timeless wisdom and 21st century self-doubt, Kiran Desai combines in herself the naturalness of Tolstoy and the depth and resonance of Dickens laced with post modern ambivalence. Thus, we can see that although Desai's second novel, "focusses on the fate of a few powerless individuals, it manages to explore, with intimacy and sight, just about every contemporary international issue; globalization, multiculturism, economic inequality and terrorist violence."[19] A confident and talented writer, Desai's novels are full of wisdom and subtle parallels; it is both funny and bitterly sad, but generally optimistic. Never preachy, never predictable, Desai's scope is broad, looking at the consequences of large cultural and political forces for both people and individuals.

NOTES AND REFERENCES

1. Kiran Desai told BBC after being declared winner of Man Booker Prize, 2006.
2. Desai, Kiran: An interview in an issue of Bold Type.
3. Kiran Desai's comments in an interview from BookBrowse.com 2006.
4. Desai, Kiran: An interview in an issue of Bold Type.
5. Desai, Kiran: *Hullabaloo in the Guava Orchard* (Penguin/Viking), p. 2.
6. Loose, Julian: the editorial director Faber and Faber: (India Today).
7. Shakespeare, William: *Hamlet*.
8. Desai, Kiran: An interview in an issue of Bold Type.
9. *Ibid.*
10. Kiran Desai told BBC after being declared winner of Man Booker Prize, 2006.
11. Hermione Lee, head judge Man Booker 2006 at awards dinner in London broadcast live on BBC.
12. John Sutherland, last years chairman for Man Booker, comments on Desai's novel *The Inheritance of Loss*.
13. Rushdie, Salman: On *The Inheritance of Loss*.
14. Harper's Bazaar: Review.

15. Baltimore Sun: Review.
16. Publishers Weekly: Starred Review.
17. Desai, Anita: In an interview with Magda Costa in Barcelona 30 Jan. 2001.
18. Desai, Kiran: *The Inheritance of Loss* (Penguin/Viking.), p. 9.
19. Pankaj Mishra's review of Feb. 12th, 2006.

'Journey of Self Discovery' in Anita Nair's *Ladies Coupe*

> "Feminism is a recognition of the domination of men over women and attempts by women to end male privilege.... It is a theory, a method, and a practice which seeks to transform human relations."
>
> —*Cynthia Orozco*
>
> Writing in the anthology Chicano Voices: Intersections of Class, Race & Gender, 1993

From aspiring to be a psychiatrist to almost being sure of becoming a journalist, to finding a hold in the world of advertising, to actually becoming a writer, Anita Nair has come a long way. Having bid goodbye to her advertising career she opted to concentrate on her "addiction," writing. As she herself remarks, "Being a writer, is a necessity for me, an addiction. The best thing about being a writer is to be anonymous in one's writing, being genderless, ageless, classless, writing about people completely different from myself,"[1] The first Indian writer based in India to be on the Picador USA select list for Spring 2000, which was earlier dominated by Jim Crace's *Quarantine*, Blake Morrison's *And When Did You Last See Your Father*? and Ted Hughes' *Difficulties of a Bridegroom*, Anita Nair emerges as "a discovery, a born storyteller with a style of narration which compels reading."[2]

Her debut novel, *The Better Man*, a novel of great promise, tipped her as one of the better young writers of the time and has established Nair as "a fine writer with a great sense of character, vivid knowledge of South Indian culture and an eye for telling detail."[3] Set in contemporary India in a little fictitious village, called Kaikurussi, in northern part of Kerala, *The Better Man* features Mukundan Nair, an elderly bachelor who retires to his village after years of government service. He is haunted by a sense of failure for having abandoned his mother and for not measuring up to the expectations of his still alive and domineering father. However, towards the end, he emerges from the shadow of his father's personality to become a better man. Nair has successfully unravelled the deepest recesses of man's psyche in *The Better Man*. She not only shows a wonderful knowledge of life in a village and like Narayan's Malgudi has created in Kaikurussi another homestead that could become just as famous but also shows an almost Dostoevskian feeling for the undercurrents of consciousness, as Mukundan seeks and finds redemption. Thus, *The Better Man* describes every individual's attempt to find a degree of inner peace and manner.

"The ink had barely dried on Nair's first one, *The Better Man*, that trawled with intent through fiction's latest heart of darkness, the matrilineal murkdum of Kerala, when she's produced another one."[4] Her second novel, *Ladies Coupe*, deals with multiple lives and multiple voices, where Nair answers few questions that every woman would have faced in her life—questions related to her role in society. Unperturbed by mixed reactions that the novel evinced, Nair explains that she "writes for herself"[5] and her sole attempt is to "understand what disturbs me, be it things in me or things and people around me. And by the time, I finish writing a book I know there are some answers that I'll have."[6] "Looking for answers through fiction"[7] was the raison d'être in Anita Nair's fiction. *Ladies Coupe* unravels the misinterpretations about the role of women in contemporary post-colonial feminist literature. The question was about the vulnerable position of women and whether she could survive alone. The answer that the novel provided her was that "there was a certain strength deep inside that every individual has"[8] and that "women must be courageous and claim their own lives and possibilities."[9]

Nair's India suffers from a patriarchal system which has tried in many ways to repress, humiliate and debase women. The questions she poses in the novel not only shake the ideological ground of man's patriarchal role in our traditional society but also imply the existence of an alternative reality. It presents an opposition between ideological appearance represented in mythic and metaphysical understanding of the material world and reality represented in the material oppression of women of low caste and their sexuality. What was striking about her debut novel, *The Better Man* was that it was a woman writer exploring unusual territory—the man's world. Critics wondered if she was "only secondarily concerned with her gender and the like."[10] The answer was her next novel, *Ladies Coupe*—a story of a woman's search for strength and independence. Unlike, *The Better Man*, which was criticised for the lack of woman characters, *Ladies Coupe* is "very different from *The Better Man*, in that it deals with women. There was some criticism of *The Better Man* because it had so much to do with men and very little to do with women. This new book is a woman's book."[11] Thus Nair appears to be "a rag picker, with an eagle eye she observes the ordinary lives of maid servants masseurs, vendors and other women who course through daily life. It is the strength and resilience of the everyday woman that Nair brings out...Nair's women are fleshed out to the last detail. You can visualize them clearly—their faces, their bones, their desires...."[12]

Though hailed as "one of the most important feminist novels to come out of South India,"[13] Nair says "I am not a feminist. I enjoy being in the house. I like to be treated nicely and pampered. I don't think this book is about feminism. It's about that inner strength which I see in so many women that overwhelms me."[14] Talking to Aruna Chandaraju, she says that, to consider *Ladies Coupe* a work of feminism is sheer "lazy generalization." She finds the term feminism "outdated," besides, as she continues, "the word feminism implies a striving to be equal, a desperation almost, to get equal with men, while what is important is to know that you are equal and exercise that equality. To experience that equality knowing it is yours, naturally." She similarly dismisses the word liberated woman. "I don't like these labels. I don't need these words to introduce myself to another person or to make myself understood."[15] She traces the origin of her book to 1998, when at the Bangalore station; there was always a separate line for ladies, senior citizens and the handicapped. I often used to wonder why they are being clubbed together, why women have to be treated like this.... The book is about...when fifteen years ago I was travelling in a *Ladies Coupe* the women around me began talking.... People talk more openly to strangers—There is no judgment."[16]

Chaucer's *The Canterbury Tales* told by a band of pilgrims on way to the shrine of St. Thomas at Canterbury are a collection of stories in Frame. *Ladies Coupe* too, depicts six women in a railway compartment, each having a story to tell. As the stories unfold, the central character rediscovers the possibilities of life. Like Chaucer again, her characters stand for the affirmation of life. By narrating the stories of six women, Nair "moves from a state of passivity and absence into a state of active presence, from the kitchen and the bedroom to the street and the world at large. These are the stories which together make a single story, of women rediscovering their bodies. These are the stories which become a metaphor for a utopian world that is liberated from patriarchy, one that is not characterised by false binaries."[17]

Evoking experiences from everyday life and endowing it with epic dimensions, *Ladies Coupe* relates the saga of a woman's search for strength and independence. Nair beautifully fleshes out the minutest details of her women characters, bring alive their everyday dilemmas, desires and thoughts. As Christina Koning remarks—"Nair conveys her protagonists' dilemmas with a freshness and charm that makes her story more than just the predictable feminist homily it might appear. She is particularly good on the domestic details such as lazy Sunday lunches, a family row, the sights, sounds and smells of a busy railway station, which make up her characters' lives. These give her writing a sharpness and immediacy that lifts it above the commonplace."[18] These stories delve into the expectations of married Indian women and the choices they make, the relationships they are entangled in and convey a strong message of hope through change.

Crammed in a three tiered women's compartment of a train travelling from Bangalore to Kanyakumari, six women who have nothing in common between them except their gender—a woman's life is presented alike wherever we go—a mother, a daughter, a sister and a wife. She is the same compassionate, caring, affectionate and erosive women. The life stories of these women give an insight into the expectation of married Indian women, the choices they make and the choices made for them. Each of the females is finely drawn, each caught in a net of relationship partly of her own making and partly one that is made for her. Though they do not confess their life stories publicly to each other, while sitting in the ladies coupe, the manner in which Nair has them sharing their experiences with the protagonist, Akhila, shows them on the threshold of self-discovery, filled with the incantatory power to see a new destination and to burn up the tracks. Nair believed that—"There is a lot of strength in a woman that does not come out naturally, it has to be forced out of them."[19]

In the *Ladies Coupe*, Nair uses the fictional strategy of the ladies compartment to bring her six characters, each relating their own story—though each story is separate. However, each story illuminates the central story of Akhila, alone at forty-five and wondering whether a woman can survive alone. Born in a middle class Brahmin family struggling to keep itself afloat in Chennai, hanging on to the rigid pattern of their lives, Akhila is a frustrated spinster who has spent all her younger years looking after her parents, siblings and their offspring. After her father's death, she assumes the role of family head, her own wishes and desires are forgotten by everyone and they shamelessly keep living off her. Fed up with the multiple roles of a daughter, a sister, an aunt, she decides to go on a train journey, away from family and responsibilities—seeking an escape from them, hoping to discover her identity.

"This is the way it has always been: The smell of a railway platform at night fills Akhila with a sense of escape"[20] (p. 1). Nair beautifully sums up her protagonist, Akhila—"So this is Akhila. Forty-five years old Sans rose—coloured spectacles. Sans husband, children, home and family. Dreaming of escape and space. Hungry for life and experience. Aching to connect" (p. 2). Finding herself adrift with no life of her own, she expects the answers to her questions to emerge from the sea at Kanyakumari—the land's end where she intends to go. Just as, "Vivekananda flung himself into the churning waters and the salts of the three seas and swam to a rock upon which he sat resolutely, waiting for answers that had eluded him all his life. She had read that at Kanyakumari, the goddess, like her had put her life on hold" (p. 3). Waiting for her train to come she sees, "Reunions. Farewells. A smile. Tears. Anger. Irritation. Anxiety. Boredom. Stillness. Akhila sees them all" (p. 2)—very much a part of her life too. She also saw a man who carried on his shoulders the burden of other people's dreams. That she knew all about. That she could understand (p. 9)—very much like her again. As she had never travelled alone before, she is gripped by a sense of panic fear—"Panic fans the flames of fear. Panic dulls. Panic stills. Panic tugs at soaring dreams and hurls them down to earth. Panic destroys" (p. 39). She gives in and finds herself in a train with four other women—Janaki Prabhakar, Prabha Devi, Margaret Paulraj, Sheela Vasudevan and Marikolanthu. Her fellow travellers are both curious and giving and share not only their tiffin but also their lives with her. After her initial resistance, Akhila begins to tell and in the process to learn—"Akhila knew she could tell these women whatever she chose to. Her secrets, desires and fears. In turn, she could ask them whatever she wanted. They would never see each other again" (p. 20). She wants to convince herself that a woman can live alone. Various apprehensions and unanswered questions paralyse her by a nameless fear—"How can I who have never spent a week away from my family survive a future alone? What do I know of running a household? ...What do I know of life? How am I going to cope? Then I thought that maybe if I met other women who were single, or just...any women, ...if I talked to them...maybe it could help me make up my mind..." (p. 21). She is told by her fellow travellers that she must decide for herself. Initially, somewhat upset, she later recognizes the wisdom of this advice—"Akhila had thought they had established a connection. Foetuses jostling within the walls of a womb, drawing sustenance from each others lives aided by the darkness outside and the fact that what was shared within the walls wouldn't go beyond this night or the contained space" (p. 22).

Janaki Prabhakar, the oldest of the women has been married forty years—her relation with her husband is a "friendly love." She is a pampered wife—"I am a woman who has always been looked after. First there was my father and my brothers; then my husband. When my husband is gone, there will my son. ...Women like me end up being fragile. Our men treat us like princesses. And because of that we look down upon women who are strong and who can cope by themselves" (pp. 22-23). To Janaki, a women's duty was to get married—"I believed in that tired old cliché that a home was a woman's kingdom" (p. 23). She also talks of her sudden disinterest in that same home, of her sudden urge to be a confident being, no longer fragile. But at the end, she says that even if she were alone and even though she managed to cope alone, "it wouldn't be the same if he wasn't there with me" (p. 23). Janaki's story disturbs her a lot and Akhila is left wondering if she had made a mistake by wishing to escape, escape from loneliness. Her fellow travellers couldn't help her make up her mind—"Your lives are different from mine. And it is silly of me to think that if you told me about yourselves, your lives, that would guide me in my decision. And yet..." (p. 40).

However, Prabha Devi asks Akhila not to give it up so easily having heard just Janaki's story. Travelling in the train and lulled asleep, Akhila slips occasionally into the past, into the family setup with flitting images of her family members. Nair tenderly draws Akhila's family scenes and builds up her story into something very absorbing. Appa, her father was an income tax office clerk, who in his office was the butt of jokes because of the way he walked, he dressed, the food he ate. He never reacted to the insults hurled at him, thinking if he didn't react, they would leave him alone. He denied being a part of the corruption, had no interest in bribes and therefore was passed over for promotion by his senior, the very corrupt, Koshy. At home he was the head of the family and Sundays were a "full fledged weekly dress rehearsal for that day when he could retire and could live life on his own" (p. 42).

Being a mistress of minutae, Nair details everything that happens in Akhila's household—Appa's walk to the corner shop to buy the Hindu, Amma attending to his food till "he belched to signal that he was replete" (p. 45). The rest of the family would stay out of his hearing distance lest their rumbling stomachs would force Appa to hurry his meal. On Sundays, the radio was switched on by Akhila and we see the vying interests of the family members opting sometimes for Bournvita Quiz Show or Horlicks Family Show. Then there is Sarasa Mami's invitation for Akhila to make vadaam, the anger of Tamil teacher scolding Akhila for faltering while reciting Thiruvalluvar and finally Appa's death and the image of Amma dressed as a bride, when other widows stripped her of her marks of marriage. Akhila is deeply hurt to see her Amma like that and realizes "what it meant to be a woman" (p. 59).

The story switches over to present again. The next portrait is that of Sheela Vasudevan, a fourteen year old girl who had the ability to perceive what others could not. Sheela had a perfect understanding for her dead grandmother—Ammumma, as she called her. "Ammumma hated imperfections of any kind. In her home there was no room for a cracked plate, a blotched towel or a faded cushion. And now she was going to a hospital that would in all probability decree that a part of her be removed and thus condemn her to be flawed for life" (p. 67). So when her grandmother dies, she dresses up her body, because she can't bear to have her face the world looking so unprepared. She says "I'm not going to let the world see you like this" (p. 73). She brushes her hair, applies foundation and talcum on her body, puts kohl in her eyes and decorated her with costume jewellery. Her parents disapproved of all this as if she had committed a sacrilege but, "She didn't care. She knew Ammumma would have been pleased" (p. 74). Her understanding for her dead grandmother paves the way for her own future liberation.

The story again takes us back to Akhila's story. After her father's death, she "had become the head of the household. Someone who would chart and steer the course of the family's destiny to safe shores" (p. 76). After her two brothers found jobs, they decided to get married not once asking—"What about you? You've been the head of this family ever since Appa died. Don't you want a husband, children, a home of your own" (p. 77). Padma her younger sister came next. She had to get married as the "little one" had changed into a "woman."—Amma had told her. Akhila, at thirty-four is single and lonely. Her singular form of revolt uptil now is seen when she wants to taste a boiled egg brought by an Anglo Indian colleague Katherine Webber, who teaches her how to eat an egg. "My mother always says that eating an egg without salt is like kissing a man without a moustache" (p. 88). Akhila however, is not a woman without desires. Her desire to unshackle herself from the responsibilities of others and from her sacrificing self is implicit when in the coupe, she dreams of a lustful encounter with a stranger. The dream ends with her family calling her "shameless creature," a "brazen slut." Akhila wakes startle and ashamed of her behaviour.

The next figure to emerge is that of Margaret Paulraj, a chemistry teacher who reduces everything into combinations of acids, alkalines and gases. She explains to Akhila that Prabha Devi and Janaki were women "who don't feel complete without a man.... Deep in their hearts, they think world has no use for a single woman" (p. 95). She herself believes that a woman needs a man but not to make her complete. She tells Akhila that when she saw that Akhila was beginning to feel unsure after Janaki related her story, she felt very angry and vexed. A married woman talking of not needing a man is something that needs an explanation. She tries to shatter the myth of woman needing a man to be complete, by relating the story of Ebenezer Paulraj and herself. Her husband is a narcissistic, self-opinionated prig who wants to reduce her to being a simple housekeeper and a cook. When she conceives he said it wasn't the right time for a baby and convinces her to undergo an abortion. When she expresses her doubt if the church would approve the act he argues—"First of all, the Bible never mentions the word abortion...If you had a boil that turned septic wouldn't you have it lanced? Just think of this as a tumour that has to be removed"

(p. 106). Ebenezer Paulraj liked her to cook lavish meals to entertain sycophants. "The coterie was his audience and he enjoyed enthralling them with his mellifluous voice and malice disguised as humour" (p. 114). She boils with rage against her drawing of genitalia in library books, husband Ebenezer for his many conceits but remains silent. Finally she found her own unique weapon—she starts feeding him to a state of benign fatness. Her efforts paid at last and he loses his athletic figure—"Ebe slowly became a fat man. A quiet man. An easy man. A man who no longer needed the coterie or defaced books.... He needed me like he had never before. And Ebe became a man I could live with once again" (p. 134). Margaret knew how to come over the male egoism.

Prabha Devi is one woman who doesn't go by the norms set by men. She has her own opinions and plans for her life. She does something out of routine to make her life interesting, who likes to be the way she is, who knows what she wants and what she doesn't. Rather flirtatious and lively when first married, is frightened into a lifeless conformism until she rediscovers her own possibilities and learns how to float symbolically and otherwise. The glimpse of a swimming pool made her decide that she would learn how to swim. Her whole life is transformed—"She felt the years slip away from her.... From the tips of her toes to the tips of her fingers, a straight line a slow triumph.... My body no longer matters. I have this. I have conquered fear" (p. 195). Thus, Prabha is portrayed as a rich submissive wife who loves swimming because it metaphorically gives her a sense of achievement.

Thus, at the end only one passenger is left with Akhila the sixth passenger the rest have got off the train, offering her advice. The sixth passenger was Marikolanthu a woman "from whom anger poured forth like a stream of lava?" (p. 209). She was angry about the fuss the other travellers made about what she thought were little things. She wonders what they would ever do if real tragedy confronted them. She believes they couldn't fathom how cruel the world could be to women. "Women" she said however, "are strong. Women can do every thing as well as men. Women can do much more. But a woman has to seek that vein of strength in herself. It does not show itself naturally" (p. 210). Hers was the most horrifying story—of a woman raped, cast out abandoned, beyond hope, a thirty one year old woman with a son and no husband. After ugly experiences in a series of jobs, her rape coupled with extreme poverty and class exploitation is the culmination of all other stories—"I was a restless spirit warped and bitter. Sometimes I would think of the past and I would feel a quickening in the vacuum that existed within me now" (p. 266). After the rape, unsurprisingly, it is Marikolanthu who is to be blamed—Why does a young woman walk alone? In the end, on reaching Kanyakumari, she finds herself in a hotel Sea Breeze and decides to make her own private rebellion. She is empowered to reclaim her lost love and releases herself from the hold of conventions and family expectations. Now she can go back to her life but with the knowledge that she is free of some of the shackles at least. "But Akhila is certain that she won't let her family use her any more.... For within me is a woman I have discovered" (p. 270).

The lives of the women that she encounters in the ladies coupe, form a kind of mirror in which Akhila may see her reflection and grasp the happiness she has a right to—All these women who wear their own self sufficiency as a halo are trying to make some sense of their own existence by talking about it to anyone who would listen. She wants to live as she chose with neither restraint, nor fear of censure, because as she says—"Happiness is being allowed to choose one's life to live the way one wants." The women travelling with her are bound by their common human experience, their voyage of self-discovery. Like Arundhati Roy's *The God of Small Things*, Anita Nair's *Ladies Coupe* has taken her places. "It made me think" says Nair about what writing can do, what I can do as a writer."[21] Exploring certain issues that were important to her, "the author takes the readers through the remaking of a man in a quite manner, which far from being dissatisfying is truly the reason for its success."[22] What is remarkable in the novel is the strong message of hope through change and even the ending is revealed as a new beginning.

NOTES AND REFERENCES

1. Menon, Bindu: Interview with Anita Nair, cafedilli.com.
2. Singh Khushwant: Article—Travelling in a woman's compartment, *Tribune*, Saturday, March 2nd, 2002.
3. Mathai, Sujatha Anna: A review—Fellow Travellers, *The Hindu*, June 17th, 2001.
4. Doctor, Geeta: A review in *India Today*.
5. Behal, Suchitra: An interview. Writing for Oneself, *The Hindu*.
6. Raturi, Prachi: Article—In Person A talent for discovery, Financial Express. Also quoted in an interview by Sheela Reddy in Outlook.
7. Behal, Suchitra: An interview. Writing for Oneself, *The Hindu*.
8. An interview by Sheela Reddy in Outlook.
9. Mathai, Sujatha Anna: A review—Fellow Travellers, *The Hindu*, June 17th, 2001.
10. *Gentleman Magazine*.
11. Conservation with Anita Nair: Imagining Keralas, www.chennaibest.com, Jan 23rd, 2007.
12. *The Telegraph*.
13. *Daily Telegraph*.
14. Behal, Suchitra: An interview. Writing for Oneself, *The Hindu*.
15. Nair, Anita: In conversation with Aruna Chandaraju.
16. Behal, Suchitra: An interview. Writing for Oneself, *The Hindu*.
17. Nair, Anita: London: Chatto and Windus (Random House).
18. Koning, Christina remarked in The Times.
19. Menon, Bindu: Interview with Anita Nair, cafedilli.com.
20. Nair, Anita: *Ladies Coupe*, Penguin Books India 2001: All references from this book are from this edition.
21. Conversation with Anita Nair: Imagining Keralas, www.chennaibest.com, Jan. 23rd, 2007.
22. *The New Indian Express*.

'Discovery of Daring and Desire' in Manju Kapur's Fiction

"Tell us what it is to be a woman so that we may know what it is to be a man. What moves at the margin. What it is to have no home in this place. To be set adrift from the one you knew. What it is to live at the edge of towns that cannot bear your company."

—*Toni Morrison*

(Nobel Lecture, 1993)

Women writers today are talking about sex, about men, and are expressing their feelings in no uncertain terms. In the seventies, when Mridula Garg talked of a thinking woman's dichotomy between the body and mind in her novel, *Chitcobra*, she was arrested and charged with Obscenities Act. Today, women writers are blazing a new trail and blurring all the boundaries. The image of the 'New Woman' and her quest for identity, her determination to 'realize' personality, and to achieve self-definition through life, growth and experience, is portrayed convincingly and very forcefully by the Indian woman writers of the nineties. The emerging image is one of a woman unfettered—"Here she comes running, out of prison and off the pedestal; chains off, crown off, halo off, just a live woman."[1]

Women's writing in the 20th century moved towards a medium of modernism in which womanist and feminist statements were combined with political messages. In contrast to the persistent orientalist constructions of the Indian woman as a passive victim, women writers from the Indian subcontinent have written prolifically and movingly, of women negotiating and restricting the multiple patriarchies that determine and shape their lives in diverse post-colonial situations. Women writers today seek to posit the independent existence of women, focusing mainly on the question of identity crisis for women in a parochial society. Exploring a wide range of female experiences that question the recurring face of patriarchy, the recent women writers depict both the diversity of women and diversity within each woman. Among the writers who have portrayed the 'new woman' who is inclined to take the 'road not taken,' and walking on their 'own road,' Manju Kapur undoubtedly arrests attention.

The novels emerging in the twenty-first century furnish examples of a whole range of attitudes towards the imposition of tradition and offer an analysis of the joint family system, with its particular gendered spaces and hierarchies of power, exploring how these dictates the interaction of its members. The issues dealt by the women writers today are no longer feminist or chauvinistic, they are everyday issues faced by everyday people. Many times the daily chores of the household, the immediate family, the relationships and the joys and the sorrows become the setting of their works. Manju Kapur is one Indian writer who prefers reality to magic realism and recreates an intimate world where "family groups sleep in the open air on the roof and wash themselves in the yard...where love making is furtive and urgent because another wife may be listening and women's lives move to a complex choreography of cooking, washing, weaving and mending, growing, picking, chopping and blending."[2]

Kapur's fiction stresses on the woman's need for self fulfilment autonomy, self-realisation, independence individuality and self actualization. "I am interested," says Kapur, "in the lives of women, whether in the political arena or in domestic spaces. One of the main preoccupations in all my books is how women manage to negotiate both inner and outer spaces in their lives—what sacrifices do they have to make in order to keep the home fires burning and at what cost to their personal lives do they find some kind of fulfilment outside the home."[3] As it has been aptly remarked—"In depicting the inner subtlety of a woman mind, Kapur displays a mature understanding of the female psyche. Most of all, Kapur manages to blend the personal with the external."[4]

In *Difficult Daughters*, her first novel, published in 1998, and located primarily in the India of the 1940's, Manju Kapur speaks of the idea of independence—independence aspired to and obtained by a nation and also independence yearned after by a woman. Here, a personal jouissance, a woman's self expression is put in a marginal position though, in relation to the authoritative narrative of the traditional family on the one hand and the coming into being of the nation on the other. "Over the past decade, in fiction and autobiography, South Asian woman have begun to explore the stories of their pasts in an efflorescence of writings. Among others, Mrinal Pande, Manju Kapur and Suguna Iyer have accomplished this through the medium of fiction, while Sara Suleri, Yasmin Alibhai Brown and Mira Kamdar stand out in their memoirs."[5] Based partially on the life of Kapur's own mother, the novel movingly evokes the multiple frustrations encountered by the central character, Virmati, in her efforts to educate herself and establish a domestic space, she can call home. Born in Amritsar in the Punjab in 1940, Virmati, the daughter of a father of progressive ideas and a traditionalist mother seeks human relations that would allow her to be herself. Her desire for self expression and self realisation is condemned to failure by her own family as well as that of the man she marries.

"Set against the bloody backdrop of partition, in the cities of Amritsar and Lahore, *Difficult Daughters* remains a powerful portrait of a society where shame is more important than grief, pragmatism goes hand in hand with superstition and a pregnant wife has to share a bed with her mother in law."[6] The novel spans three generations of women and unveils their sense of disillusionment. The three generation of women symbolize the three stages of Indian independence. Kasturi, the mother represents the pre independence period and is shown as a victim of the offensive control of patriarchy; Virmati the daughter represents the country's struggle for independence, as she too rebels against conventions of morality. Ida, Virmati's daughter is the product of post independence era and establishes herself as an independent woman. The novel reveals that it is not only the daughters but the mothers as well who are difficult to please. Simone de Beauvoir's remarks are quite revealing in this context—"Sometimes she tries to impose on the child exactly her own fate. What was good enough for me is good enough for you, I was brought up this way, you shall share my lot."[7] Herself a conformist, Kasturi, Virmati's mother is content to inhabit the world where she was not ever allowed to forget that "marriage was her destiny. Her mother tried to ensure her future happiness by the impeccable nature of her daughter's qualifications. She was going to please her in laws."[8]

The novel traces Virmati's quest for freedom and identity, her desperation for a space of her own to study, her desire to shed the surrogate motherhood, imposed on her. Being the eldest daughter she is burdened with family duties because of her mother's incessant pregnancies—"Ever since Virmati could remember...it wasn't only baby Parvati to whom she was indispensable, to her younger siblings she was second mother as well" (p. 6). A constant sufferer, herself: Virmati, nurses a desire of being as independent, defiant and assertive as her cousin Shakuntala, and even Swarnalata her room mate in Lahore. Both combine in themselves the fiery enthusiasm of struggle for independence and for equal rights for women, thus epitomizing the post colonial emancipated "New Woman" Shakuntala's participation in the political Gandhian movement even after marriage attracts Virmati—"Virmati listened...drawn towards Shakuntala, to one whose responsibilities went beyond a husband and children" (p. 17). Further Swarnalata too, Virmati's friend, is an ultra committed feminist who takes her to a meeting of Punjab Women's Student Conference where "Heavy applause broke out as Swarna finished speaking" (p. 145). Swarnalata comes up an assertive character—"I was very clear that I wanted to do something, besides getting married. I told my parents, that if they would support me for two more years I would be grateful. Otherwise I would be forced to offer Satyagraha along with other.... But they agreed because they knew. I meant what I meant" (pp. 107-08).

Further, Virmati, like so many other sub-continental women is asked to accept a typical arranged marriage. She rebels against that destiny and insisting on her, right to be educated, she manages to leave home to study in Lahore. Nonetheless, she falls in love with Harish, a professor, a married man who first appears in her life as her parent's tenant. The professor was married as a child to an illiterate woman, whom he had tried to educate and had miserably failed. This wife has no name till the end of the book—she is the woman whose life's mission was to cook for and feed her family and keep the house clean. So the professor falls in love with his student Virmati who is passionately interested in studies. The professor professes his love for her and seduces her through culture, sending her petrarchan sonnets and through referring to Machiavelli and the Greek tragedy until he gains complete control over her mind. Virmati is only happy to enter into this scandalous relationship with the man she loves. The professor wants to have Virmati not as his wife but as a woman to gratify the intellectual needs. However, although Virmati believes that she and Professor are bound together by the bonds of intellectual compatibility, it is physical lust that overpowers them, whenever they are together. Virmati refuses to marry the man selected by her family, tries to commit suicide, is saved and is locked up and finally packed off to Lahore to study further.

After a series of vicissitudes, including a period as a school principal in a small Himalayan state she finally marries the man she loves and returns to Amritsar to live with him. However, he refuses to leave his first wife and she has to live like an outsider in the family; marginalised by her in laws. The professor becomes quite insensitive to her problems. Her mother in law holds her solely responsible for the marriage—"if she had not gone after him, he would not have strayed" (p. 192) and she also believes that, "He was a good son. How was it his fault if he was caught in the trap of some shameless young Punjabi" (p. 193). Virmati wilts under the hostile gaze of Ganga, her husband's first wife, with whom she has to live. She loses all sense of identity: the continuation of her education feels no more dreams of independence. Virmati undergoes the humiliation of being the second wife of the professor and decides to "walk tight-lipped, mute, on the path her destiny had created out for her" (p. 196). In the end, her story disappears and becomes irrelevant swallowed in the greater tragedy of partition. It is only after Virmati's death that her daughter, Ida sees her as a lonely woman who had committed the unforgivable sin of carving an identity of her own. Virmati's tale is told, from a present day perspective, by Ida, her only daughter, who seeks to reconstruct her late mother's life story, against the background of the Independence Movement of the 1940's and the trauma of partition.

The book is interesting for reasons that are not just literary but because, "Kapur has an unusual angle on the involvement of women in Gandhi's Swaraj agitations."[9] Amidst cries of 'Lal Quila tod do, azad fauj chhod do, Muslim league *murdabad*, coalition ministry *zindabad*,' Kapur "emphasizes the efforts made at that time by numerous women, who while demanding equal opportunities, equal access to education and life-opportunities going beyond convention, were a visible force in the non-violent resistance to the British."[10] The story *Difficult Daughters* tells the tale not only of Virmati but of other difficult daughters who succeed better than she did in their parallel struggles for independence in their lives. Virmati's daughter Ida is shown as leading a freer life than her mothers in external terms, yet inside her she feels the same anxieties as her mother. Ida is the narrator through whose voice Kapur speaks—"In Difficult Daughters we do not listen to Virmati's voice. She could not speak out, being certainly situated at the juncture of two oppressions: colonialism and patriarchy. "What we have is her daughter's reconstruction and representation."[11] Though at the centre of the narrative we see a woman who fights but falls and fails Kapur's novel shows that what happens to Virmati is the representative destiny of Indian woman. However, Gur Pyari Jandial correctly points out that it is a mistake to devalue Virmati's struggle just because she failed, for what mattered was to have made the attempt, "to break the patriarchal mould, and for Virmati to have tried to do that in the forties was a great achievement."[12]

Manju Kapur's second novel, *A Married Woman* deals with the socially critical and women oriented themes quite as powerfully as its predecessor and is thematically even more challenging. In contrast to the other Indian fiction writers who focus on a historical view, Kapur stresses on the complex portrayal of the social and communal unrest. The focus here shifts from a woman's rebellion against society shackled in traditions, torn between duty and desire, to an exploration of the positioning of women in sexual orientation. In the Indian Homophobic socio-cultural context, where any overt expression of sexuality by women is considered as promiscuity, Kapur's novel explores the twin explosive subjects of sexual intimacy between women and Hindu Muslim confrontation, against a backdrop of respectable middle class Delhi life.

With women as its central theme once again, Kapur raises the question of identity which has been related to the representation of lesbians in literature and culture. Even Shobha De in *Starry Nights* and *Strange Obsession* has extensively dealt with the theme of lesbianism, Deepa Mehta too, in her film *Fire* focused and projected the world of lesbian utopia. However, though the novel approaches this "women-identified experience,"[13] it does not specifically address lesbians or present an ideal role model in the protagonist who "could be emulated by the invisible lesbian community in Indian society."[14] The novel should not simply be assessed as a rendition of lesbian relationship. Set at a time of socio-political upheaval, "A Married Woman is a well balanced depiction of a country's inner development—its strengths and its failures and anguish of a women's unrest, which is as complicated as the social and political upheaval going around her."[15] Manju Kapur has beautifully combined love, family values, communal riots, a married woman's life and how she finds love in a person of the same sex. The novel beautifully chronicles the socialist generation of India's post-independence, dealing with self-imposed limitations, socio economic privations and a yearning for much more. Cast in the rising independence of urban women from the shackles of feminist rhetoric, *A Married Woman* expects the acknowledgement of oppression and the inability of the individual, to effect change in the circumstances, despite the antagonistic forces and expectations of the family and society.

Kapur's preoccupation with displacement of individual and repression is culturally universal. The novels preoccupation with the displacement and repression felt by tradition bound women is evident from the opening of the novel,—"Astha was brought up properly as befits a woman with large supplements of fear"[16] (p. 1), Astha, a young romantic girl drawn to the idea of a love marriage succumbs to the desperation of her perpetually anxious parents, who wish to see her safely married, as they were on the verge of retirement. She rebelliously refuses every suitor, until she meets Hemant whose time at university in the states has turned him into a liberal thinker. Or so she hopes. But as Hemant becomes increasingly involved in his business, Astha finds herself consigned to a traditional female role and discontent slips in. Astha has reached a state of ennui, with her comfortable middle class existence and yearns for more than the quotidian woman's role as a helpmate or a sexual object succumbing to the pressures of society and her family, she never acknowledged her inner desires and aspirations. Astha has little to complain about, and yet she operates as if it is society's greatest crime to limit an individual's passions merely because she is a woman.

Her growing dissatisfaction is played out against a background of Indian political and social unrest. Hit by existential angst, she begins an internal rebellion against the life of repression and anguish. Her convictions are put to the test when she finds not one, but two outlets for her passions. Following the death of a street theatre activist Aijaz in a communal riot in the troubled early nineties, in the wake of the Hindu Muslim clashes over the Babri Masjid in Ayodhya, Astha connects with a social group. She makes a few paintings to be sold in an exhibition sponsored by the Manch and begins to express her creativity through painting, filling her self imposed loneliness with art. Ironically Astha passes on the same limiting value that her mother in law passed on her "thus teaching her daughter how to devalue her work and passing on the tradition from woman to woman." Later in Ayodhya itself, Astha encounters Pipeelika Khan, a woman qualified in sociology and economics and with a background that is Hindu, on her mother's side, South Indian, who works for a Delhi NGO and who turns out to be Aijaz's widow, having boldly married him across the racial divide. A rapport is quickly established between them. The two connect at multiple levels and are drawn to each other. Against all social norms, the friendship between the two women develops into a fully intimate same sex relationship. Astha is enlivened by their romance, to the point that she begins to fantasize of an independent, unfettered existence, together with Pipeelika. She steals time away to be with her lover, until her husband begins to suspect, so that she might have an independent life.

However, due to the generation gap between them, the younger woman Pipeelika realizes the implausibility of any lasting permanent coexistence and finally she leaves for the US to study for a doctorate and Astha is left with nothing but to return emotionally to her marriage to Hemant. Thus, Astha leaps into the fold, unable to take the leap. *A Married Woman* thus explores Astha's longing for a purpose to her life other than being a wife and mother against a vividly realized backdrop of Indian sectarian politics. The author makes Pipeelika leave for the US is a narrative strategy which Patricia Juliana Smith calls, "lesbian panic"[17] a strategy which could be traced in the works of Virginia Woolf, Ellen Moers, Elaine Showalter. As Smith remarks—"the condition of lesbian panic have long been inscribed in narratives by and about women."[18] The novel therefore, "is not a lesbian text because lesbian sexuality is depoliticalised and reduced to a matter of private preference."[19] Astha's choice of heterosexual family, marriage and children along with her private preference for lesbian sexuality, makes one wonder if it is a lesbian text. We are also told that even in the most intimate moments that Astha spends with Pipee she cannot help worrying about her kids. We see her straddling between two worlds—the heterosexual world she opts for and the lesbian world which she enjoys but does not acknowledge, her relation with Pipee, was not the outcome of her sexual desire to be with a woman, it was more an incidental happening resulting from her predicament—"like a woman of straw, her inner life dead, with a man who noticed nothing" (p. 287). 'Emotionally starved' and 'throttled', she seeks her jouissance in the lesbian continuum, but the female bonding managed to provide her only a temporary release, not a permanent solution.

The mode employed here is, as in *Difficult Daughters*, social realism of the classical type, with no Rushdiesque recourse to fabulation or magic realism. Throughout Kapur's writing delineates the human relations and their social context with great sensibility and close attention to the details of daily life. Blending the personal with the external, Kapur beautifully entwined the major historical event with the lives of her characters and depicts the political situation with the same fervour and graphic detail as she describes the protagonist Astha's turmoil. Anita Nair's remarks beautifully sum up the essence of the novel—"If one's looking for a metaphor, here it is. A nation falling apart because of religious differences and the dynamics of power politics; a marriage falling apart because of difference that somehow cannot be bridged."[20]

Like her earlier two novels, Manju Kapur's latest novel *Home* beautifully weaves "conflicting loyalties, intrigues, triumphs"[21] as well as the "small rebellious and intense power struggles"[22] which constitutes the universal human experience. Here, too, the canvas is the familiar one: the ordinary middle class joint family and the subject is, the exploration of the lives of ordinary women, and the ways in which they connect to and resist other women, as it had been in *Difficult Daughters* and *A Married Woman*. A novel about the pressures and rewards of living in a traditional extended but close knit Indian family of shopkeepers: brothers and their families living in the same house, the story presents the women characters as mistresses of a joint kitchen in the day time and their husband's bed at night. Destined to be married off at a marriageable age they accept every brunt easily as something controlled totally by Fate. Kapur's novel describes the submissiveness of women to their mother in law when these show their resentment of their daughters in law; the pressures on wives to produce children—boys for preference—and the disgrace if they fail to do so; and the women in the novel are shown spending their energies left over from cooking and housework in being jealous of each other and being particularly status conscious in nagging their husbands who are softer than their wives. The shifts in relationships the power struggles within a family, the suppressing individuality are all very minutely captured by Manju Kapur.

A saga of Indian family life featuring endearing characters and vivid portrayals, *Home* spans three generations whose destiny and dreams are glued to the Banwarilal Cloth Shop. The patriarch of the family, Lala Banwarilal, a refugee from Pakistan sets up his cloth shop in Karol Bagh and implements a work ethics which dictates focus, unity and complete surrender to the family's commerce. His two sons, Yashpal and Pyarelal ably assist their father in running the business smoothly. Everything is perfectly balanced till Yashpal falls in love with a girl, Sona, who came to their shop to buy cloth. Though coming from a very ordinary family Sona manages to be Yashpal's wife after he convinces his parents for the marriage. Sona is very beautiful while Pyarelal's wife Sushila is rather ordinary looking. The novel opens with the two sisters Sona and Rupa—"Mrs. Sona Lal and Mrs. Rupa Gupta.... One was rich, the other poor, one the eldest daughter in law of a cloth shop owner, the other the wife of an educated badly paid government servant"[23] (p. 2). Whereas, Sushila quickly has the required sons, Ajay and Vijay, Sona is childless for the first ten years of her marriage and therefore, an object of resentment and pity among the women folk of the family as she was unable to perform a women's prime function as a means of bringing forth the next generation.

The tale then shifts the focus from the two sisters to the happenings in the Banwarilal family. The respected, benign and conservative patriarch maintains some kind of unity in the family but when he dies, tensions multiply. The patriarch had stood in ways of modernisation and after his death the second generation modernises the shop and pulls down the old house and builds a modern one. The story diversifies into the second generation people when Sona gives birth to children Nisha and Raju after a decade of barrenness. Since the time Sona had conceived, her mother in law had started doting on her, thus antagonizing Rupa who had earlier been Sona's confidante in her gossips about her mother in law. In a parallel thread, we are introduced to Yashpal's sister, Sunita, who was married to a drunkard and dies a suspicious death. Her young son Vicky is brought to Delhi to stay with the Banwari Lal's, where confused and uncared for, Vicky ends up abusing his little cousin sister, Nisha. Since Nisha's childhood is scarred by incestuous abuse, the victimized girl is sent to stay at Aunt Rupa's home in order to preserve the honour of the family. Kapur handles the theme in a matter of fact manner and draws our attention to the fact that the scary incident is considered unthinkable to be discussed and brought to the open. These are our social realities, even if we normally keep them under wraps and the family tries to suppress the matter and gathers around the girl to comfort her. At Rupa's place Nisha is brought up as a brilliant student and she comes back to her own family ultimately. She is the first girl to go to college and the first to fall in love with a boy of another caste but when the family finds about it, their relationship is quickly snubbed out. Manglik Nisha can't find a husband and remains a spinster in the house till she decides to set up her own business of making readymade clothes and also finally gets married to a childless widower. The book ends with her pregnancy and her decision to leave the readymade clothes business. The second-half of the book concentrates on Nisha and excludes everybody else. Though Nisha emerges as a woman who dreams outside of matrimony and maternity and falls for a boy of lower class, she goes on to develop eczema and loses her beauty and eventually makes a sorry marriage with a widower. The novel has a headstrong female protagonist but she shows up as one only till two-thirds of the novel: later she gives up her desire for assertion.

The novel shows modernity threatening the solidarity of the joint family and every hint of individual expression is substituted with deadened conformity. The book explains the issues of the patriarchal society and one of the daughters breaks the rules with the changing social equations. Despite individual ambitions and legal restrictions, there is a growth of the old house and cloth shop because the novel asserts emphatically, that the interests of a business family came before personal concerns.

Entitled with the "full freedom to create a circumstance, a character, a twist, a turn" Kapur, however, ends up documenting the lives of people she is most familiar with—the lives of woman. Hugely human and engaging, *Home* is a masterful novel of the acts of kindness, compromise, and secrecy that lies at the heart of every family. Kapur does a wonderful job dissecting the everyday of an ordinary life, showing how even the ordinary in this generation can be claustrophobic. Kapur's women were made to believe that anything outside the small world created for them was not normal.

Thus, whether it is the unusual angle on the involvement of women in Gandhi's Swaraj agitation as in her first novel, *Difficult Daughters*, or exploring the positioning of women in the context of sexual orientation as in *A Married Women*, and further, the saga of traditional Indian business family in *Home*, Manju Kapur displays a mature understanding of the female psyche. Striking a balance between a natural coexistence and unfettered freedom and space on the other, Kapur's eloquent narration of women's issues is nevertheless, both Indian and universal.

NOTES AND REFERENCES

1. Gilman, Charlotte Perkins' remarks in an article on the New Woman.
2. Lee, Maggie in *Sunday Times*.
3. Kapur, Manju in conversation with Kiran Nagarkar, 7th June, 2006, Love Marriages "Too Much Adjustment."
4. Banerji, Mithu. C.: *The Observer*, 23 Feb. 2003.
5. Rajan, Rajeshwari Sunder, review of Shards of memory: Woven Lives in Four Generations.
6. Quoted in *The Observer*.
7. Beauvoir, Simone de: *The Second Sex* translated and edited by H.M. Parshly, pp. 533-34.
8. Kapur, Manju: *Difficult Daughters* (1998), London: Faber and Faber, 1999, p. 57.
9. Singh, Amardeep, review of Difficult Daughters.
10. Salvador, Dora Sales, translators note to Hijas dificiles (q. v.), 356.
11. Salvador, Dora Sales, in her essay on the novel in English.
12. Jandial, Gur Pyari, "Evolving a Feminist Tradition: The Novels of Shashi Deshpande and Manju Kapur."

13. Rich Adrienne, "Complete Heterosexuality and Lesbian Existence" in signs: Journal of Women in Culture and Society, pp. 631-60.
14. Chandra, Subhash in a review: Intersections: Gender, History and Culture in the Asian Context, Issue 14 Nov. 2006.
15. Banerji, Mithu. C, in a review in *The Observer*, dated 23 Feb. 2002.
16. Kapur, Manju: A Married Woman, London: Faber and Faber, 2003.
17. Smith, Patricia Juliana: "And I wondered if she might kiss me": lesbian, panic as narrative strategy in British women's fiction in Modern Fiction Studies.
18. *Ibid.*, p. 572.
19. Hoogland, Renee C.: Lesbian Configuration, New York: Columbia University Press, 1997, p. 21.
20. Nair, Anita in the Book Review of Manju Kapur's A Married Woman.
21. Nagarkar, Kiran: On the blurb of Home, Published by Random House, India, 2006.
22. Roy, Nilanjana: On the blurb of Home, Published by Random House, India, 2006.
23. Kapur, Manju: *Home*, Published by Random House, India, 2006.

'Seeking the Self' in Shashi Deshpande's *That Long Silence*

13

> "When she stopped conforming to the conventional picture of femininity she finally began to enjoy being a woman."
>
> —*Betty Friedan*

In the context of contemporary Indian writing in English, Shashi Deshpande is one of the most understated yet confident voices exploring the individual and universal predicaments through the female psyche. In her 'quest for the human self within the woman,' Deshpande lays bare their trails and tribulations under the impact of the conflicting influence of tradition and modernity. Through myth and modernity, Shashi Deshpande has emerged as an icon for the younger writers. Writing for Femina Eve's Weekly and other Indian magazines while nurturing her two younger sons in Mumbai, she recalls: "I feel I came through only because I had faith in myself. The desire to say something was so strong. That was hard, when my whole life was considered unimportant, even writing by women was considered unimportant. Many women are silenced by lack of time. If I admire anything in myself, it's only that I kept on. It's easy to give up."[1] Her work reflects the whole gamut of Indian cultural issues, the thickly populated world of her novels, the working out of relationships within families and marriages, the fine insight into human character as well as her boldness in the treatment of sex and class barriers which have been the major concern of her fiction.

Instead of portraying India as an exotic land full of magic and mysticism, Deshpande chooses to tell stories about the quotidian life of the average Indian. What is extraordinary is the way she questions the everyday existence and helps to see through the evolution of well etched characters, the frailties and possibilities of human life. "So unerring is Deshpande's grip on social reality that, whatever comes through as gendered does so as natural almost undistorted record of reality...without lapping into sectarian shrillness"[2]—says Jasbir Jain. For, Shashi Deshpande, writing was a means to self discovery. She was exasperated being known as somebody's daughter, somebody's wife and somebody's mother, she speaks her truth gently but firmly and her words linger on. Betty Friedan's, *The Problem Without a Name* proved to be the turning point in her life. She felt—"I'm not only a woman. I'm not only a mother. I'm not only a wife. I'm not only a female. I'm a human being with a mind. It gave me a lot of unhappiness that my intellect was not being connected to my female self. I was always Mrs. Deshpande, Raghunandan's mother, Vikram's mother...that anger ultimately translates into feminism."[3]

Through her writings, she fights for the recognition of women as individuals and with tremendous feeling she pleads: "You've got to read woman's writings differently.... It's about a human being trying to place herself within relationships, peoples and ideas."[4] Her fiction besides six short story collections includes *Roots and Shadows* (1983), *The Dark Holds No Terrors* (1980), *That Long Silence* (1988), *The Binding Vine* (1993), *A Matter of Time* (1996) and *Small Remedies* (2000). Though all her novels work through feminine consciousness, Shashi Deshpande never attempts at focusing only on the feminine perspective. "I am not a feminist," insists Shashi Deshpande. "I am a human being and I write about other human beings who happen to be women," she said. However, she places her writings within an overtly feminist framework when she states—"My own writing comes out of a deep involvement with the society I live in, especially with women. My novels are about women trying to understand themselves, their history, their roles and their place in this society. I rejected stereotypes and requestioned the myths which have so shaped the image of women, in this country. In a way, through my writing, I have tried to break the long silence of women in our country."[5] Deshpande thus lends her effort to a major aspect of the feminist project, which is to transform a predominantly androcentric symbolic order. Exploring the patriarchal set up of India, Deshpande's protagonist reaches out to define the 'self' in an attempt to free themselves. In there quest for self-realization, each protagonist breaks free of the religious and social codes that circumscribe and undermine a woman's spirit and deny her an identity of her own. However, it would not be correct to term her a feminist, because there is nothing doctrinaire about her fiction; she simply portrays the meaning of being a woman in modern India.

Her work provides a pointer to the catatonic status of women in the tradition bound, male dominated middle-class society of contemporary India, and concentrates on the struggle of women to overcome the constricting dilemmas of prefixed gendered definitions and behavioural norms. Hers is not the strident and militant kind of feminism as she has stressed again in a free wheeling interview—"I don't like to call myself a feminist writer. I'm a feminist but I don't write to propagate an ism."[6] However, she does believe, "that the female of the species has the same right to be born and survive, to fulfil herself and shape her life according to her needs and the potential that lies within her as the male has. And how can feminism be anti-men when it is really working for a better, a more meaningful and companionable relationship between man and woman."[7] Her feminine perspective does not entirely oppose the patriarchal strictures but also perceives men themselves as victims of patriarchy. Her men and women analyse their failures and problems in order to work their way out of the state of crisis. Deshpande's chief concern is the human relations, not the rationalized, but the felt, perceived and real, not the traditional but redefined human relations, especially the relationship between man and woman. In all these, the central figure is woman. Women narrators in her fiction transcend their gender in order to explore the male psyche and avoid stereotypical projections of patriarchal strictures. Women's lives in India, their problems and the domestic sphere have been consuming themes of most of Deshpande's oeuvre. Shashi Deshpande's novels explore the patriarchal social set up of India and her protagonists, located within this social reality, reach out to define the 'self' in an attempt to free themselves. In their quest for self realisation, each protagonist breaks free of the religious and social codes that circumscribe and undermine a woman's spirit and deny her an identity of her own. These alternative narratives of women's history are transformed into narratives of resistance as resistance forms a strong subtext of the novels.

Shashi Deshpande's sure footed literary voice explores predicaments through the female psyche. Her novels reveal the inability of the woman to speak and the positive movement is always the movement towards the breaking of 'That Long Silence'. *That Long Silence* re-emphasizes Deshpande's passion for these issues as she weaves a simple ingenious tale of the contradictions of male ambivalence and cruelty, female stoicism and shame and human desire and desertion. The title brings to our mind a British Feminist Manifesto quoted in the epigraphy (American actress Elizabeth: Robin's speech to WWSL in 1907)—"If I were a man and cared to know the world I lived in, I almost think it would make me a shade uneasy—The weight of that long silence of one half of the world."[8] It is against this backdrop that the novel describes the patriarchal impositions on women to the extent of cramping their space. The novel realistically articulates the silence of the feminine world. Talking about *That Long Silence*, Shashi Deshpande herself says—"And then I wrote *That Long Silence* almost entirely a woman's novel nevertheless, a book about the silencing of one half of humanity. A lifetime of introspection went into the novel, the one closest to me personally; the thinking and ideas in this are closest to my own."[9]

The narrator of this novel is a writer for whom the stripping of accumulated layers of self deceptive constructions yields the present fiction. Jaya, the narrator writer, commences the novel with an acknowledgement of the ruthless process entailed in the self revelations of the autobiographical mode she employs.

There is the literal silence of the many women of Jaya's circle whose stories are never told or if they are, have too limited a currency to make any impact on the symbolic field. In *That Long Silence*, Shashi Deshpande reveals an intriguing picture of an ordinary middle class woman. The protagonist, Jaya, lives with her husband Mohan and two children Rahul and Rati. The author describes the travails of being a middle class woman educated yet confined to restrictions posed by the conservative society. Shashi Deshpande describes and dissects the life inside the cage, behind the veil, under the bell jar from the vantage point of inner space. The novel centres on the inner perception of a woman who is subtly drawn from inside, a woman who finds her normal routine so disrupted that for the first time she can look at her life and attempt to decide who she really is. In the stifling and suffocating domestic ambience and patriarchal set up, she finds her female identity effaced. As Spivak writes in her article, 'Can, the subaltern speak,' "Between patriarchy and imperialism subject—constitution and object formation the figure of the woman disappears, not into a pristine nothingness, but into a violent shuttling which is the displaced figuration of the 'Third World Woman' caught between tradition and modernisation."[10]

The novel is shrewdly presented by Shashi Deshpande as Jaya's own series of memories, a first person account of both her past and present life, written only for herself, and thus as a direct and truthful statement on one woman's introspective analysis, her concrete existence. In evoking, 'the original gushing forth of existence,' Shashi Deshpande renders a spell inducing tale not in the complete naturalistic style but with some magical realism we have come to associate with Gabriel Garcia Marquez, filling her protagonist's world with ghosts and luscious imagery that suggests meaning hidden even in the most ordinary things. Deshpande reveals the consciousness of Jaya, the protagonist through an exposition of here mind in the process of thinking, feeling and reacting to the stimuli of the moment and situation. Playing the role of an ideal wife, Jaya follows her husband into exile. They shift into their old small flat in Dadar. In the silence of this flat and in the absence of her usual domestic routine, Jaya broods over her situation and fondly recalls her past. The move to Dadar flat destabilizes the fictions upon which Jaya had based her life till then, and wrote herself in the roles of mother and wife. But with Mohan's job in jeopardy, which precipitates the move to Dadar, the middle class dream is endangered and Jaya has to re-evaluate her comfortable personae as wife and mother of a middle class family when these are threatened by her husband's involvement in fraudulent activities. The Dadar flat becomes the inspiration for further intrusions upon Jaya and mock her precarious self constructions. The lesson the Dadar flat offers to Jaya is the possibility of inscribing an authentically worded text through the roles one must necessarily assume with reference to others. Though, she is a writer, Jaya has not achieved true self-expression. As Jaya, goes over the past, she realizes in how many different ways Mohan has pushed her and appropriated her space and her relationships, and also in how many different ways he has limited her, inhibiting even the free expression of her natural generosity and fellow feeling. Even on most crucial domestic issues, she was silent. Veena Sheshadari aptly comments: "One ends up by wondering whether Jaya has imposed that long silence on herself not out of a sense of duty or to emulate the ideal Hindu woman of the ages gone by, but in order to camouflage the streaks of ugliness within her."[11]

Jaya silently recollects how her husband gave her a new name 'Suhasini' on her wedding day. Though she remains silent, she does not use the name Suhasini she remains Jaya, the name given to her by her father, meaning victory. Suhasini meaning—"a soft smiling placid motherly woman"[12] is not accepted by Jaya. Her not accepting the new name is the manifestation of her resistance as well as assertiveness. However, even when hurt at being accused she stays dumb and also wonders—"Oh God, Why couldn't I speak? Why couldn't I say something?... I could say nothing" (p. 120). Her husband described woman being treated very cruelly by their husbands and he calls it strength. She comments—"He saw strength in the woman sitting silently in front of the fires, but I saw despair.... I saw a struggle so bitter that silence was the only weapon. Silence and surrender" (p. 36). When she scrutinizes her life closely, she realizes that to achieve this state of fulfilment as wife, she had deliberately suppressed many traits of her personality. However, Jaya doesn't suppress her writing career and her relationship with Kamat, her neighbour at one time.

In the early years, Jaya's writing was a matter of pride for her husband Mohan. But a particular story, about—"a couple, a man who could not reach out to his wife except through her body" (p. 144) makes Mohan intolerant. Jaya's imaginative writing is condemned by her husband who asks—"How could you have done it? How can you reveal our lives to the world in this way?" (p. 144) Jaya loses her identity as a writer, she compromises with writing silly things for a woman's magazine which doesn't satisfy her intellectual hunger. She had neglected her real self but now at the end, she decides to come out of the nest, because life has become intolerable for her. She suffers from alienation and mutters in anguish: "I was Jaya. But I had been Suhasini as well, the Suhasini who was distinct from Jaya, a soft, smiling placid motherly woman. A woman who coped (p. 16).

She reappraises her own role-enactment placing the sacred icons of marriage and family life under the light of a mercilessly honest scrutiny. Through her protagonist, Deshpande is fulfilling an implicitly feminist's function, a consciousness—raising similar to one carried on by women's groups in American in the 1960's during the early years of the radical feminist movement. The protagonist Jaya had to suppress her emotions as Mohan warns her—"My mother never raised her voice against my father, however badly he behaved to her" (p. 83). Another striking trait of Jaya's personality which comes into conflict with her role as wife and mother is her association with Kamat, a widower, who lives in an apartment above Jaya's flat at Dadar. An advertiser by profession, Kamat analyses Jaya's problems objectively. Jaya confides all her problems to him: "Jaya's thwarted creativity and attempts to acquiesce to Mohan's desires generate a feeling of guilt in her, which makes her social poise somewhat artificial. Her relationship with Kamat, which is never very precisely defined in the novel, is an escapade to find some humane empathy and sharing. This relationship imparts an inner fulfilment to Jaya which her relationship with Mohan had failed to provide" (p. 94). She feels physically attracted to Kamat but she felt that by "the equally overwhelming certainty of my mind that I could not do so" (p. 157). Even when Kamat dies, she doesn't pay homage to him, remains silent as it might have resulted in threatening her marriage.

Jaya is a modern predicament and the flood of consciousness that ensures out of it is a silent stream of thoughts and feelings. Jaya succumbs and surrenders to Mohan without revolting silently. She wills to his will. She never says, 'Yes,' when her husband asks her whether he has hurt her. She endures everything, tolerates all kinds of masculine oppression silently in the emotion that governed her behaviour to him, there was still the habit of being a wife of sustaining and supporting him. Shashi Deshpande uses a beautiful image to describe Jaya's married life—"A pair of bullocks yoked together" (p. 8). Jaya wants to escape from the confines of an incarcerated domestic life in her quest for selfhood. There is no communication between Mohan and Jaya—"Nothing between us...nothing between me and Mohan. We live together but there had been only emptiness between us" (p. 185). In Jaya, Deshpande presents not a woman who has a desire to revolt but one who has reconciled to her lot. Having been unable to discover the truth, Jaya remains silent and reveals her personal emotion in her writings. To Mohan, to be angry was something absolutely unfeminine: "A woman can never be angry she can only be neurotic, hysterical frustrated. There is no room for despair, either. There is only order and routine, today. I have to change the sheets tomorrow, scrub the bathrooms, the day after, and clean the fridge..." (pp. 147-48). Enmeshed in the Indian family system, Jaya has lost her authenticity as a human being. She has shaped herself to the wishes of Mohan. She has given up the job she wanted to take, the baby she wanted to adopt and the anti price campaign she had wanted to take part in. Since Mohan accuses her of not caring about the children, she has stopped writing. She learns at last, "no questions, no retorts, only silence" Unable to communicate her anxieties to the unapproachable, incommunicable, indifferent Mohan, she is engulfed by a sense of seclusion. Ever since she gets married she has done nothing but wait: "Waiting for Mohan to come home, waiting for children to be born, for them to start school, waiting for them to come home, waiting for the milk, the servant, the lunch carrier man" (p. 30).

Jaya's sexual life too gives her no satisfaction. Unable to endure, "a silent wordless lovemaking", she says—"I could stay apart from him without a twinge, I could sleep with him too, without desire" (p. 97). Mohan's indifference after sex often fills her with a sense of loneliness and of illusion: "But, lying there my body still warm and throbbing from the contact with his, it had come to me in one awful moment that I was alone" (p. 98). Gradually, Jaya's identity is completely lost into her role of a wife and mother and from a fiercely independent woman that she once was, Jaya is ultimately reduced to a mere stereotype of a woman: nervous, incompetent, needing male help and support" (p. 76). Her silent suffering reaches its climax when Mohan leaves home silently and stealthily without a word to his wife after she has uncontrollably laughed at him. His absence unnerved her and she begins to ruminate. As she does not want her family to disintegrate, she is rather longing to break her silence. Wandering in the streets of Mumbai she could not bear the crushing burden of her marriage and the responsibility of her children on her shoulders alone. She couldn't bear the thought of losing her husband—"The thought of living without him had twisted my insides. His death had seemed to me the final catastrophe. The very idea of his dying had made me feel so bereft that tears had flowed effortlessly down my cheeks. If he had been a little late coming home, I had been sure he was dead. By the time he retuned, I had in my imagination, shaped my life to a desolate widowhood" (pp. 96-97).

Towards the end of the novel Jaya emerges as a bold and mature woman. She has decided not to look for clues in Mohan's face and then "give him the answer I know he wants." She wants to break out of the yoke. At length she resolves to break that silence by putting down on paper all that she has suppressed in her seventeen years silence—that long silence which had reduced her to fragments. She erases the silence and asserts herself. (p. 192)—"I will have to speak, to listen, I will have to erase the silence between us"—says Jaya. She breaks the silence, writes her story and concludes: "We can always hope without that life would be impossible. And if there is anything I know now it is this; life has always to be made possible" (p. 193). She stands for hope, for change—"We don't change overnight it's possible that we may not change even over long periods of time. But we can always hope without that life would be impossible" (p. 193). The long silence which had reduced her to fragments is broken at last. She realizes that fragmentation of "self" is not possible—"I am not afraid...any more. The panic has gone. I am Mohan's wife. I had thought and cut off the bits of me that had refused to be Mohan's wife. Now I know that kind of fragmentation is not possible. The child hands in pocket have been with me through the years. She is with me still" (p. 191).

The novel is beautifully summed up thus; "The novel which is more a woman's novel than any other novel of Deshpande's, and which is full of minute details of every day life, the hopes and dreams and the insignificant happenings, end on a positive note. The crisis has forced a whole lot of rethinking. And there is hope for a new beginning. Jaya has recovered her lost self and along with that her capacity to dream. She has decided to get rid of the silence which women have lived with for ages."[13] *That Long Silence,* therefore, remains "a muted and essentially sympathetic treatment of the problems of marital relationship, maintaining a credible balance between the sexes."[14] For a writer, the most significant thing is to find a voice and Deshpande through her fiction breaks the silence of women and redeems them from their linguistic exile. All her women protagonists—Indu, Saru, Jaya, Urmila and Sumi reorganize themselves in new kinship patterns with every change, and when their woman's space is eroded within these changing patterns, they revolt against the traditions and in their quest for liberation.

NOTES AND REFERENCES

1. Deshpande, Shashi: Quoted in the online edition of *The Hindu*, Aug. 28, 2003: Breaking That Long Silence.
2. Jain, Jasbir: Rawat Publication, p. 318.
3. Deshpande, Shashi: Quoted in the online edition of *The Hindu*, Aug. 28, 2003: Breaking That Long Silence.
4. *Ibid.*
5. Deshpande, Shashi in an interview with *The Times of India,* 22nd July 2001.
6. Deshpande, Shashi: In a free wheeling interview.
7. Deshpande, Shashi: "Why I am a feminist" (a collection of her essays), p. 83.
8. Deshpande, Shashi: 'Epigraph,' *That Long Silence* (New Delhi: Penguin, 1989).
9. Deshpande, Shashi: Quoted in Creative Theory: Writers on writing. (Ed.) Jasbir Jain (Delhi: Pencraft International, 2000), p. 210.
10. Spivak, Gayatri Chakravorty: "Can the Subaltern speak." From Colonial Discourse and Post Colonial Theory (Harvest Wheat Sheaf, 1994).
11. Sheshadari, Veena: *That Long Silence Literature Alive.* 2. 1. (1988), p. 94.
12. Deshpande, Shashi: *That Long Silence* (New Delhi: Penguin, 1989), p. 16. Subsequent references are to this edition.
13. Jain, Jasbir: 'Shashi Deshpande,' *A Companion to Indian Fiction in English* ed. Pier Paolo Piciucco.
14. Nambiar, K.C.: "Eve in an Urban Jungle," Review of That Long Silence, *The Hindu*, 6th March, 1990.

'The Sense of Exile, Alienation and Assimilation' in Jhumpa Lahiri's Fiction

> "As is frequently the case with immigrants in general, the Indian diaspora is also keen on taking pride—some self respect and dignity—in the culture and tradition of the original homeland. This frequently takes the form of some kind of 'national' or civilizational appreciation of being Indian in origin."
>
> —*Amartya Sen*
>
> In the Argumentative Indian.

While Indian writers have been making a significant contribution to world literature since Independence, the past few years have seen a massive flourishing of Indian fiction in the global market. Though there is a great deal of difference between Indian writers, there are a few themes that loosely link them together—the issues of identity and language for example, and the themes of exile and diaspora which have been a focal point of much Indian fiction.

The immigrant experience, the question of identity and the expatriate experience continues to furnish terrific material for fiction and can be traced in the works of various South Asian women writers too. For instance, Monica Ali's *Brick Lane* which won the Granta's Best of Young British Novelists of the decade, Newcomer of the Year at the 2004 British Book Awards and was also short listed for Booker Prize, reveals tellingly that the truest part of Ali's writings is about the experience of exile, the pain of un-belonging. Zadie Smith, another non-white novelist blasted into the literacy scene with *White Teeth*—the

Booker nominated bestseller about immigrant culture in London. Last but not the least, Kiran Desai's 2006, Man Booker prize winning title, *The Inheritance of loss*, also illuminates the pain of exile and the ambiguities of post-colonialism. What sets Lahiri apart is the combination of her absorbing concern for the moral and psychological truth related to the immigrant's discontentment with the outstanding literary qualities which makes her writings—supple, elegant, economical, ironic and compassionate, marvellously capturing the nuances and minutely observed details. "Though endowed with a distinct universal speech, her stories do bring out rather successfully the predicament of the Indians who trapeze between and across two traditions, one inherited and left behind, and the other, encountered but not necessarily assimilated."[1]—remarks Aruti Nayar.

With its characters poised between the old world of India and the unnerving newness of America, Jhumpa Lahiri's prize winning collection of short stories, *The Interpreter of Maladies*, reveals her commendable grasp of biculturism and authoritative grace. Having won critical acclaim for "its grace, acuity and compassion in detailing lives, transported from India to America,"[2] the book remains a subtle evocation of the warm and complex portrayal of family life and Indian immigrants trying to saddle two cultures—their Indian heritage and the American Dream. Lahiri introduces us to people who left behind family and friends and the familiar heat and bustle of India to build a new life in America—a cold, bleak land of strangers and new customs. Lahiri's subject is the loneliness of dislocation, cultural displacement, sense of identity and belonging with one foot in two worlds. Imbued with the fine details of both Indian and American cultures, Lahiri's stories describe with universal compassion, the fragmentation of identities, the alienation and sense of loneliness experienced by all immigrants, giving voice to their anguish and probing into their complex psychoses. Lahiri, "hits her stride closer to home on the uncertain ground of the immigrant, the sense of loss and longing that permeates other Indians abroad...with a rare eye for the details of displacement."[3]

In a recent interview to Newsweek, Lahiri pointed out that the older she gets, the more aware she is, that she has "inherited a sense of exile"[4] which strongly pervades her major writings. Lahiri's major concern is the "question of identity which is always a difficult one, but more so for those who are culturally displaced, like the immigrants are, or those who grow up simultaneously."[5] When asked how she felt growing up as the child of immigrants, Lahiri explained, "It was always a question of allegiance, of choice. I wanted to please my parents.... I also wanted to meet the expectations of my American peers.... It was a classic case of divided entity."[6] Thus, we can see that it is the complications of being a hyphenated American that informs her work completely. Lahiri's true genius resides in capturing the ordinary moments in the life of her characters and transforming them into works of art. She combined her authentic familiarity with the lives of the Indian Diaspora and her gift for inhabiting the space of her characters while describing the most mundane experiences, thus making the readers identify with the characters.

Unlike the landscape artist with an imposing canvas and sweeping bold strokes, a short story writer is a miniaturist. With deft and precise strokes Lahiri too, like a true miniaturist, straddles between two worlds of Boston and Bengal with great ease. Her collection of short stories *The Interpreter of Maladies* negotiates dilemmas of the cultural spaces, with a master's touch. Lahiri's success is in the fact that she has emerged as an interpreter of exile in its various nuances and manifestation. *The Interpreter of Maladies* is a collection of nine stories, depicting the trauma and angst of the first generation and second generation Indian migrants to the United States. The themes range from emotional struggle of love to immigrants battling new worlds. Her stories are marked by a sense of alienation, longing, loss and hope which so often mark the immigrant experience, and which form a part of what she, her parents and friends too experienced as fellow immigrants. As she says in an interview, "I always say that I feel that I have inherited a sense of that loss from my parents because it was palpable all the time I was growing up, the sense of what my parents had sacrificed in moving to the US and in so many ways."[7]

Though most of the stories in this collection have an American setting, India, especially Calcutta keeps rearing its head in the memory of its characters. Her earliest stories—*A Real Durvan, The Treatment of Bibi Haldar* and *The Interpreter of Maladies*, are set in India. The first-two stories centre around women living on the fringes of the society, and are exploited by their own people. India continues to form a part of the fictional landscape, as Lahiri draws heavily on the memories of her parents to depict an India, she did not know. Her stories though set in America, are full of details of traditional Indian name, food, cooking and wardrobe giving character and an Indian flavour to her stories. *A Real Durvan* tells of Boori Ma, a stairwell sweeper deported to Calcutta after Partition. We see her bemoaning her fate in a voice "brittle with sorrows, as tarts as curds, and shrill enough to grate meat from a coconut."[8] Lahiri brings out the pathos of her situation with gentle sympathy. In a mite infested quilt, broom and keys, tied along with her life's savings to the free end of her sari, Boori Ma loved to reminisce the earlier easier times. She would enumerate, the losses suffered since her deportation, narrating the fictional account of her days spent in a clover. "crouched instead in doorways and hallways and observing gestures and manners in the same way a person tends to watch traffic in a foreign city," Boori Ma is thrown out by the residents, after a theft because now the building needed a "Real Durwan."

The title story, *The Interpreter of Maladies* is about a young affluent American couple tracing their Indian heritage under the guidance of Mr. Kapasi, their English speaking Indian guide. The focus keeps shifting between the guide's observation about this family of non-resident Indians and the visitor's impressions of this vast, unruly, fascinating country. Essentially an interlude between Mina Das and Mr. Kapsi, the tourist guide who doubles up as an interpreter of the maladies afflicting patients for a doctor since there are lots of Gujaratis, Mr. Kapsi acts as a channel between a doctor and his patients. The polarity of vision is achieved by Lahiri with the help of her own impressions of India, when she used to come to India along with her parents as a child. As she says in an interview, "when I began writing fiction seriously, my first attempts were...always set in Calcutta, which is a city I know quite well as a result of repeated visits with my family, sometimes for several months at a time. These trips, to a vast, unruly, fascinating city so different from the small New England town where I was raised.... The reason my first stories were set in Calcutta is due to...that necessary combination of distance and intimacy with a place.... The terrain is very much the terrain of my own life—new England and New York, with Calcutta always hovering in the background."[9]

The Treatment of Bibi Haldar presents again, a maltreated shop girl who dreams of winning a husband and surprises us with her unusual tenacity. The story has much to say about the idea of sexuality, and specifically one's own agency in establishing it. It is determined that Bibi, an older woman with seemingly incurable disease that causes fits of seizures, should marry in an attempt at a cure. The community sees her as a sexual object for the first time after doctors make this suggestion. They, "imagined the contours below her house coat, and attempted to appraise the pleasures she could offer a man."[10]

Lahiri's stories reflected the minutest details of displacement, as she had experienced it first hand. Probing into the psyche of culturally displaced individuals she says, "I think that for immigrants, the challenges of exile, the loneliness, the constant sense of alienation, the knowledge of and longing for a lost world is more explicit and distressing than for their children. On the other hand, the problem for the children of immigrants—those with strong ties to their country of origin—is that they feel neither one thing nor the other."[11] Her next category of stories, *When Mr. Pirzada Came to Dine, Mrs. Sen* and *The Third and the Final Continent* present the immigrant's struggle to survive in this world where they try to fight their homesickness, and also convey the nostalgia for their own country which they have left behind. These stories provocatively present Lahiri's concern for the fading of origins.

The Third and Final Continent has as its protagonist, an immigrant from India who exclaims about his survival in New World: "I know that my achievement is quite ordinary," he admits, "I am not the only man to seek his fortune far from home and certainly I am not the first. Still there are times I am bewildered by each mile I have travelled, each meal I have eaten, each person I have known, each room in which I have slept. As ordinary as it all appears, there are times when it is beyond my imagination."[12] These lines express a universal experience—the experience of all immigrants who yearn for a home, who yearn to belong and who yearn to be rooted. Based on the life of her own father, *The Third and Final Continent* tells of a young man who came to US, has an arranged marriage in India and writes about his new wife and their life together. Through the eyes of a young Indian, the narrator experiences the cultural difference between the young man and his aging landlady.

Mrs. Sen and *When Mr. Pirzada Came to Dine* both have child observers—it is an American child Eliot, in *Mrs. Sen* and Lilia in *When Mr. Pirzada Came to Dine*, who inevitably remind us of Lahiri's own experiences of growing up as an immigrants, child. As she says—"I feel that I have inherited a sense of that loss because it was so palpable all the time I was growing up, the sense of what my parents sacrificed in moving to the United States."[13] Mrs. Sen has reluctantly accompanied her professor husband who has come to teach mathematics at an American University shares her isolation with young Eliot.—Mrs. Sen the baby sitter is seen through the eyes of Eliot, an eleven year old left in her charge. Back home in Calcutta, people think that she lives like a queen in a palace. Her refusal to learn driving which she needs to learn if she is to keep her job is a gesture of resistance she offers to a new life. Her loneliness is conveyed through the manner in which she waits for the letters and listens to cassettes of Bengali speaking people and narrates accounts of Calcutta life to Eliot.

When Mr. Pirzada Came to Dine, is about an Indian American Lilia, who sees the similarity between her Bengali parents and Mr. Pirzada, a Pakistani from Dacca. She is intrigued by the visitor whose watch is set to Dacca time. In search of compatriots, her parents used to trail their fingers at the start of each new semester, through the columns of the university directory, circling surnames familiar to their part of the world oblivious of the war between India and Pakistan, she is equally oblivious of the differences between a Bengali Muslim and a Hindu. Her world concerns just the American history and geography and so engrossed was she with the maps of the thirteen colonies that she couldn't have even imagined how the intrigues thousands of miles away could affect her parents.

A Temporary Matter, Sexy and *This Blessed House* bear a great closeness to Lahiri's own personal experiences. *A Temporary Matter* is a story of a young couple, Shukumar and Shobha, who have drifted apart after losing their child in a miscarriage. Neither of them have the capacity to provide emotional anchorage to the other. Both deliberately avoid each other. One day they find a small note in their mail box, indicating that the electricity would remain disconnected for a few hours, everyday for a week. In the enforced darkness the couple finds a pretext for discovering their latent, subconscious fears and dark secrets, and also about their 'little betrayals'. By the time the week is over, the couple reaches a point of no return and Shobha, the bread winner walks out on Shukumar who at thirty-five hasn't progressed beyond being a student. There is a reversal of gender roles here with Shukumar doing all the cooking and cleaning, and being blamed for the miscarriage, whereas in India the mother would bear all the responsibility.

Sexy chronicles the extra marital love affair of an Indian with a Caucasian woman, told from a non-Indian perspective. Miranda, a mid western woman has an affair with a married Bengali. Miranda's childhood memory of a reaction to a painting of goddess Kali, evoking trepidation and horror does not deter her in anyway. She tries to learn all about Bengali culture and even makes an abortive bid to learn Bengali, though before her marriage she had ridiculed his family as the only Indian family in the neighbourhood.

This Blessed House presents Twinkle, a second generation immigrant, who along with her husband moves into a new house in US. Twinkle is too attached to the articles found in the house, connected to Christianity. Sanjeev, the husband, however, wants her to do away with all such objects though Twinkle does not want to part with them. She ironically calls herself a "good little Hindu" and places "a kiss on top of Christ's head and then placed the statue on the fire place."[14] Lahiri captures the *joie-de vivre* of Twinkle beautifully and realistically.

Despite her immigration from the subcontinent of short story to the hectic mainland of the novel, Lahiri's much awaited novel; *The Namesake* marks no special advance over *The Interpreter of Maladies*. It appears like an extended short story developing and exploring further the themes already made familiar through her short story collection, *The Interpreter of Maladies*. A finely wrought, deeply moving family drama, *The Namesake* illuminates Lahiri's signature themes: the immigrant experience, the clash of cultures and the tangled ties between generations. A veteran in the short story form, Lahiri in *The Namesake* attempts the novel form and says that, "from the purity and intensity of short story to the broader canvas of a novel felt liberating and at times overwhelming."[15] Though, she feels that, "Writing a novel is certainly more demanding than writing a story, and the stakes are higher,"[16] she finds that the novels, nevertheless, are "roomier, messier and more tolerant than a short story."[17] Reviewing *The Interpreter of Maladies* in *The New York Times*, Michiko Kakutani wrote: "Ms. Lahiri chronicles her characters' lives with both objectivity and compassion while charting the emotional temperature of their lives with tactile precision. She is a writer of uncommon, elegance and poise, and with 'Interpreter of Maladies', she has made a precocious debut."[18]

A coming of age novel, *The Namesake* is built around the theme, already made familiar by Lahiri in her debut short story collection, *The Interpreter of Maladies*—the theme of the uneasy status of the immigrant, rediscovery of his roots and finding an identity in a country that will treat you as an alien even if you were born there. The terrain Lahiri trespasses here is one she knows like the back of her hand—the limited spaces of Bengali immigrants in the Boston area, their peculiarly lonely lives with extended families made up of fellow expatriates. C.J. Gillen in the review of Lahiri's *The Namesake* traces the semblance of the novel to a Jan Vermeer painting, in its choice of a limited canvas concentrating on a modest tale of a first generation Bengali American boy and his family. Vermeer too owes the immediacy of his appeal to his concentration on domestic scenes and a limited canvas.

A cross-cultural multigenerational saga of a Hindu Bengali family's journey to self acceptance in Boston, *The Namesake* is a novel that offers a "Chekhovian exploration of father and sons, parents and children, as it is resonant in its exploration of what is acquired and lost by immigrants and their children in pursuit of American Dream."[19] *The Namesake* chronicles the life of Gogol Ganguli from his birth in the1960's to the present. The novel begins by tracing the emotional struggles, of an Indian couple trying to make a new life in America. Ashima Ganguli, the pregnant wife longs to be with the family during childbirth. When she goes to the hospital for her delivery, she feels the cravings for her country, "Nothing feels normal to Ashima, it's not so much the pain, which she knows, somehow she will survive. It's the consequence: motherhood in a foreign land... unmonitored by those she loved...she is terrified to raise a child in a country where she knows so little, where life seems so tentative and spare."[20] Ashoke, Ashima's husband wants to provide a better life for his new son by earning a doctorate degree from a prestigious American University but Ashima's love of family makes her create a close knit web of immigrants, who share a common language and practice common customs. Whereas, Ashima is reluctant to accept the American culture and resists all things American, Ashoke adapts himself less warily to the American culture.

His memories of life in India are less peaceful and remind him of the terrible train accident that left him both physically and emotionally shattered. This incident is instrumental in making him leave India and choose an unusual name for his son in memory of the catastrophe. When a letter from his great grandmother suggesting a formal Indian name for him, fails to arrive from India, Ashoke impulsively settles for the name Gogol, after the famous Russian writer whose book of short stories helped save his life during that accident when his train got derailed he was reading that book and rescuers spotted him only because they saw a page flutter from his hands in the dark. Ashoke, like his wife embraces his past in India but their son Gogol and his sister Sonia resent childhood trips to India, which denies them the material comforts of US. Both of them are more comfortable with the American culture than the Bengali culture which is a major part of his parent's past. As Gogol grows older, his attempts to eradicate his heritage become more pronounced. Hence, when it comes to joining college, he accepts a position at Yale, not at his father's alma mater. Gogol hates his name which is neither American nor Indian and has some old depressing associations—"He hates that his name is both absurd and obscure, that it has nothing to do with who he is, that it is neither Indian nor American but of all things Russian. At times his name, an entity shapeless and weightless, manages nevertheless to distress him physically, like the scratchy tag of a shirt he has been forced permanently to wear" (p. 76).

Soon Gogol changes his name to Nikhil, yet he is not able to shake his past life off. Gogol grows up, moves out and goes through life suffering personal tragedies that also shape his identity. After graduating and going through a number of relationships with American girls, his father's sudden death, forces Gogol to look back into his own culture that he dismissed. In order to please his mother and friends, he agrees to marry a fellow Bengali American Moushumi Majoomdar. The marriage ends in a disaster as he struggles to balance the American and the Bengali parts of his life. Gogol learns that his clumsy attempts to create a coherent identity for himself are what in the end, define him—"Thing that should never have happened, that seemed out of place and wrong, these were what prevailed, what endured in the end" (p. 287). Eventually, Gogol reaches some sort of compromise, but it is never entirely satisfactory—there is always a sense of sadness that he is neither fully of one world or the other. Gogol's inner thoughts are the vehicle through which the author explores the other characters, including his sister and mother. Hemmed by the twists and turns across two continents Gogol thinks to himself, towards the end of the novel—"His family's life feels like a string of incidents, before seen, unintended" (p. 286).

The end of the book however is quite liberating as we see young Nikhil, finally coming into his own. Despite all his efforts, Gogol couldn't ignore the memories of his past—his name, his parents his Indian heritage. After his father's death, he realizes that he can't simply walk away from who he is and begins to feel that his efforts to create an entirely new persona are just reactions against the past. In order to make peace with his past, he accepts his heritage, becomes a student of his past. And the lesson he learns as a student paves the way for a peaceful future. He finds himself increasingly drawn to his heritage. The omission of a concrete ending serves as a final reminder of Lahiri's focus on the tension between the past and present. Thus, the story of Gogol develops progressively through the novel into the allegorical saga of diasporic decentredness. With penetrating insight, Lahiri reveals not only the defining power of names and expectations bestowed upon us by our parents but also the means by which we slowly redefine ourselves. What we reclaim was our past, what we can claim is our present? Where we live, we do not belong and where we belong we can not live. Thus, *The Namesake* remains Lahiri's quietly dazzling novel which justifiably places her in the distinguished league of William Faulkner, Pearl S. Buck and Saul Bellow. *The New York Times*, aptly describes it as a "debut novel that is as assured and eloquent as the work of a long-time master of the craft."[21] Salman Rushdie had stated, that Americans want to read only about themselves, hence Indian authors have a better response in England than in US, but by bringing home the Pulitzer, Jhumpa Lahiri seems to have proved Rushdie wrong.

NOTES AND REFERENCES

1. Nayar, Aruti in her review of *The Namesake*.
2. A review by Subhamoy Das titled; "A Hindu Family's American Journey."
3. Hajari, Nisid: The Promising Land, Times International, 13 September, 1999, p. 49.
4. Lahiri, Jhumpa: in a Newsweek interview.
5. *Ibid.*
6. Lahiri, Jhumpa: in an interview to *Hindustan*.

7. Lahiri, Jhumpa: in an interview with Elizabeth Farnsworth.
8. Lahiri, Jhumpa: "A Real Durvan" from *The Interpreter of Maladies*, Delhi: Harper Collins, 1999.
9. Lahiri, Jhumpa: in an interview with R.S. Shanker of Rediff.com.
10. Lahiri, Jhumpa: *The Treatment of Bibi Haldar* from *The Interpreter of Maladies*, Delhi: Harper Collins, 1999, p. 162.
11. Lahiri, Jhumpa: in an interview with Elizabeth Farnsworth for online News hour.
12. Lahiri, Jhumpa: *The Third and Final Continent* from *The Interpreter of Maladies*, Delhi: Harper Collins, 1999.
13. Lahiri, Jhumpa: in an interview with Elizabeth Farnsworth for online News hour.
14. Lahiri, Jhumpa: *The Blessed House* from *The Interpreter of Maladies*, Delhi: Harper Collins, 1999, p. 137.
15. Lahiri, Jhumpa: in an interview.
16. *Ibid.*
17. *Ibid.*
18. Kakutani, Michiko's review of Interpreter of Maladies in *The New York Times*.
19. Kakutani, Michiko: in a review published in 2nd September, 2003.
20. Lahiri, Jhumpa: *The Namesake*, London: Harper Collins, 2003, p. 6. All quotations from *The Namesake* adhere to this edition.
21. Quoted in *The New York Times*.

'Changing Images of Women' in the Fiction of Bapsi Sidhwa and Taslima Nasrin

> "This has always been a man's world, and none of the reasons that have been offered in explanation have seemed adequate."
>
> —*Simone de Beauvoir*

In the context of feminine consciousness, Irene de Claremont Castillejo's remark in her book, *Knowing Women: A Feminine Psychology* seems quite revealing: "When Adam ate the apple offered to him by Eve, he had stolen the power to choose."[1] It was Eve who freed Adam from the blindness of nature and now it was Adam who "stretching out his hand to the same tree, has plucked a second apple and this time it is he who has offered it to her. He has discovered the contraceptive."[2] "Eve," says Claremont "had been avid in her eating of this newest stolen fruit. Her energy once locked in an endless chain of bearing and rearing children, has been freed for pursuits of every kind. She has both soared and elbowed her way through thick and thin, filling her lungs with her new found freedom till Adam, and sometimes Eve herself must have wondered if he had been wise to let her taste that second apple."[3]

Women today, after hundreds of years of struggle are in a negotiating position and they do have choices. Even in literature as in any other art, the role of women is no longer only to inspire but also to create. Various women writers have become story tellers, poets, prophets, the authors of dreams and ideas, and the voices to whom we listen. In almost all the languages of the world, expression of women's liberation, of feminist concern is noticeable, whether it is British, Nigerian, Canadian or South Asian. The South Asian literature is remarkable for the prominence of women writers who are transcending their traditional boundaries and making their presence felt on the international scene. Their fiction reveals how the apparition of power by women could be conducted according to the principles of self interest and self definition.

The images of women in South Asian novels have undergone a change in the last three decades. Earlier, women were conceived as a symbol of self sacrifice and suffering. Though, according to Margaret Egnor, 'a special positive power comes from suffering and self sacrifice which can be defined as the ability to act, to make others act, to make things happen and as action itself....'[4] Such a complex concept of suffering and spiritual power explains why the Sita Savitri image has persisted in literature until recently. But, in due course of time, women writers affected by Western Feminism have explored the alternative ideal of self assertion. From the suffering woman in Kamala Markandaya's *Nectar in a Sieve* and Meera Mahadevan's *Shulamith* to the recent subversions of the traditional image in the works of Chitra Fernando, Anita Desai, Sara Suleri, Anees Jung, Arundhati Roy, Bapsi Sidhwa and Taslima Nasrin, the women have come a long way.

Unlike Markandaya's evil Kunthi in *Nectar in a Sieve*, Anita Desai's characters seem justified when they act out of self preservation. Furthermore, unlike Markandaya's Rukmani and Ira who appear justified for their rebellion yet offer punishment anyway, Fernando and Desai's women, successfully defy traditional mores. This characters' self justification has continued in recent years as women writers tell their own stories and that of other women. Desai shocks us near the end of the novel, *In Custody*, when she presents Nur's young wife's point of view: "Are you not guilty of assuming that because you are a male you have a right to brains, talent, reputation and achievement, while I because I was born a female, am condemned to find what satisfaction I can, in being maligned, mocked, ignored and neglected?"[5] Thus, in *Image of Women in Indo-Anglian Novel*, Meena Shirwadkar claims that "Tradition, transition and modernity are the stages through which the woman in Indo-Anglian novel is passing." Kamala Das' *My Story* or Sara Suleri's *Meatless Days* and Anees Jung's *Unveiling India: A Woman's Journey* explore an educated women's search for identity.

The recent women writers from India, Pakistan, Sri Lanka and Bangladesh exemplify the issue of gendered self representation and feminist concern. Their works realize not only the diversity of women but the diversity within each woman. They are incorporating their experience to make new, empowering image for women, instead of limiting the lives of woman to one ideal, they push the ideal towards, the full expression of each woman's potential. Anees Jung, an eminent woman writer in search of new values for woman explores the wonderful consequences of Indian women renaming self and experience—"Individually, they have gained a name, collectively an identity.... Their new strength stems from personalities defining their own terms, lending grace to living."[6] She further explains the change that has taken place in Indian society, so that now women will tell their own stories, "Not long ago a woman who spoke about herself was considered a loose woman. To voice a pain, to divulge a secret, was considered sacrilege, a breach of family trust. Today voices are raised without fear, and are heard outside the walls of homes that once kept a woman protected, also isolated. Some of the women who speak have stepped out. Others who have not are beginning to be aware, eager to find expression, but let them speak for themselves."[7] The most important contribution that Anees Jung's vision of survival and grace makes to developing literary tradition lies in the way it moves beyond the Sita—Savitri ideal of women as wife. The feminist writers, the world over, are emphasizing a new perspective of women. Be it Margaret Laurence or her contemporary, Japanese women writer, Minako Oba, they have both rebelled against stern patriarchy or male chauvinism. The inevitable theme is beautifully captured in Margaret Laurence's words—"The theme of survival, not just physical survival but the preservation of some human dignity and in the end some human warmth and ability to reach out and touch others."[8]

Even in the fledgeling Nepalese English literature, Manjushree Thapa in her book, *The Tutor of History*, talks of a young widow, her protagonist, who chooses loneliness over subservience.

One of Pakistan's most prominent fiction writers, Bapsi Sidhwa is certainly one of the finest Anglophone novelists of South Asia. As there was no tradition either of women's literature or of English language literature in Pakistan at the time when Bapsi Sidhwa started writing, she may be considered a pioneer in both the fields. Many critics believe that the appearance of Sidhwa's work signals even before Rusdhie's, the belated coming of age of South Asian fiction in the eighties and nineties. Though she doesn't see herself as a writer writing for women, her protagonist, of course, are mainly women and they invariably win against men in their struggle for survival and honour. Greatly influenced by Western Feminism, her novels chronicle the history of the Indian subcontinent with particular focus on women. Sidhwa's women are strong willed, assertive and courageous, capable of resolving their crises in their own way. They try to cope with the parental, societal and cultural pressure in their life as much as they can, but when their very life or identity is endangered, they protest and fight against injustice and oppression with women and show the way for other women.

It is noteworthy that no woman character dies in any of her novels. In her first novel, *The Crow Eaters*, Faredoon Junglewalla tries to kill Jerbanoo by setting fire to the house, but she is rescued by the fireman. She in fact outlives her tormentor, Faredoon. In *Cracking India*, the abducted Ayah, who was forced into prostitution is saved by her Godmother from Hira Mandi and sent back to her family in Amritsar. In *The American Brat*, Firoza, inspite of the enormous pressure of her family, to return to Lahore and her failure in her first love, decides to settle in America. Firoza has tasted freedom in America and now cannot give it up. Having learnt her lesson she won't let anyone meddle in her affairs. Sidhwa's latest novel, *Water* based on Deepa Mehta's controversial film depicts the lives of widows in 1930's Benaras. Talking of *Water*, Sidhwa says, "Besides being a gripping story, the plot deals with a subject close to my heart, that of the oppressive hold traditions had on women...it tells of oppression and constraints that govern even a girl child life in a patriarchal society."[9] Sara Suleri Goodyear beautifully sums up the unsettling quietude that the novel evokes: "Sidhwa historicizes the images, lends greater poignancy to faces and provides speech where the film must leave the women silent."[10]

Though all her novels are gynocentric, *The Pakistani Bride*, is an exclusive paean to women's zest for life, their adaptability and indomitable courage. In this novel, no women character is a defeatist, they never yield. Whether it is Zaitoon, Carol or Afshan, the prime concern of Sidhwa's women is preservation of life. Despite being brutally treated by her husband, Zaitoon does not commit suicide. Her instinct for self preservation keeps her going. Her only hope is that she would be in Lahore before the end of nine months for child birth, so she patiently bears the brutality of her husband. But, in the meantime, an incident takes place that forces Zaitoon to leave the place much before. Her husband's beastly reaction for the innocent act of waving to an army jeep proves to be the last straw. Zaitoon resolves to run away because in flight alone lay the hope of her survival.

It is the same love for life that compels another Pakistani bride, the American girl Carol, who is married to a Pakistani, Farukh, to dissolve her marriage and go to America. Though she tries to adjust to the Pakistani social conventions, she soon finds it quite strenuous to bear its restrictions. In retaliation to Farukh's over possessiveness, she indulges in an affair with Major Mushtaq, who however, expresses his inability to obtain a divorce from his wife in order to marry her—Carol goes back to Farukh. But all her resolutions are shaken when she comes to know that Zaitoon's husband with his tribesmen is tracking her down to kill her just because she has run away. Carol asks the Major what he could do to save Zaitoon. He gives a calm reply—"Very little, unless she manages to get across.... Don't worry, she'll probably be okay.... It happens all the time."[11] Carol asks him what he meant by saying, "happens all the time."[12] The Major says, "Oh, women get killed for one reason or other...imagined insults, family honour, infidelity...."[13] She asks the Major, if Farukh would kill her for her infidelity, the

Major says, "I might if you were my wife."[14] Carol feels restless and takes Farukh out for a walk. On seeing a tribal woman's head floating in the water, Farukh remarks—"Probably asked for it."[15] Again, while lying sleepless in her room at night, Carol remembers Farukh's words and thinks about women's condition in the world, especially in Pakistan—"Women, the world over, through the ages, asked to be murdered, raped, exploited, enslaved, importunately impregnated, beaten up, bullied and disinherited."[16] Carol gets convinced that she cannot take it any more. She suddenly remembers Zaitoon. Zaitoon had exercised her "Khudi" and now it is time for her to do the same—"I think I'm finally beginning to realize something.... Your civilization... has ways that can really hurt me.... I'm going home."[17] With this pronouncement, Carol goes to America.

Thus, Sidhwa seems to give a message to women that life must be preserved at all cost, since one can fight oppression only when one is alive. Through her various marginalised narrators and through the experiences of the many marginalised characters in her first-three novels, Sidhwa gives voice to hitherto silenced groups of India and Pakistan.

The feminine protest against the phallocratic set up which present women as colonised were also made in Bangladeshi literature. The emergence of Taslima Nasrin's feminist writings inaugurates one of the most controversial moments in the scene of Bangladeshi literature. Although, the feminist movement in Bangladesh has fallen short of achieving its goal, certainly there has been a growing awareness of male domination which should be recognized. It is against the backdrop of such growing awareness of gender subordination as systemic that Taslima emerges on the scene of Bangladeshi literature. The pain and rage of Taslima's writings are unique in the history of Bangladeshi literature and representative of countless other women's lives in Bangladesh. "Within the bounds of our closed society, darkness reigns so strongly that there is no fissure to let in light or air."[18] Hence, Meer Nurul Islam in his review focuses on Taslima's rage as a crucial necessity to transform society.

The pivotal importance of Taslima's novels is the heroines' ability to reclaim the power over her body, tearing apart the ethical cover up of the subordinating practices of Bangladeshi patriarchy, where the girl is not called by her name but "bou" (bride) of a certain man, a certain "bari" (house) or a certain "poribar" (family).[19] One of the recurrent themes of Bangladeshi literature is the transformation of a girl who initially embodies the spirit of freedom into a "normal wife," so that the girl follows the new programme of renunciation to achieve that status of good wife. Taslima Nasrin's rebellious tirade against the patriarchal society is voiced in a passionate fearless voice, full of outrage and betrayal, yet also simply human. The onslaught unleashed by Taslima makes both men and women grit their teeth. There is such unarguable fact and so much honesty of conviction in her words that all but the brave or the grossly insensitive are left cringing in the corner as Taslima sweeps by. Irene de Claremont Castillejo has very aptly remarked, "There is nothing so ruthless as a woman with a cause between her teeth."[20]

Her first novel *Aparpokkho* remains Taslima's vote of no confidence to the patriarchal institution of marriage and a bold critique of the institution of divorce. The story of *Aparpokkho* narrated by Taslima to her sister represents Jamuna's shifting predicament and her progressively intensifying struggle and divorce. Jamuna is divorced from her husband Saber, for allegedly having an illicit relationship with Saber's friend. Now, reduced to the position of further devaluation on account of her divorce, Jamuna remarries. Unhappy with her second husband, she becomes passionately involved with a lover and conceives. She boldly decides to have the baby and envisions a child outside of patriarchal descent. "I want a child over whom man has no entitlement...like me, my child will be free of the offensive control of patriarchy."[21] When asked about the paternity of the unborn child, Jamuna retorts, "I'm nobody's land for cultivation, nor can a man use me as he wishes."[22]

Taslima's novels present marriage as exploitative and it inevitably ends in divorce preceded by husband's polygamous marriage. It is through the perspective of displaced woman that the institutions and practices of marriage and divorce are examined. She uses daily events as evidence for the conclusion that subordination and economic exploitation of women are embedded in patriarchal marital relationships. One day Humayun, Jamuna's second husband demands his food but Jamuna remains motionless. Taslima offers the following dialogue: Humayun asks, "Give me rice." I said, "I didn't cook." "What?" "I didn't cook means I didn't cook." "Why?" "I did not want to."[23] The above lines appear like a domestic quarrel but they inaugurate Taslima's next novel, *Shodh*. Here Taslima's resistance to patriarchal marriage "rites" is brought into focus. Illegitimate pregnancy still figures as a key theme in this story.

Jhumur, the central character in *Shodh,* subverts the patriarchal agenda of appropriation and effacement of female by conceiving a child outside of marriage and passing him off as her husband's legitimate son. After one and half months of marriage as Jhumur finds out that she is pregnant, she turns to her husband for affection. But he asks her to get the child aborted and denies that it is his child. As a male, it is her husband's prerogative to define what is licit and what is illicit? Driven by anger and pain, and determined to take revenge, Jhumur secretly makes love to an artist named Afsal and becomes pregnant again but on her own terms and establishes her legitimacy by giving birth to a son. Jhumur says—"this is not my desired baby. This is a baby of protest and revenge...."[24] Jhumur and Jamuna become the spokespersons of the author, Taslima Nasrin. Their complete defiance of patriarchal prohibitions against illegitimate pregnancy derives its power from the author whose passion for change against the system of patrineality is wellknown through her fictional writings.

Thus, Taslima's novels document the failure of the institution of marriage to protect women in a culture which is based on a concept of women's dependence on the male protector. By unveiling the patriarchal agenda of subordinating women and by introducing overt and covert strategies to subvert this agenda, Taslima has pioneered the feminist discourse in Bangladeshi society. We can conclude, therefore, that the South Asian women writers have opened up areas for new exploration and debate in post-colonial feminist studies. They create stories which deal with women who understand what survival is—a story with grace.

NOTES AND REFERENCES

1. Castillejo, Irene de Claremont: *Knowing Women: A Feminine Psychology*, p. 91.
2. *Ibid.*, p. 92.
3. *Ibid.*, pp. 92-93.
4. "On the Meaning of Sakti to Women in Tamil Nadu" The Powers of Tamil Women, ed. Susan. S. Wadley (New York: Syracuse University, 1980), p. 22.
5. Desai, Anita: *In Custody*, p. 196.
6. Jung, Anees: *Unveiling India: A Woman's Journey* (New Delhi: Penguin Books, 1988), p. 122.
7. *Ibid.*, p. 109.
8. Laurence, Margaret, in an interview.
9. Sidhwa, Bapsi: (in the case of writing *Water* in an interview).
10. Goodyear, Sara Suleri: Blurb of Water (Penguin Books, India, 2006).
11. Sidhwa, Bapsi: *The Pakistani Bride* (Penguin Books, 1990), p. 223.
12. *Ibid.*
13. *Ibid.*, p. 224.
14. *Ibid.*
15. *Ibid.*, p. 225.
16. *Ibid.*, p. 226.
17. *Ibid.*, p. 229.
18. Islam, Meer Nurul: "Bhinnya Dristir Annyarakam Akjon Kabi"—Taslima Nasrin. Pakkhe Bapakkhe, Vol. 1, ed. Mesbahuddin Ahmed.
19. Ahmed, Naseem: Women in Bangladesh Universities Field Staff International, 36, p. 2.
20. Castillejo, Irene de Claremont: *Knowing Women: A Feminine Psychology*, p. 56.
21. Nasrin, Taslima: *Aparpokkho*, p. 63.
22. *Ibid.*, p. 66.
23. *Ibid.*, p. 29.
24. Nasrin, Taslima: *Shodh*, p. 181.

'Delineation of Inner Spaces and the Angst Within' in Anita Desai's Fiction

16

> "The only way for a woman, as for a man, to find herself, to know herself as a person, is by creative work of her own. There is no other way."
>
> —*Betty Friedan*

Women have been unofficial storytellers to generations, but when it came to documenting literature, men historically dominated the role of authors. Early South Asian literature had been largely dominated by male writers like R.K. Narayan, Mulk Raj Anand and Raja Rao, when Anita Desai, a distinct contemporary Indian English novelist appeared on the literary horizon of the sixties. As Sagarika Ghose remarks, "Even before Desai, in the fifties; women writers had been writing for quite a while, like Nayantara Sahgal, Kamala Markandaya, Ruth Prawar Jhabwala and Attia Hosain. From Ismat Chugtai, Krishna Sobti, Kusum Ansal, Kamala Das, Mahasweta Devi, Nabaneeta Dev Sen, Anita Desai, Nayantara Saghal, Indian women writers have been writing for decades."[1]

Desai's fiction has invited much critical attention. Whereas, the postcolonial literary scholars have focused on Desai's use of Indian settings in the majority of her works, contending that colonial appropriation of Indian cultural values remains an obstacle for post-colonial writers, others have explored the effects of English culture and the feminist critics have assessed the psychological development of Desai's female characters in terms of the patriarchal Indian family structure while evaluating

Desai's representation of the Indian feminine within the context of other Indian literature written by women. Although most of these critics have praised the complexity of the family relationships depicted in Desai's novels, several have objected to their resolutions as either too simplistic or perpetuating patriarchal values.

What cannot be denied however is the fact that all her novels gravitate around women who come of age in homes heavy with patriarchal oppression and offer an insight depiction of the "inner spaces" of her female protagonists in the writings. In Desai's fiction, women are carved in the traditional role of a woman whose 'silence' is to Desai the consequence of the marginal living condition for the traditional Indian women. In contrast to the Japanese feminist writer, Joy Nozomi Kogawa, whose 'silence' focusses on the states of "emptiness" and "nil," Desai's 'silence' resists sexual discrimination, and the silent women that she creates in her fiction, revolt against their marginal position. By no means 'silent,' Desai's silence is rather resounding.

Anita Desai's fictional oeuvre has undoubtedly carved her a distinct niche in the contemporary fictional world. What makes her remarkable is her attempt to shift the focus from socio-political realities as is evident in the novels of Kamala Markandaya, Ruth Prawar Jhabwala and Nayantara Saghal to the exploration of the inner reality—the unexplored realm of the female psyche, the poignant evocation of human predicament and the sensitive apprehension of the existentialist vision of "anguish, abandonment and despair."[2]

An innovative writer, Desai found the contemporary fiction writers falling short due to "a lack of imagination, courage, nerve or gusto—the satirical edge, the ironic tone, the inspired criticism or the pyrrhic response that alone might have been content to record and document...."[3] Writing to Desai was a "process of discovering the truth—the truth that is nine tenth of the iceberg that lies submerged beneath the one tenth visible portion we call Reality. Writing is my way of plunging to the depths and exploring this underlying truth. All my writing is an effort to discover, to underline and convey the true significance of things."[4]

In her attempt to explore the underlying truth, Desai probes into the human psyche and offers a psychological delineation of characters and an exploration of their sensibilities. Her forte being, "the exploration of sensibility—the particular kind of modern Indian sensibility that is ill at ease," to the "inner climate, the climate of sensibility that colours or clears or rumbles like thunder or suddenly blazes fourth like lightening, is more compelling than the outer weather, the physical geography or the visible action."[5]

Throughout her novels and short stories, Desai focuses on the personal struggles of Anglicized, middle-class women in contemporary India as they attempt to overcome the societal limitations imposed by a tradition-bound patriarchal culture. Set amid the cultural and social changes that have swept India since its independence from Britain in 1947, most of Desai's narratives validate the importance of familial bonds and explore the tensions that exist between different generations. In her later works, Desai has addressed such themes as German anti-Semitism, the dissolution of traditional Indian values, and Western stereotypes of India. Most of Desai's works engage the complexities of modern Indian culture from a feminine perspective while highlighting the female Indian predicament of maintaining self-identity as an individual woman.

Her early novels including *Cry, The Peacock, Voices in the City, Where Shall We Go This Summer?* reveal her feminine concern for women's oppression, a quest for fulfilling identity, family relationships and the crumbling of traditions. Desai's fiction reveals the changing images of women in the South Asian literature. Whereas, Kamala Markandaya's *Nectar in a Sieve* or Meera Mahadevan's *Shulamith* portray its positive women characters as ideal sufferers and nurturers, Desai's fiction portrays women who want their individual worth realized and break through the suffering that traditional society offers them. In her article, *A Secret Connivance* Desai describes the fate of Indian women who have had to confine themselves to the domestic scene—few women have had any experience of the world outside their homes and families. Desai's women characters may not be heroic in the traditional sense and are often swept away by historical and social forces and are unable to control them. What makes her characters heroic, however, is the fact that they show a kind of heroism of survival, of coming out through the experience of life without compromising.

Her later novels like *Fire on a Mountain*, *In Custody*, *Baumgartner's Bombay* and *Clear Light of Day*, reveal her persistent concern with the existentialist angst of a modern man trapped in the islands of loneliness. Her concern with Alienation—the strange disease of modern life, her poignant evocation of human predicament, inevitably brings to our mind, the distinguished contemporary British novelist, Graham Greene. As in the Preface to *Ways of Escape*, Graham Greene has a revealing sentence—"Writing is a form of therapy; sometimes I wonder how all those who do not write, compose or paint can manage to escape the madness, the melancholia, the panic fear which is inherent in the human situation."[6] Greene's obsession with the human situation—La Condition Humanitie remains the nucleus of his entire artistic vision, assiduously tracing existentialist motifs of thought like betrayal, choice, loneliness and despair. Desai's fiction too, probes into the psyche of 'isolates and exiles,' enmeshed in despair. Closer home, in Indian English literature, Desai's fiction draws comparisons with Arun Joshi, whose fiction focusses on the predicament of modern man, a certain awareness of rootlessness and a sense of estrangement. Desai, in her first novel, *Cry, The Peacock* and Joshi in *Foreigner* expound the philosophy of detachment to probe into the psyche of his characters.

Desai's novels try to tackle the central aesthetic problem of the modern writer—the problem of rendering, "complete human personality...in an age of lost values, lost men and lost Gods."[7] "The twentieth century is called the age of alienation and man suffers from an acute sense of rootlessness which manifests itself as, the alienation from oneself, from one's fellow men and from nature; the awareness that life runs out of one's hand like sand...."[8] Desai's characters are presented as facing the dilemmas of self alienation in each successive novel.

Her debut novel, *Cry, The Peacock*, presents Maya, the protagonist as a hypersensitive woman, on the verge of turning into a neurotic, obsessed from the very beginning of the novel, with the awesome prophecy of an albino astrologer. According to the prophecy, Maya or her husband Gautam would die during the fourth year of their marriage. The novel deals with the theme of marital discord resulting from the dichotomy between diametrically opposed view points of the partners. The emotional incompatibility with her husband Gautam stands in absolute contrast to the memories of her happy childhood. The introverted favourite daughter of a wealthy artistic father, Maya is unable to cope with the tensions of normal existence. She herself confesses to have been "a wayward and high strung child and to have "lived as a toy princess in a toy world"[9] (pp. 53-89). The world appears to her to be uninhabitable and finds herself reduced to "a body without a heart, a heart without a body" (p. 196).

With the fear of the prophecy coming true, the communication gap between herself and Gautam, her own childless state, the "bleak comfortless figure of her husband makes her yearn—Had there been a bond between us, he would have felt its pull.... But, of course, there was none.... There was no bond, no love, hardly any love" (p. 108).

Maya's alienation is unbearable—"All order is gone out of my life, no peace, nothing to keep me within the pattern of familiar, everyday, living and doing that becomes those whom God means to live on earth. Thoughts come, incidents occur, then they are scattered, and disappear. Past, present, future, Truth and Untruth. They shuttle back and forth, a shifting Chiaroscuro of light and shade.... Those are no longer my eyes, nor this my mouth.... The pattern for an order of lines and designs, a symmetry...has deserted my own life...strangers surround me" (p. 179).

Maya's growing disintegration is beautifully conveyed through instances of fever, headaches, mounting fears of death, thoughts of murder and violent outbursts. The theme of marital discord and incompatibility is also effectively built through a succession of events of everyday occurrence. For instance, in the very opening scene, the death of Maya's dog is an unbearable event for Maya but for Gautam it is just an everyday incident. Her frustration reaches its completion and in a fit of insane fury she pushes him down from the terrace. Her madness becomes more explicit when she starts justifying her act in front of Gautam's mother and sister. The novel ends with the author reporting the tragic death of Maya as she jumps out of the balcony.

Her next novel, *Voices in the City*, is a story about the siblings, Amla, Nirode and Monisha and their different ways of life in Calcutta. Amla sees the city as a monster. Nirode sacrifices everything for her career and Monisha cannot bear her stifling existence in the household of a wealthy old Calcutta family. The novel offers a brilliant exposition of the alienation suffered by these dislocated individuals trapped in the "monster city" (p. 150), and it is again the inner climate that is important.

As in *Cry, The Peacock*, Desai again has as her theme, the problem of non communication between husband and wife, Monisha and Jiban. Monisha commits suicide unable to stand the strain of living with Jiban. Nirode the rootless nihilist, is alienated even from his mother whom he calls "that old she cannibal" (p. 103). Ultimately, Nirode ends up being a "shadowy cipher," a drifter, crusted with his 'anonymity' and certitude, and is reduced according to his elder sister Monisha to a "shrunken, etiolated, wasted thing" (p. 139). Nirode wants to escape from this world—"Better to leap out of window and end it all instead of smearing this endless sticky glue of senselessness over the world: Better not to live" (p. 18).

His escapist attitude is borne out of his lack of commitment and moves on from one failure to the other. Monisha identifies Calcutta with "the city of Kali—Goddess of Death" (p. 138). Marital discord coupled with her sense of alienation finally leads her to commit suicide too. Thus, each character here encounters grief. Nirode ends up as a drifting Bohemian, Monisha commits suicide and Amla is heartbroken when her love is rejected.

Hence here again Anita Desai's focus is on the "inner climate," of her characters. Iyengar's comparative estimate of these two novels is quite revealing—"Voices in the City, although its canvas is larger, the detail fuller and the diction richer is never the less satisfying than Cry, the Peacock because it is not contained by a single sensibility like Maya's in the earlier novel. What is wanting is the controlling act that contains and gives form and unifying impression to the pressures of dispension? Voices in the City for all its powerful articulation, leaves on impression of incompleteness behind, of action and characterization, idea and symbol, not being fully integrated into artistic form."[10]

Her next novel, *Bye-Bye Blackbird* is an authentic study of human relationships subject to a sense of human relationships, subject to a sense of non belonging, displacement, dilemma and deracination. Of all the novels by Desai, *Bye-Bye Blackbird* is most intimately related to her own experience—"Of all my novels, it is most rooted in experience and the least literary in derivation."[11] It reconfirms Desai's reputation as a psychologist, when she renders the raging rows of her characters in the situations which they don't want to be in. The novel gives expression to disillusionment at racial prejudice, indifference leading to an anguish of loneliness and search for identity.

It is a story of an Indian immigrant, Adit Sen, who works as a small clerk in a tourist agency in London. Married to an English girl Sarah, he has adapted himself to the intermittent current of hatred and contempt that the Britishers nurse for the immigrants. Though he feels a kinship with England, as he had been acquainted with English literature, lifestyle as well as manners, yet he experiences the yearnings, anxieties and aspirations for a reunion with his own people. This longing becomes more intense with the arrival of Dev, a young Bengali student who has come to London to seek admission into London School of Economics. Dev unlike a usual immigrant looks at British way of life contemptuously initially but later he is reluctant to leave, once he gets acclimatized to the British culture. Dev reminds Adit of his complacency and his contemptuous state by his caustic remarks—"Laugh, go on.

That's all you people can do—you lazy immigrants. God. You should go mad, when you find that London docks have three kinds of lavatories—Ladies, Gents and Asiatics. But what did you do? You laughed" (p. 19). He expresses his anger candidly —"I wouldn't live in a country where I was insulted and unwanted" (p. 18).

Adit Sen and his English wife Sarah share a relationship which is subject to tension by cultural schism between them. Sarah finds Adit crude and loud and Adit finds her silence unfriendly and her reserve chilling. Unwashed dishes horrify Adit and he is often possessed by a yearning to go home. Sarah hates her Indian husband but struggles to cope with her loneliness. She is ostracized by her people for marring Adit. Thus, Adit feels stifled by the basic disharmony and returns to his homeland was the last remedy for him. Ironically, Dev stays behind with a conflict raging in his mind. When Adit decides to leave for India, Sarah too goes with him. Though the central theme varies in Desai's novels, the undercurrent in these novels is one of loneliness and alienation of a human being stranded in the isolated island of human destiny.

Anita Desai's fourth novel, *Where Shall We Go This Summer?* Is her shortest novel but "an interesting addition to Anita Desai's achievement as an Indian novelist writing in English."[12] Here, Desai returns to the theme of alienation and lack of communication which results in marital discord. It is the story of a sensitive, over emotional, middle aged woman, Sita. A mother of four children she experiences an aching void in her life as she faces loneliness, boredom and madness of a woman, a wife and a mother.

Suddenly, she realizes that she is pregnant for the fifth time and is full of rage, fear and revolt. Her reluctance to let her fifth child be born expresses her feeling of protest but her husband's frightening approach forces her to retain the pregnancy. Suffocated by the vegetarian complacence, stolidity, insularity and unimaginative way of life of her husband she escapes to Manori—"the island of miracles" (p. 31). The island "concretizes the feeling of isolation of Sita. She retreats into it as an obsessive desire to recapture once again her childhood innocence and purity."

She saw the island as a piece of magic, a magic mirror and her father a legend who lived on the island, its black magic, its subtle glamour and sought relief in coming to the mainland after her marriage to Raman, as the mainland implied solidity, security, the solidity of streets, the security of houses (p. 58). But as the light of the ordinary world grew stiff, static and petrified around her, "as the streets and walls ceased to offer security and safety but implied threats of murder" (p. 100). Living in the mainland was just "a crust of drill tedium of hopeless disappointment" (p. 58), "Bored, dull, unhappy, frantic," she is painfully distressed at "the tedium and ugliness of a meaningless life" (pp. 144-45). She finds her existence meaningless. "Life seemed complete, full, without her, there was no reason for her to exist" (p. 84). She goes to the island with her children in an act of defiance bringing to a climax the conflict with her husband. She goes to the island, not to give birth but in order to achieve the miracle of not giving birth because Manori was the island of miracles, "her father had made it an island of magic once and he might work another miracle posthumously" (p. 31). However, she is shocked to see that the island has totally changed and it worsened her isolation. It was bereft of its glamour, its magic, and proved to be an unpalatable substitute for the hostile forces of an incompatible marital life.

Towards the end of the novel, "tired, dishevelled and vacant like a player at the end of the performance, clearing the stage, picking the costume, in equal parts saddened and relieved" (p. 152), she realizes that escapism isn't an answer to life's problems—"She had escaped from duties and responsibilities, from order and routine, from life and the city" (p. 139). The answer that life gives is—"Life must be continued and all its business..." (pp. 138-39). The tragedy of Sita is obviously due to her constitutional inability to accept the values and attitudes of society and her irreconcilable temperament."[13]

Exploring the effectiveness of escapism as a coping mechanism, her next novel, *Fire on the Mountain,* underlines the theme of alienation in the lives of the three females and their complex experiences in life. The main protagonist is Nanda Kaul, an old widow and an elderly matriarch who has retreated to a reclusive life in the Kasuli mountains in Carignano, after a life time of dutiful servitude to her family into an old house that looks down at the Punjab plains. She leads a life that is recoil to her, hectic and tiring life as the Vice Chancellor's wife who ran her house as a perfect hostess and a dutiful mother of many children. The starkness and barrenness of Carignano with its three pines reflect the minimalist lifestyle shorn of entanglements, relationships and responsibilities that she opted for herself. At Carignano, "she had held herself religiously aloof, jealous of this privacy achieved, only at the end of her life" (pp. 35-36) like a "recluse out of vengeance for a long life of duty and obligation" (p. 4). All she wanted was "to be left to the pines and cicadas alone" (p. 4). The quietness of her life, however is shattered when her great granddaughter comes to live with her, she dreads the arrival of the ten year old child Raka, wondering how to accommodate the child in her bare home and life. Raka, the second female character is a natural recluse, whereas Nanda Kaul was a forced recluse. Raka is completely indifferent to Nanda Kaul and this makes the latter wish to establish some kind of link with the unusual child. Her indifference was "a challenge" to Nanda Kaul (pp. 98-99). How totally unconcerned she was would be clear from these lines—"Solitude never disturbed her she was the only child Nanda Kaul had ever known who preferred to stand apart...to being loved, cared for..." (pp. 79-80). The novel shows the clash of generations between Raka and Nanda, the division of classes between Nanda's isolated hill community and the nearby village and the conflict between educational programmes of Central Government and the traditions of local villages.

Ila Das, the third woman in the story is a spinster, much disliked due to her campaign as a social worker. Her anti-dowry and family planning programme which provoked the anger of the villagers and ultimately got her strangled and raped by Preet Singh. Slightly comical, she is a pathetic figure—"All her life mobs have taunted and derided her" (p. 110). Her voice was her tragedy—"Such a voice no human being ought to have had, it was antisocial to possess" (p. 111). Ila's death reminds Nanda of the barrenness of her own life. Her husband had loved another woman and even her children didn't understand or love her. The novel ends with Raka announcing that she had set the forest to fire. The fire purges the dark secrets that the characters carry, annuls the pretensions and razes the hill to a scarred terrain.

Thus, *Fire on the Mountain* portrays three different types of alienated figures and tries to bring out their interrelations and differences. *Fire on the Mountain* is one novel which can be compared to her daughter, Kiran Desai's, "The Inheritance of Loss". Both the novels were written when the authors were between thirty-five and forty and both consolidate the author's position, in the realm of serious writing in Indian and world scene. As far as the characters are concerned, *Fire on the Mountain* is centered around a reclusive old widow and her great granddaughter. The Inheritance of Loss tells the tale of a retired judge and his granddaughter.

After *Fire on the Mountain*, Desai's fiction moves out of her psychological mode towards a "widening out of human concerns" and integrating concrete historical and specific cultural dimensions in the creation of interior landscape."[14] Set against the historical backdrop of Delhi before the Partition of 1947, *Clear Light of Day* recounts the saga of the Das family, a Hindu clan from Old Delhi. The main characters are three of the four Das siblings: Bim, who is unmarried and teaches history at a women's college; her younger sister, Tara, who lives in America with her diplomat husband, Bakul, and their two teenage daughters; and their elder brother, Raja, who has given up his aspiration to become a poet and lives as a rich, fat businessman in Hyderabad with his Muslim-heiress wife, Benazir, and their five children. The story begins with Tara's visit to the now run-down family homestead in a suburb of Old Delhi, where Bim continues to live and to take care of their autistic younger brother, Baba. Tara has come to India to attend the wedding of Raja's eldest daughter, an event that Bim is boycotting, having long been estranged from her once beloved brother.

Clear Light of Day presents Bim, who marks a clear advance over Desai's earlier female protagonist. It presents the tragedy of Bim, a victim of life's adverse circumstances, who towards the end of the novel arrives at a realisation that is something very positive. Unlike Maya in *Cry, The Peacock*, who is unable to shake off the fears and obsessions, Bim doesn't leave her house, she doesn't seek any escape—she "rejects all modes of escape, both physical and emotional and continues to stay amidst the drabness of Delhi, in the cemetery like silence of the family house."[15]

A novella for young people, *The Village by the Sea* tells the story of a family beset by misfortune in the traditional fishing village of Thul, on the west coast of India near Bombay. With the mother ill and bedridden and the father an unemployed, abusive alcoholic, the brunt of the family responsibilities devolve upon the elder children, the adolescents Lila and Hari, both of whom have stopped attending school in order to fulfil these duties and care for their two younger siblings.

Since the mid-1980s, Desai has shown a definite shift in her narrative voice, favouring dialogue over interior monologue and focusing on underprivileged characters rather than her usually bourgeois protagonists. *In Custody* revolves around Deven Sharma, a middle-aged man who once dreamt of becoming a poet but who was forced to take a job teaching Hindi in order to support his wife and child. A sharply incisive social comedy, *In Custody* dramatizes the tensions between worldly and spiritual concerns through Deven's almost-obsessive attempts to interview Nur, the greatest living Urdu poet. Based on Desai's own Eurasian heritage but narrated from a male perspective. An ironic story about literary traditions and academic illusions, *In Custody* views very closely the life of the unprivileged and criticises the traditional society. The central characters are Nur, an Urdu poet who has fallen on hard times and Deven, a Professor of Hindi who realizes that the beloved poet isn't the magical genius he imagined. Desai's women characters in this novel emerge as liberating, creative forces. Desai makes clear in the novel that just as the male characters are trapped in a world that offers no possibility for success, the female characters have even more right to feel frustrated with the society that reduces them to clinging to these men who can't provide them what they want. The Urdu poet's wife rages at her own limitations: "Are you not guilty of assuming that because you are a male, you have a right to brains, talent reputation and achievement, while I because I was born a female, am condemned to find what satisfaction I can, in being maligned, mocked, ignored and neglected?" (p. 196). Devan also comes to a realisation that is again very positive: "Perhaps when everyone has cut him off and he was absolutely alone he would begin to find himself and his own strength" (pp. 189-90).

Baumgartner's Bombay like *In Custody* deals with men characters because Desai wanted to write on something else other than her family and neighbours. To find more range. She chose to write of Hugo Baumgartner in *Baumgartner's Bombay* a German Jew in India who flees Nazi Germany for India, only to be imprisoned as a hostile alien and then released to Bombay at wars end. The novel has as its background, the author's own German half of the parental heritage and *In Custody* too shows a college lecturer Deven, go in search of a famous poet, Nur. A beautifully written and haunting story, *Baumgartner's Bombay* is Anita Desai's classic novel of the Holocaust era describing the wounds inflicted by the war and exiles. Thus, the story opens with Hugo's murder and the ensuing chapters alternate between scenes of his last hours and flashbacks that take us chronologically through his life.

The first half of Desai's next novel *Journey to Ithaca* focuses on Matteo, an idealistic Italian, and his temperamental girlfriend, Sophie, a hard-bitten realist German. The countercultural pair marry in 1975 and immediately set off for India, chiefly in pursuit of Matteo's dream of enlightenment, which has been inspired by his reading of Hermann Hesse's *Journey to the East.* They eventually arrive at an ashram in northern India that is led by a charismatic, elderly woman who calls herself the "Mother." Although Sophie remains unimpressed by the "Mother," Matteo is enthralled by what he finds to be the spiritually edifying environment, and they remain for several years, during which time they have two children. Most of the novel's second half consists of Sophie's retracing of the "Mother's" life, which is presented in the form of flashbacks to the early 1920s.

Fasting, Feasting relates the disastrous attempts of an Indian daughter to leave her parents' home and achieve independence without marriage. Her parents, referred to as the indivisible unit Mama Papa, barely notice their daughter's aspirations as they lavish all of their attention on their only son and presents a contrast of American and Indian culture of male and female roles. It is the story of an unmarried woman who is forced to care for her demanding elderly parents, while her adored younger brother is sent to study in America. Uma's attempt to leave home and marry ends in disaster.

Her new novel, *The Zigzag Way* is set in Mexico and is narrated by a young American writer, a man who travels to Sierra Madre without knowing why. Desai says that this novel reveals more and more, her own experience. Thus, we can conclude that Anita Desai emerges as an evolving artist in Indian English fiction. Unlike her earlier novels the canvas is no longer confined to probe into the interior landscape of characters but Desai, in her later novels deals with themes like German anti-Semitism, the demise of tradition and western stereotypical views of India. In her long, distinguished career, Anita Desai has focused her capacious vision on questions of culture and identity. Her next novel, *The Zigzag Way*, brings her fiction to an unexpected region of the world: mythical, lush Mexico. In this seductive landscape, a young American stumbles upon an unlikely path to self-discovery. Eric is a newly minted historian who pursues his own private quest, tracing his family's history to a Mexican ghost town, where, a hundred years earlier, young Cornish miners toiled to the death. With vivid sympathy, Desai conjures the struggles of Eric's grandparents and their community. Haunting and atmospheric, with splashes of exuberant colour and darker violence, *The Zigzag Way* is a magical novel of elegiac beauty.

Despite the varying themes, her novels all of them, are unified by the persistent strain of existentialism. She herself makes her intentions clear—"My novels are no reflections of Indian society, politics or characters. They are a part of my private effort to seize upon the raw material of life—its shapelessness its meaninglessness."[16]

NOTES AND REFERENCES

1. Sagarika Ghose comments in an article on Indian English literature.
2. Jean-Paul Sartre: "Existentialism is a Humanism," Existentialism from Dostoevsky to Sartre, pp. 350-57.
3. Quest, 65 (April – June 1970), p. 43.
4. Anita Desai comments, "Contemporary Novelists, James Vinson, ed. (New York: St. Martin's Press, 1972), p. 348.
5. K.R. Srinivasa Iyengar: Indian Writing in English, New Delhi: Sterling Publishers Pvt. Ltd., p. 464.
6. Graham Greene in Preface to Ways of Escape. The Bodley Head London (1980), p. 9.
7. Harry J. Moony Jr. and Thomas F. Stanley, eds., Shapeless Gods (Pittsburgh, 1968), p. 3.
8. Erich Fromm *et al.*, Zen Buddhism and Psychoanalysis (New York, 1970), p. 86.
9. All textual quotations have been taken from the following editions of Anita Desai's novels:
   (1) *Cry, The Peacock* (New Delhi: Orient Paper Backs, 1980).
   (2) *Voices in the City* (Delhi: Hind Pocket Books, 1965).
   (3) *Bye-Bye Blackbird* (Delhi: Hind Pocket Books, 1971).
   (4) *Where Shall We Go This Summer?* (New Delhi: Orient Paper Backs, 1982).
   (5) *Fire on the Mountain* (New Delhi: Allied Publishers, 1977).
   (6) *Clear Light of Day* (New Delhi: Allied Publishers, 1980).
   (7) *In Custody* (London: Heinemann, 1984).
10. K.R. Srinivasa Iyengar: Indian Writing in English, New Delhi: Sterling Publishers Pvt. Ltd., p. 470.
11. Atma Ram: "Anita Desai: The Novelist who writes for Herself," The Journal of Indian Writing in English (July 1977), p. 40.
12. Vimla Rao: "Anita Desai's Where Shall We Go This Summer? An Analysis" Commonwealth Quarterly, 3/9 (December 1978), p. 50.
13. B. Ramchandra Rao: The Novels of Anita Desai (Kalyani Publishers 1977), pp. 49-50.
14. Meenakshi Mukherjee: Review of In Custody, The Indian Express (7th October 1984), p. 5.

15. Jasbir Jain: In her article, In Pursuit of Wholeness: Trancendence of the Self in the Novels of Anita Desai. Studies in Contemporary Indian Fiction in English ed. By Dr. A.N. Dwivedi, p. 300.
16. Anita Desai comments, "Contemporary Novelists," James Vinson ed. (New York: St. Martins Press, 1972).

'Paradigms of Feminist Statement' in the Novels of Nayantara Sahgal

17

"Feminism is an attack upon social opinion, wherever it discriminates in its attitude toward man and woman on the basis of sex."

—*George Middleton*
Early 20th-century playwright,
speaking in 1914.

In an attempt to make new empowering image for women, the Indo Anglian writers, particularly the women writers affected by Western feminism have explored the alternative ideal of self assertion. "One might say that in spite of the fact that some Indo Anglian novelists are still attempting to recapture a recent historical part, the majority of writers since 1950, have turned inwards to more private and personal problems."[1] Betty Friedan in, *The Feminine Mystique* voices the prevalent trend: "For women as for men, the need for self-fulfilment, autonomy, self realization independence, individuality, self actualization is as important as the sexual need, with as serious consequences when it is thwarted."[2] In her book, *Image of Woman in the Indo Anglian Novel*, Meena Shirwadkar claims that "Tradition, transition and modernity' are the stages through which the woman in Indo Anglian novel is passing."[3] Following the changes in the Indian society, the Indo Anglian novelists have moved away from presenting the traditional, enduring, self sacrificing women towards conflicted female characters searching for identity.

Nayantara Sahgal is one such prominent Indian English

novelist who has tried to depict women suffering due to sexist bias in patriarchal society and she envisions a world which should be based on equality and harmony between the two sexes. Compared to her contemporaries, Sahgal's stand on women and female sexuality and the concern with woman's right to her body is both unconventional and subversive. From amongst her early contemporaries of the fifties,—Kamala Markandaya, Santha Rama Ram and Attia Hosain—she can be singled out for her boldness in relating the issue of sex, to individual freedom and the desire to free a woman from being treated as a possession. Thus, placed within the context of the writing of the fifties and sixties, Sahgal displays a highly developed consciousness of the gendered nature of morality and social structures. Primarily, seen as a feminist, her feminism is rooted in the larger framework of human rights, of personal freedom and right to body. Talking of feminist awakening in herself, Sahgal confesses in her letter to Neena Arora: "I have come to this awakening rather late, although I have personally always been independent minded. That is not enough. I think, if one cares, one must project and ally oneself with one's beliefs. I think I do this more now as regards feminism."[4]

Her novels stress on the independent existence of women and atrophy all the attempts to exclude them from the centre stage of human existence focusing chiefly on the question of identity on crisis for women, Sahgal believes—"Through the rewriting women do, new Sitas and Savitris will arise, stripped of false sanctity and crowned with the human virtue of courage. Then at last we will know why they did what they did, and their lone remote struggles can help our search for identity and emancipation."[5] Her fiction reveals the conflict between Tradition and Modernity in India in the late 20th century. Her women are generally traditional but they revolt against those traditions which question their identity and endanger woman's pivotal role in the family and society. Sahgal's work has been critiqued from different perspectives—a feminist, a political writer, an advocate of Gandhian ideologies and as a writer of social documentaries.

Along with colonial and post colonial issues Nayantara Sahgal's novels fore grounded the emotional incompatibility between partners in arranged marriages and voiced the woman's need for space in a patriarchal society. As a result of the patriarchal society woman has become—"The subdued sex, creatures not yet emerged from the chrysalis, for the adventure of self expression had not yet begun. Whatever, womanhood had once meant in India had been lost in the mist of antiquity. In its place there has long been a figure of humility, neck bent eyes downcast, living flesh consigned to oblivion."[6] Nayantara Sahgal has emphasized in her novels on freedom and a new definition of "the virtuous woman." Her sensibility got sharpened during her study in America. She finds: "Freedom was a cherished possession, belligerently defended. In India, it has been haunting in its lack, a distant star on the horizon, something to work and ache for, often at stupendous personal cost. In America it was in one's lap, on one's tongue, where, I suddenly discovered, it belonged. It was one's very own.... The freedom to think, to write, to be, was what life was all about."[7]

In most of her novels, the heroines are aware of the injustice done to them in their marriage and they walk out of their homes. They reflect the changing social conditions. In spite of being deep-rooted in Indian culture, they care and yearn for personal freedom and have their own identities. Civil liberties for women are another cause that Nayantara Sahgal's characters vociferously advocate. The curbing of liberties during emergency period of Mrs. Indira Gandhi's time has found detailed description in Sahgal's novels. Freedom for women, according to Nayantara Sahgal, implies awareness of her identity and raising the voice against injustice. Sometimes they revolt against the exploitations of men and sometimes compromise with this social reality and Nayantara Sahgal has portrayed women mostly from the upper strata and often a political backdrop is created. Harin Majithia opines: "In the eight novels to her credit from the first one *A Time to Be Happy* (1957) up to her latest one *Mistaken Identity* (1988), she emphasizes the value of freedom so essential to inner and outer development of individuals and the country. Her characters are often entrapped in trying situation but being honest to themselves, they emerge victorious, morally upright, taking revolutionary stand."[8]

Cocooned within domesticity, Sahgal's early heroines gradually move on to wider spaces, areas of competition and face problems of survival. Sahgal's first-two women, Maya in *A Time to Be Happy* and Rashmi in *This Time of Morning* are still women in stasis, but the next three protagonists of Sahgal, namely Saroj, Simrit and Devi mark a clear advancement from the point of view of any determination. The second phase of Sahgal's career opens with *Storm in Chandigarh*. Whereas, the heroines of her early novels were products of a parochial society, and it was not without a sense of guilt, that they struggled for emancipation, the heroines of the second phase like Simrit and Saroj break free from the shackles of oppression, with no sense of guilt, no sense of remorse. Saroj in *Storm in Chandigarh* represents the majority of people who are instrumental in letting violence spread and engulf them. Her marriage to Inder is not built upon love, patience and truth which to Inder are superfluous things. He can never treat his wife as a friend with whom he can "be naked in spirit."[9] With a man like him who applies a double moral code, her openness spells only disaster. He is obsessed with her pre marital lapse and uses chastity as a weapon to humble her. Her act, he feels has no place "in an order that clearly demarcated the roles of men and women."[10] Saroj on her part does not consider herself guilty of any lapse. She is warmly and wholly involved in her marriage to Inder but he persists in raking up the past making Saroj beat against his "numbness like a bird against a windowpane trapped in a futile frenzy."[11] Saroj, "wants to build up a relationship on that basis where as Inder treats her merely as a wife—a possession, not a person."[12] Offering a remedy to this state of inaction and paralysis Sahgal makes Saroj act at the right moment. Saroj walks out of the home that had ceased to be a home.

Simrit, in *The Day in Shadow* truly represents those women of the Indian Hindu society who are inspired by a sense of good and ideal values of life and who yearn for understanding, sympathy and friendships to blossom between them, but the cruel, materialistic and selfish husband finds it melodramatic. Som, Simrit's husband is interested in accumulating wealth, in making money, in his male heir and his ammunition deals. Due to the incompatibility of their world views, Simrit's marriage with Som is a failure, despite having children, despite having wealth. Simrit wants to nurture, to build, to cherish, but Som represents materialism. Som's insensitivity and differences of opinions fills Simrit's life with distress. Thus, forced by circumstances, when Simrit asks for divorce, he vindictively places her under a financial arrangement which cripples her by the tax problem but nobody recognizes it as an exploitation Simrit came to represent for the writer the average, acquiescent woman who allows herself to be exploited because she "is not part of the creating active world."[13] She is symbolic of the Hindu race; she is not an individual, she is, "a culture, a tradition, a patient, enduring passivity."[14]

But towards the end of the novel, like a true feminist, Simrit moves out of her husband's home. She becomes aware of her own identity existence and rights. Ram Krishan, an intelligent philosopher becomes instrumental in solving her problems. Instead of renunciation she opts for struggle to find her way out, instead of self pity she is guided by a sense of adventure. She tells Raj, a Christian who evokes the avidity and confidence of Simrit to a great extent—"D you know why I came? It was to tell you. I'd got rid of my guilts. It was gone without a trace and in its place there was a strong positive feeling. If feelings have smells, this one was a clean, carbolic, disinfectant smell."[15] Thus, when Simrit marries Raj, her problem disappears and in the end Simrit appears as a woman who very bravely came out of her shell.

Rich like us marks the third and the most mature phase of Sahgal's career. The women belonging to this phase are strong willed, courageous and emotionally independent. In the previous phase, the women struggled for self realization with the support of their male friends—Vishal Dubey motivates Saroj in *Storm in Chandigarh* and Raj motivates Simrit in *The Day in Shadow*. But Sonali Ranade in *Rich like us* dares to challenge male superiority successfully unaided by any man. Her survival instinct is very strong and instead of giving in she gives up. An uncompromising I.A.S. officer she resigns as she could not compromise. Her resignation, however is not her defeat it is her refusal, her defiance against oppression. She says: "I hadn't merely been transferred without warning, I had been demoted, punished, and humiliated, and I had no inkling why."[16] She wrote about herself: "And then I had become the kind of woman, who highly concentrated on the subject in hand, is supposed to have 'a man's mind' and who disappoints the flirtations and flippant."[17] She has a strong individuality, is brave and opposes dictatorship; "not even of the proletariat, not even as a passing phase because who knows the phase might get struck and never pass."[18]

Sonali's views about love, friendship and marriage are also quite revolutionary as she does not consider marriage to be the ultimate end of love and friendship. Marriage is not necessary. One can do very well without it. When Ravi admits his love for her and tells her that he had to marry someone else because of his mother, he tells her: "It's too late now, but if we had our time over again I'd work it out differently."[19] The remark of Sonali is significant: "This admission of waste, of years gone and opportunity lost filled me with a sweet relief. Isolated from all that had happened outside our private creation it had the wonder for me of broken ends mending, of Kachru becoming Ravi again, of friendship resuming of love having been really love and not a mistake he had been trying to forget."[20] Sonali, ir spite of being unsuccessful in her personal and professional life, is not at all pessimistic. The remark with which the novel closes reveals the metal of which she is made; "I went to work immersed in the past; I was preparing all the while for the future beyond Brian's century and his exhibition. Marcella had reminded me of it, made a gift of it to me. Though it was really Rose's legacy again, the paths that had crossed hers now crossing mine, reminding me I was young and alive, with my own century stretched out before me, waiting to be lived."[21] Sonali escapes marriage by asserting her individuality. She remains unmarried till the end, though she unhesitatingly gives her self to Ravi Kachru, but is free of guilt. Thus in Sonali Ranade we see the feminist in Nayantara Sahgal coming of age.

In *Rich like us* the woman question is presented through multiplicities ranging over nearly a century—the great grandmother who commits Sati, the Kashmiri mother who is aggressively expressive, Rose who knowingly walks into second marriage, but does not betray her ideals, Mona who endures but not passively, Nishi who submits to Dev for she comes from a many daughtered family. Sahgal examines with keen sensibility and perception the sufferings and problems of women in marriage who feel completely entrapped. Mona is the typical Hindu woman who submits herself to Ram. When her husband brings home the second wife Rose, she doesn't utter a word but weeps in silence. The husband inflicts great emotional violence on both the women, he marries. When Rose, the second wife questions, "How can we get married when you're married?"[22] He has the audacity to answer—"My religion lets a man have more than one wife."[23] Both women being dependent on him are exploited by him and he just continues doing whatever he likes. Thus, in *Rich like us*, Sahgal deals with two kinds of women, the first group of women is of those who are confined to a life of Hindu orthodoxy and the other of those who have a strong sense of individuality and an analytical mind.

Anna Hansen of *Plans for Departure* is a Danish woman, who wants to break out and be herself, she knows not only what she wants, but also how to achieve it. Her travels were "part of her quest for freedom and meaning"[24] thinking of her epitaph, she is full of despair: "Here lies Anna, beloved wife, who died without having made much effort to live, and nobody noticed the difference, since being a beloved wife was supposed to be reward enough."[25] Her thirst for identity forces her to leave her home and her country.

In *Mistaken Identity*, culminates Sahgal's quest for emancipation of woman. Here, is a woman, the Ranee of Vijaygarh, who is living in 1920's-30's, is uneducated, has an apathetic husband, has nothing to look forward to, and yet she dares to shun her husband from her life, when she discovers the man does not respect her. When her husband marries for the third time, this woman behind the veil breaks all ties with her husband. She does so without anybody's support. In the end, she breaks free from all inhibitions and marries comrade Yusuf. She doesn't need support even from her son, Bhushan. Thus, Ranee of Vijaygarh though a nameless character, marks the culmination of the march of Sahgal's 'new women' towards freedom.

From *A Time to Be Happy* to *Mistaken Identity*, Sahgal's novels show her deep concern with the parlous state of woman in the parochial society. From prototype Maya to Ranee of Vijaygarh her women characters try to become themselves by staying within the limits of the Indian traditions and values. Sahgal never aims to set one sex against the other. Her major concern is to present the problems that the contemporary women face in society and in their struggle towards self definition.

NOTES AND REFERENCES

1. Mukherjee, M.: Twice Born Fiction (Delhi, 1971), p. 206.
2. Friedan, Betty: 1963, 1971. *The Feminine Mystique*, Harmondsworth: Penguin.
3. Shirwadkar, Meena: *Image of Woman in Indo Anglian Novel* (New Delhi: Sterling, 1979), pp. 153-54.
4. Arora, Neena: Nayantara Sahgal and Doris Lessing (A Feminist Study in Comparison), New Delhi: Prestige, 1991, p. 115.
5. Sahgal, Nayantara: Point of View, New Delhi: Prestige, p. 33.
6. *Ibid.*, *Storm in Chandigarh*, p. 195.
7. *Ibid.*, Point of View, New Delhi: Prestige, p. 28.
8. Majithia, Harin: 'The Novels of Nayantara Sahgal's: A Prismatic View,' Jaipur: RBSA Publishers, 2000, p. 19.
9. Sahgal, Nayantara: *Storm in Chandigarh*, p. 69.
10. *Ibid.*, p. 96.
11. *Ibid.*, p. 97.
12. Jain, Jasbir: N.S., New Delhi: Arnold Heinemann, 1978, p. 52.
13. Sahgal, Nayantara: "My New Novel," *Hindustan Times*, 18 Dec., 1971.
14. *Ibid.*, Point of View, p. 18.
15. *Ibid.*, *The Day in Shadow*, p. 208.
16. *Ibid.*, *Rich like us*, p. 27.
17. *Ibid.*, p. 193.
18. *Ibid.*
19. *Ibid.*, p. 295.
20. *Ibid.*

21. *Ibid.*, p. 301.
22. *Ibid.*, p. 42.
23. *Ibid.*
24. Jain, Jasbir: N.S., Jaipur Printwell, 1999, p. 146.
25. Sahgal, Nayantara: *Plans for Departure*, p. 62.

'The Immigrant's Voyage' in Monica Ali's *Brick Lane* 18

"I think that for immigrants, the challenges of exile, the loneliness, the constant sense of alienation, the knowledge of and longing for a lost world is more explicit and distressing than for their children. On the other hand, the problem for the children of immigrants—those with strong ties to their country of origin—is that they feel neither one thing nor the other."

—*Jhumpa Lahiri*

Hailed by the London Observer as "one of the most significant British novelists of her generation,"[1] Monica Ali emerges as a writer "who found right at the beginning of her career and with absolute confidence her own voice."[2] A new exciting voice of post-colonial Britain, Ali opens up the experience of minority groups to a much wider readership. Depicting an 'outsider's quest to find her voice,' Ali has extended the migrant voice in British fiction, particularly through her representation of gender and focus on history and dislocation. In her stunningly accomplished debut novel, *Brick Lane* we hear a voice "not always fully mature," but spoken in a tone "that was humorous and humane and managed to bring to life with marvellous precision a particular emotional journey in a particular milieu."[3]

Monica Ali was selected by a panel of judges as one of Granta's magazine's Best of British Young Novelists in 2003, merely on the basis of the manuscript of the novel. She had not published a single word then, but the judges unanimously agreed about her selection in the panel. A thrilling new voice in fiction, "one of those dangerous writers who sees everything,"[4] Monica Ali's *Brick Lane* won the 2003 Discover Award for Fiction and was short listed for the Man Booker Prize. However, the Bangladeshi community leaders have called her debut novel, a 'despicable insult' and The Greater Sylhet Development and Welfare Council, representing many Bangladeshis in the UK called the book "Shameful."[5] The council complained the book treated Bangladeshis as "economic migrants" and portrayed them as ignorant. However, Larry Finlay, the managing director of Transworld Publishers, said—"Monica Ali's *Brick Lane* is a novel that we are enormously proud to have published—we find both the accusations against it and any demand for censorship ludicrous, as it was a work of fiction."[6]

Monica Ali's debut novel has also earned the acclaim of The New York Times—"Writers are prone to false starts and slumps, and some of them always run the same race, incapable of changing stride. It usually takes two or three books to establish their form—and yet Monica Ali already has a sense of technical assurance and cannot be learned."[7] What inspired Ali to write this novel were a number of factors. As she says—"My experience, for instance, of conflict between first and second generation immigrants. The stories that my father used to tell about village life. A book of case studies about Bangladeshi women garment workers in Dhaka and the East End of London, disparate lives drawn together by the common goal of self empowerment."[8] *Brick Lane* has always been a temporary interzone for immigrants who haven't fully settled in England, whose lives are defined by the past but who want to seize the future. It was for centuries a part of Roman burial ground, an unclean extremity lying beyond the walls of the City of London. In 1603, a quarter of a century after bricks began to be manufactured here, John Stow described its buildings as 'filthy cottages.' Since then the area...has been a byword for poverty and violence."[9] Monica Ali appears to be telling a story about what she knows best in her novel, *Brick Lane*. Born in Bangladesh and grown up in London, she offers a deep insight into that land and culture. Not only does she focus on life in

Tower Hamlets, giving us a glimpse of gender and class relations there, but she also tries to impart life in contemporary urban Bangladeshi life in rural Bangladesh and even history of Bangladesh to some extent.

British critics have called her the next Zadie Smith presumably because they are both young, nonwhite females who blasted onto the literary scene with Booker—nominated bestsellers about immigrant culture in London. The Times (London) placed Monica Ali with Zadie Smith as a significant author in contemporary post-colonial fiction—"Britain's brightest young literary stars range from...Zadie Smith whose debut novel White Teeth sold one million copies and Monica Ali, who has yet to see her work in print."[10] Ali joins Zadie Smith in the panel of 20 British writers of the next decade chosen by Granta's Magazine and the two have a great deal in common, not only because of their cross-cultural backgrounds (Ali is the child of a British mother and a Bengali father), their intimate knowledge of what it feels like to be an outsider in Britain, and their Oxbridge educations. The thematic comparisons to Smith's first book are clear and abundant: the immigrants' unfulfilled dreams in an adopted country; the generational conflicts between parents and the children who all too easily assimilate to the new land; the yearnings for a home. Yet while Smith's brilliance is in her vibrant depiction of the multicultural society that is now London, Ali gives us a slice of that world. In White Teeth, Smith chronicled a particular down-at-heel corner of North London from the perspective of two multi-racial families, while Ali focuses on an equally shabby estate near east London's Brick Lane, occupied almost exclusively by Bengalis. Both of them have highlighted a city that is largely foreign territory for most of its citizens, heralding a welcome new "state of England" novel, which is what the Granta judges purport to seek? But where "White Teeth" teemed with a cast of characters careening across one another's lives in tangled subplots, "Brick Lane" is a stoutly simple tale, chronicling the fortunes of a Bangladeshi woman named Nazneen, who immigrates to England to consummate the marriage her father has arranged with a middle-aged civil servant she has never met named Chanu.

Thus, the immigrant world Ali chronicles in this penetrating, unsentimental debut has much in common with Zadie Smith's scrappy, multicultural London, though its sheltered protagonist rarely leaves her rundown East End apartment block where she is surrounded by fellow Bangladeshis. But apart from the demographics, they have little in common. Smith's comedy is more frantic and while her prose is exhilarating, it is also self dramatizing. Ali's eloquence is more firmly restrained. In fact, *Brick Lane* comes closer to Timothy Mo's *Sour Sweet*—a similarly naturalistic account of immigrant life. Yet another comparison would be with Anita Brookner, that non-young blisteringly white matron of British fiction whose quiet incisive novels scrutinize the plight of lonely people.

Beginning in 1967, in Mymensingh district of East Pakistan, which seven years later would become Bangladesh, the book gives a rich insight into Bengali culture. A tender and touching story, the novel captures the struggles, the cultural clash and the frustrations of a family caught between two worlds. Though Monica Ali is not the first person to write about the Bangladeshi communities who live in *Brick Lane*, Syed Manzurul Islam's *The Mapmakers of Spitalfields* (1997) and Farukh Dhondy's *East End at Your Feet* (1976) and *Come to Mecca* (1978) being the previous books dealing with the Bangladeshi communities, Monica Ali's *Brick Lane* is the first novel to focus almost exclusively on the lives of Bangladeshi women in Tower Hamlets. It tries to take us beyond the yellowing net curtains of their cramped tower—block flats and into their living rooms and bedrooms. It articulates their fears and desires and offers a finely textured corrective to those accounts which portray them as elective mutes, unthinking purveyors of Third World Tradition.

The truest part of Ali's writing is about the experience of exile, the pain of unbelonging. Monica's mother born in Bolton married a Bangladeshi man she met at Dhaka. However, as a result of the Pakistani crackdown in March 1971, when Monica was three years old, the family ended up living in Bolton in a run down area. She had a very bitter experience in mid 2003 when the Bangladeshi High Commission refused her a visa to visit her birthplace. Ali's voice is "distinctive compassionate, wry, sharply observant,"[11] expressing the struggles, that the new migrants face.

In setting and theme, *Brick Lane* is a remarkably old fashioned tale, as Ali herself says it is, "an old fashioned saga about the struggle between fate and free—will, endurance and self help."[12] The novel reminds us inevitably of the opening page of Israel Zangwill's children of the Ghetto (1892)—'This London Ghetto of ours is a region where, amid uncleanliness and squalor, the rose of romance blows, yet a little longer in the raw air of English reality; a world which hides beneath its stony and unlovely surface an inner world of dreams, fantastic and poetic as the mirage of the Orient where they were woven.'[13] To that 19th century model, he adds the more contemporary theme of a floundering woman's coming—to—(feminist) consciousness. Though, "the story of migrant women, newly married wives to non resident South Asian men are not new to the genre of South Asian writing in English," but what is remarkable is the manner in which Monica Ali "has tackled this particular task of fleshing out on the page, the life of a young woman who's grown up in a village who knows only a couple of English words, 'sorry' and 'thank you,' who must negotiate an alien country, feel out entirely new relationships with neighbours both Bengali and English and come to terms with marriage to a stranger."[14] The young author presents a detailed if sometimes plodding depiction of a Bangladeshi woman's life in London and her metamorphosis from a voiceless village girl to a decisive woman and with great sensitivity how Nazneen lived long years of her life accepting fate, but finally—after an arranged marriage to an older man, three children and a constricted life in London—breaks free to make choices of her own.

What in past decades, Naipaul, Buchi Emacheta, Beryl Gilroy and Sam Selvos did for African and Carribean immigrants coming to Britain, Monica Ali has done for Bangladeshi immigrants especially from a woman's point of view. The narration of the plight of Bangladeshi immigrants in London's *Brick Lane* has been manipulated to be an Amazon—feminist saga of Nazneen. Ms. Ali is being celebrated for her limpid portrait of Bangladeshi characters living in London, defining the immigrant experience through the obstacles and conflicts they encounter. She has spun magic with the elan of an empathetic writer, creating the sounds, smells and sights of life as a Bengali and she paints a memorable portrait of the growing rebellion among second generation Bangladeshi Brits struggling with their identity, as do immigrants the world over.

The novel is written from the point of view of Nazneen, a Bengali girl who grew up in rural Mymensingh district and arrives in London as a young woman married to Chanu, a man who has been living in England for many years. Monica Ali successfully puts herself in Nazneen's shoes and through her eyes, she brings the reader to the world of the Bengali immigrant community in London's East End. Set in the Bangladeshi community on a council state in London's Tower Hamlets, *Brick Lane* "tracks the process by which she moves fitfully and self laceratingly from shame to tentative self possession, from a willing submission to a belief in her own agency from a silence, both voluntary and culturally conditioned to a yell of liberation."[15] Her story starts with her premature birth and to all appearances Nazneen was stillborn. She stirred to life in the very moment that a village midwife pronounced her dead. And even after her birth, as her mother loses no opportunity to remind her, Nazneen rallied to sustain herself only when her mother refused any intervention from midwives and medical professionals and placed her destiny entirely in the hands of Allah. Thought unable to survive, she is left to take its course by her mother, who later goes on to take her own life. Whilst still in her teenage years, her father arranges marriage to a much older man, Chanu. With a great deal of fatalism she accepts her father's wishes for her and leaves her village, travels to London where her life on a council state begins. Nazneen's journey is mirrored by that of her sister, Hasina back in Bangladesh. In contrast her younger sister, Hasina, has fled from the village and married her young husband for love. Monica Ali has depicted stories from Nazneen's childhood in the Bangladeshi village, stories which came from her own father's memories of life in rural Bengal. She also keeps a connection with contemporary urban Bangladesh through Nazneen's sister, Hasina, who appears in the text through her letters to Nazneen—which inform us about the world of working class women in Bangladesh. We read of Hasina's travails as Nazneen does, in episodic letters posted from the various points she provisionally settles into over the course of her glum, downward slide to the lower depths of Bangladesh society. Monica Ali shows how the choices that face the sister in Bangladesh are so much starker than Nazneen's—choices that determine Hasina's survival as well as her happiness. Appalling things happen to her over the years. A baby dies despite mother's determination to save him. Left without the protection of a husband, Hasina is raped, then forced to become a prostitute, to survive. Hasina's life is a "pedestrian tale of outrageous misfortune." Hasina's character "brings me back" says Ali, "to the Dhaka balcony; my inherited memory, my internalised folklore that tells me that life hangs by a thread."[16]

It's a home Ali brilliantly renders through the long series if often anguished letters that Nazneen receives from her sister, Hasina a girl whose beauty proves almost unbearable to own. These letters appear throughout the novel, but Ali employs a large number of them to bridge thirteen years in Nazneen's life from 1988 until 2001. Monica Ali depicts Nazneen in a variety of settings, looking out of the window of her flat in council housing, caring, for a very sick child in a London hospital, trying to sort out the changing politics around her, both of the racists and the young Muslim militants, relating to life in her flat with her husband and teenaged children swept up in a love affair with a spirited young man; and searching for her runaway daughter amidst a rebellion of Bengali youth on the streets of East London —From some one who is largely an observer, Nazneen grows into a woman gaining confidence and acting to change her circumstances. Nazneen's sudden forced isolation in a culture very different from her own is something many an immigrant can identify with. Her constant comparisons in the small flat, Ali observes are 'the muffled sounds of private lives sealed away above, below, and around her, the television on, coughing, sometimes the lavatory flushing, someone upstairs scraping a chair.' As events come to upend Nazneen's constitutional fatalism, so too do they undermine Chanu's dreams of never-ending upward mobility: His promotion is never forthcoming, and his extravagant pride compels him to resign his post, sparking his own descent into an anything but "respectable" livelihood as a cabdriver. Her husband Chanu is full of promise and eager to succeed at the outset. Finally, he gives in to a system he can't associate with, leaning on crutches that promise him the good life "back home." For several years, Nazneen drags on her life thinking of "the rolls of fat, that hung low from Chanu's stomach," wherein "it would be possible to tuck all your hundred pens and pencils under those rolls and keep them safe and tight. You could stuff a book or two up there as well"[17] (pp. 14-15). Larger forces, too, impinge on Nazneen's cloistered life, notably when the household's mounting economic distress propels her further into the world to take in piecemeal sewing work—and when the aftermath of the Sept. 11, 2001, attacks stir many Bangladeshi residents of Tower Hamlets into painful new reckonings with their Islamic identity. Ali renders these bigger events, too, in plainly wrought but affecting fashion.

As Nazneen finds her way around the contours of her new immigrant life, she is plagued by a constant sense of unease: "How difficult it was, this business of sitting still," she observes, "But there was nothing really to complain of. There was Chanu, who was kind and never beat her. And there was this shapeless, nameless thing that crawled across her shoulders and nested in her hair and poisoned her lungs that made her both restless and listless." At this time young Karim enters Nazneen's life and the docile and obedient Nazneen's life is interrupted by her rebellions thought, a rebellious side that is unveiled when the path of the attractive radical named Karim crosses her path. Almost every day, Karim drops off piece work for Nazneen's new sewing job. Ali shows how the physical attraction that explodes between them destroys their moral expectations. She captures all the little details of Karim's attractiveness to Nazneen from the citrus scent of his shirts to his eager energy when discussing politics, until, long before their first kiss, you have been convinced by a sense of absolutely inexorable desire. Nazneen sees that everybody sought but could rarely find—a place in world. Young Karim is full of ideas about the injustice shown towards the Muslims, and he seeks to galvanize the local Muslims into action against local white militants. Karim is the opposite of Chanu—young, not greying and corpulent, religious rather than multi faithed, financially secure and good looking—very much like the Millat character in Zadie Smith's *White Teeth*. The smouldering attraction between Nazneen and Karim, much against their own better judgements is one of the many beautiful aspects of *Brick Lane*.

"In the morning she said her prayers and did housework and began her sewing and there was nothing inside her that demanded more. But lunchtime when she looked for Karim out of the window her stomach began to surge with excitement" (p. 418). "In place of her husband's rolls of fat she watches the muscles in his arms tense and relax...skin golden, like honey and to her it looked like you could lick it off" (p. 419). Smelling the sweat of her lover, she is stirred and exclaims, 'Ah, you! You are the real thing.' A flashback comes to her mind in the form of conversation overheard in the early days of her marriage when she stood in her night dress in the hallway, while Chanu was on the phone—"An unspoilt girl. From the village. All things considered. I am satisfied" (p. 411). Her adultery produces a terrifying burden of guilt, but it also encourages her growing sense of outrage at her mother's passivity and wakens her to the possibility of shaping her fate rather than accepting it. In fractured English, she describes—sometimes without even realizing it—disastrous relationships and experiences that expose the horrors of misogyny back home. Her salvation comes not by doing what she's told or by choosing from the options of saint or sinner as outlined for her, but by daring to imagine a life outside those boundaries.

Where her husband drones on and on about the lack of global appreciation for Tagore, Karim is ready to strike, to march, to fight for the rights of British Muslims. The character, Karim, Monica Ali's beauty, youth and status as a non–white Englishwoman further led to comparisons to Zadie Smith who, in *White Teeth* traces the radicalization of a young man too. Ali is tender and interested in the slow immergence into consciousness of a single, humble woman, whereas Smith is hilarious, brazen and interested in the bruises the world imposes on confident young people. Different again from Smith. Ali's book is the story of a single character and unusual for that character being a wife and mother, a woman who does not, for many years, think of herself as an individual except in stolen moments.

Through the jerky murky lines of narrators, the novel halts at a point when "she had wanted to go. But now she did not know the children would suffer. Chanu would face fresh agonies of disappointment; and she was not the real thing" (p. 420) and thus a severe combat is bumped as the search for identity and freight of family ties. Thus the protagonist in her teens has proved to be successful in realizing an 'outsider's quest to find her voice.' Ali brilliantly chronicles Nazneen's isolation, her passivity and at last her gradual exploration of the outside world. In an extremist male society Nazneen must grasp at flecks of freedom, and Ali is extraordinary at capturing the female immigrant experience through her character's innocent perspective. In Ali's "subtle narration, Nazneen's mixture of traditionalism and adaptability of acceptance and restlessness, emerges as a quiet strength."[18]

Nazneen shrugs off her passivity at just the right moment and the supporting cast-Chanu, the ineffectual patriarch, Nazneen's defiant and struggling neighbour, Razia and Karim the foolish young Muslim radical with whom Nazneen eventually has an affair—are all richly drawn. Though Ali is dealing with such large themes, her tone remains deceptively light, and her comic touch saves her from any melodrama or soupiness. It is a nicely humane sense of comedy that still allows her protagonists room to live and breathe. ...The relation that Chanu has with the local doctor at first seems to be purely a comic turn...by the end even this relationship reaches a pitch of greater emotion, as Nazneen realizes quite how much love the two men have for one another.[19] The writing style is colourful and descriptive and the reader can smell the spices wafting through the hallways, view the multicultural clutter of a shabby overcrowded apartment and share the confusion in Brick Lane due to cultural, religious and racial prejudice. All the characters—Chanu with his inner doubts and disillusionment, the starchy Dr. Azad, the crafty hypochondriac, Mrs. Islam and the Britishised Razia are depicted with a deft touch.

Ali is an attentive observer of people, describing in rich detail all the odd mannerisms by which we unconsciously express ourselves. Chanu's body and absurd physical tics are meticulously catalogued: his soft, spongy corns; the way his belly nestles into his thighs when he sits down; the manner in which he "hunched to his food to abbreviate the journey between plate and mouth;" the way his eyebrows "shot up high, leaving his small eyes vulnerable, unprotected, like two snails out of their shells." His pretensions are also rendered with the same perspicacity and comic verve, but he is sometimes a little too predictable. Ali rescues him from the brink of caricature by demonstrating his fragile self-respect and ample affection for his wife and two daughters; he is, in the end, rather lovable. Nazneen's neighbours on the estate, who are her only contact with the larger world, are also lovingly evoked, and each represents a different approach to the problem of being a permanent foreigner in Britain. Razia Iqbal is a feisty, large-boned woman who abandons her *sari* in favour of trousers and embraces English life by getting a job. Her generous nature is closer in spirit to the Koran than is Mrs. Islam, a manipulative mean-minded usurer who hopes to gain God's favour by her donations to a mosque back "home" in Bangladesh.

Monica Ali's debut novel delves into the landscape of love, family and the yearning for a sense of belonging. "The novel manages to take in a great swath of immigrant experience with its vivid minor characters, its scenes of absurd local politics and its focus on individuals thrown together becoming and trying to make their way."[20] Thus we can conclude that "Brick Lane has everything, richly complex characters, a gripping story and an exploration of a community that is so quintessentially British that it has given us our national dish, but of which most of us are entirely ignorant. Plus, it is a meditation on fate and free will. Oh, and it is funny too. And painful."[21] *Brick Lane* remains "a humanely forgiving story about love.... *Brick Lane* may be Ali's first novel but it is written with wisdom and a skill that few authors attain in a life time."[22]

NOTES AND REFERENCES

1. *The London Observer.*
2. Reviewed by Natasha Walter in The Guardian, May 20, 2006.
3. *Ibid.*
4. Kirkus Reviews.
5. Review by Gaiutra Bahadur "The Village People."
6. Larry Finlay, Managing Director of Transworld Publishers.
7. *The New York Times.*
8. Quoted from essay first published in The Guardian, June 17th, 2003. Where I'm coming from. Monica Ali interviewed at Powell's.
9. Sukhdev Sandhu: reviews Brick Lane, The London Review of Books.
10. *The Times London.*
11. Margo Thomson's review in NZ Herald—6th June 2003.
12. Monica Ali quoted in *The Sunday Times*, Dec., 2003.
13. Israel Zangwill's Children of the Ghetto (1892).
14. Mahmud Rehman's review—Sawnet Book Review.
15. Sukhdev Sandhu: reviews Brick Lane, The London Review of Books.
16. Quoted in Essay which appeared in The Guardian on June 17, 2003.
17. Monica Ali: Brick Lane; Scribner, New York. All quotations from this book are from this edition.
18. The New Yorker.
19. A review from Guardian Unlimited Books Special Reports.
20. Geraldine Bedell review dated 15th June 2003 in The Guardian. Full of East End Promise.
21. *Ibid.*
22. *The Sunday Times* (London).

'Emerging Gender Identities' in Bapsi Sidhwa's Fiction

19

"Feminism is a social movement whose goal is to eliminate the oppression of women in all its forms."

—*Amy Kesselman*,
Lily D. McNair, and
Nancy Schniedewind,
eds., Women: Images & Realities, 1996

Undoubtedly, "Pakistan's finest English language novelist"[1] Bapsi Sidhwa emerges as one of the most prominent Anglophone novelists of South Asia. Stylistically dextrous and liberally laced with humour, her fiction offers a sensitive insight into the complexities of life in the subcontinent with particular focus on the lives of women. A chronicler of the history of the Indian subcontinent, Sidhwa's novels, reflect her personal experience from the days of the Raj, to the partition of India, the rise of religious fundamentalism and the impact of the modern ideas of Mahatma Gandhi on the traditions of colonial India. A born storyteller, "the appearance of Sidhwa's work signals, even before Rushdie's, the belated coming of age of South Asian fiction in English, paving the way for the blend of magic and fantasy with history that was to become the trademark of subcontinent fiction in the eighties and the nineties."[2] However, although Sidhwa sees herself as a subcontinent writer, she is a Parsi who has lived many years in Pakistan and this gives her voice a distinctive edge. Hence, a Pakistan born Parsi, and settled as Houstonian, Sidhwa describes herself as a "Punjabi-Pakistani Parsi woman, because all three societies influenced me."[3] In an interview to Bachi Karkaria, Sidhwa says—"I am a Parsi first, then a Pakistani, specifically a Punjabi. I'm woman simply by gender. I don't feel American at all. My consolidated 3 P identity has enriched my writing."[4] Thus, though settled in the United States, and combining a "whole medley of identities"[5] in herself, Sidhwa keeps returning to the Indian subcontinent every now and then.

With her first novel, *The Crow Eaters*, Sidhwa introduces us to an unfamiliar segment of Indian life, a "riotous mix of banguard humour and loving portrayal of Parsis."[6] A debut, as notable as Kiran Desai's *Hullabaloo in the Guava Orchard*, Sidhwa's portrayal of the idiosyncratic Parsis achieves the same triumph in revelry, which makes *Hullabaloo in the Guava Orchard*—"a festival of comic eccentricity," exuding "charisma, poetry and joy in language and life."[7] Sidhwa's charming portrayal of the protagonist, Faredoon Junglewalla, a hard working delightful scoundrel and his mother in law, the riotous Jerbanoo, a shrewish humourless character are the funniest and most delightful characters from among Sidhwa's deft portrayals of idiosyncratic Parsis. Like the author herself, Faredoon Junglewalla is a Parsi and his story takes us to the heart of that minority community—"The focus on the Parsis, their rites and customs not only provides a rich subject in itself, but also an ideal vehicle for observing the history of India and in particular, the events played out between Hindus, Sikhs and Muslims, from a detached yet intimate insider/outsider perspective."[8] *The Crow Eaters* ushered a new era in South Asian novelists like R.K. Narayan, Nirad Chaudhari and Mulkraj Anand were already published but *The Crow Eaters* was perhaps the first in the next wave of writing to come out of the Indian subcontinent. Her book was published a year before Rushdie's *Midnight's Children* and Sidhwa was quick to notice that—"I think the parents in *The Crow Eaters* influenced Rushdie's presentation of parents in Midnight Children, its bawdy humour...."[9] As a preserver of the collective tradition, a folk historian and myth-maker, Sidhwa has tried to immortalize the unfamiliar segment of Parsis by capturing its quintessential ethos in her first published novel *The Crow Eaters* in particular. The title of the book refers to the crow like high pitched garrulousness of the Parsis.

Faredoon Junglewalla leaves his ancestral village in Central India with his wife Putli, mother-in-law Jerbanoo, and his infant daughter, Hutoxi, to seek his fortune in Punjab. After facing many mild disasters, Freddy's bullock cart reaches Punjab. After, staying in Amritsar they move to Lahore. Altogether there were four Parsi families in Lahore and "like one large close knit family, they assisted each other, sharing success and rallying to support failure."[10] Gradually, Freddy is able to increase the sales of his provision store and he begins to live in comfort with his family. Freddy's mother in law Jerbanoo is a quarrelsome and gluttonous woman who consumes huge amounts of chocolates, biscuits and wine. She often sends Freddy's clerk on her errands, thus affecting his business. In an attempt to cure her of this, Freddy seeks the advice of a mystic who suggested him to procure a coil of his mother in law's hair. Just when he is going to snip her hair she gets up and Freddy's plan is a failure. After this incident Jerbanoo becomes very careful about her hair. She wears her *mathabana* all the time. She blackens her eyes and presses two large spots of soot on her temples to protect herself from the evil eye. She goes to the extent of dipping a tattered bit of meat membrane in turmeric and commanding her daughter to circle it seven times over her head and fling it out of the window to the crows. Thus this novel presents the Parsis not only as a progressive lot but also rooted in superstitions. Throughout the novel we see Freddy's stubborn fending mother in law, whom he cannot vanquish. Jerbanoo suddenly turns extremely religious and somehow has a premonition of portending death. What worries her is the absence of the burial place of Parsis—Dokhma or the tower of silence in Lahore. Her fears are set at rest only when Freddy promises to dispose her body in Karachi, in the Tower himself.

An otherwise not so religious a person, Freddy consults the fortune tellers, once again in desperation who blame the influence of Saturn on his stars and tell him that, "a tall, slender charmer will come your way soon. The person will have a very fortunate influence on you and change the course of your life"

(p. 53). One day Mr. Dinshaw Adenwalla, an insurance agent arrives in Lahore and motivates all the Parsi families to get insured every thing that is insurable. Suddenly, Freddy realizes that he has to pay huge amount as a premium which he is not in a condition to pay. After two months of great mental turmoil an idea dawns on him. He proposes to set his house and shop on fire, and if possible, to get rid of Jerbanoo by burning her too. He sets his house, shop and mother in law on fire but Jerbanoo somehow is rescued. However, the sizeable sum of insurance money is enough to reset Freddy. Then a series of misfortunes come his way. His son Yazdi decides to marry an Anglo Indian classmate who is a whore and had a relation with Freddy himself. On knowing this, Yazdi becomes an ascetic and leaves his family. Next, his eldest son, Soli dies unexpectedly from a minor wound. After Soli's death Freddy mellows down and finds his interests awakened in mysticism and religion. Billy, the only son left with him is entrusted the business and he does it quite well. However, his wife Tanya doesn't value the traditional customs of Parsees and values the British customs more. The family is happy with the arrival of Tanya's second issue—a son who they believe is a reincarnation of Soli.

Suddenly, at sixty-five, Freddy can foresee his death. However, he doesn't fear it as he has lived his life to its full. The story ends with the Faredoon getting stirred by the talk of independence from British rule and bursts out angrily: "I tell you we are betrayed by our own kind, by our own blood! The fools will break up the country. The Hindus will have one part, Muslims the other.... And they won't want you" (p. 283). In reply to the question posed by his son-in-law as to where would they go, Freddy softly says, "We will stay where we are...let Hindus, Muslims, Sikhs or whoever, rule. What does it matter? The sun will continue to rise—and the sun continues to set..." (p. 283). Thus, the book has made the non Parsee world familiar with the Parsees and "has opened for us all the windows of this world's inner most recesses it is a veritable to de force"[11] and "a minor masterpiece."[12] Whereas, *The Crow Eaters* ends with the horrors of Partition still to come, *The Pakistani Bride* uses those as its starting point. In this novel, Sidhwa again makes use of a detached and marginalised character from a Pakistani minority group. Sidhwa uses Qasim, a Kohistani tribe man as her window into the period of history she describes. After witnessing a brutal attack on a train of refugees, Qasim adopts a young girl orphaned by the massacre. As the years pass by, Qasim makes a fortune but he grows increasingly nostalgic about his life in the mountains. Impulsively, he promises Zaitoon in marriage to a man of his tribe. But for Zaitoon, giving up the civilized city life to become the bride of a hard inscrutable husband proves so traumatic for her that she decides to run away, though she knows that by the tribal code, the punishment for such an act is death. Sakhi her husband, sets out to hunt her along with his brother and clansmen. However, Zaitoon manages to escape from them with the help of Major Mushtaq. Sidhwa's women believe that life must be preserved at all cost, since one can fight oppression only when one is alive. Her instinct for self preservation keeps Zaitoon going. Thus, in Zaitoon, Sidhwa has created a woman who feels that she can fight against all odds, only if she is alive. It is this love for life that prevents her from disintegrating, she chooses to resent not obey.

The story also tells of an American bride, Carol, who marries a Pakistani, Farukh. Though, she tries to confirm to the Muslim conventions, she cannot resist her attraction for her husband's friend Major Mushtaq. She gets involved with Major, thus betraying her husband, but when Major refuses to marry her, because of the difficulty in getting a divorce, as he and his wife were cousins, Carol realizes her mistake. When she comes to know of Zaitoon's flight and her husband's hunt to kill her for her act, she is horrified at her own infidelity towards Farukh. When she asks the Major, "do you think Farukh would kill me?"[13] (p. 224). He says, "Who knows? I might, if you were my wife" (p. 224). "Carol becomes restless and wonders about the plight of Pakistani women—Women the world over, through the ages, asked to be murdered, raped, exploited, beaten-up, bullied and disinherited..... What had the tribal girl done to deserve such grotesque retribution" (p. 226). Carol decides to exercise her 'Khudi' and goes back to America. Thus, all

Sidhwa's women are strong willed, assertive and never yielding. Quite different from the Parsi ethos that she evoked in *The Crow Eaters*, *The Pakistani Bride* displays yet another stance of her oeuvre—the feminist stance.

With the publication of her third novel, *Ice Candy Man* or *Cracking India*, Bapsi Sidhwa established herself as a Pakistani leading English language novelist. Her first three novels are located in Pakistan and in each there is a strong sense of place and community which she uses to examine the post colonial Pakistani identity. In the *Ice Candy Man* the political and historical consciousness of her previous novels reaches a pinnacle in this novel, and the young narrator proves to be an ideal means of exposing the complexities of the period. Liona Badr's *The Eye of the Mirror* and Sidhwa's *Cracking India* present similar feminist framework through, which the traumas of war and communal violence may be addressed. Both these novels feature a girl on the verge of sexual maturation who sees the violence in the society around her to be fundamentally analogous to the inherent violence that accompanies the new social role she assumes as a woman.

Partition figures as a key theme in all her novels in general and in her most prestigious novel, *Ice Candy Man*, in particular. Though many writers like Khushwant Singh, Amrita Pritam and Chaman Nahal, Attia Hosain had written about partition, what distinguishes Sidhwa from them is the fact that she isn't a Hindu, a Muslim or a Sikh, she belongs to a non committed sect—the Parsees who owe their allegiance to the state. Thus, Sidhwa's heritage allowed her to witness, the partition from a safe distance, since Parsees held a religiously and politically neutral position. In an interview she says—"The struggle was between the Hindus and the Muslims and as a Parsee (member of a Zoroastian sect) I felt I could give a dispassionate account of this huge, momentous struggle."[14]

Sidhwa collaborated with the other South Asian leading artist Deepa Mehta, the filmmaker in the 1990's when Mehta made the film Earth, based on Sidhwa's stirring partition novel, *Cracking India*. Through *Cracking India* Sidhwa presents the dirtiness and ineffectiveness of politics—"As a Parsi," says Sidhwa "I can see things objectively, I see all the common people suffering while the politicians on either side have the fun."[15] Along with this political ineffectiveness she also sees the symbolic desecration of women, on both sides of conflict. *Cracking India* recalls the pain of hideous memories that Partition inflicted on women. The moans and shrieks of wailing women haunted Sidhwa, and she asks herself—"Why do they cry like that? Because they are delivering unwanted babies or reliving hideous memories."[16] Talking of the pitiable condition of women Sidhwa says in an interview "Victory is celebrated on a woman's body, vengeance is taken on a woman's body. That's very much the way things are, particularly in my part of the world."[17]

Cracking India is the tale of the bloody partition that led to the creation of independent Pakistan and India as the British left the sub-continent. Set in Lahore, in the time period directly before and during the Partition of India in 1947, the story is told from the point of a young Parsee Zoroastrian girl. Sidhwa, herself admits that her novels have certain autobiographical elements for instance, she based the parents in *The Crow Eaters* on her own parents and now in *Cracking India*, the child protagonist Lenny is reminiscent of Sidhwa's own childhood. Like Lenny Sidhwa too was, at the time of Partition, polio ridden as an eight year old girl living in Lahore. Talking of her personal recollections of Partition, Sidhwa says: "The roar of distance mobs was a constant of my childhood: it was a sound that terrified me.... I picked up the sense of alarm from the adults. I saw buildings on fire.... I saw dead bodies."[18]

Elsewhere she reminisces—"When I was a child living in Lahore at the time of partition, my maiden name was Bhandara, which sounded like a Hindu name. After most of the riot was over, a gang of looters came in carts into our house thinking it's an abandoned house and were quite shocked to see us there. At that time our Muslim cook came out and said, 'What do you damn people think you're doing? This is a Parsi household,' and they said 'we thought it was a Hindu household,' and they went away. I decided to write a story about Partition because this scene was vivid in my mind."[19]

When the story opens, Lenny is a four year old girl, who comes from a very well off Parsi family of Lahore. She has a brother Adi, a year younger to her. As she is polio ridden, her eighteen year old ayah, Shanta takes her out to her godmother and electric—aunts houses from time to time. The ayah draws a lot of attention due to her charming looks from everyone—the gardener, Masseur, Ice Candy Man, restaurant wrestler, a knife-sharpener. Of these the most privileged ones are Masseur and Ice Candy Man. Lenny, however, has a few ominous nightmares about a German soldier coming to take her on a motorcycle, the vision of men in uniform slicing off an arm of a child here, a leg there or of a hungry lion attacking her. These nightmares pave the way of the impending real violence in public life. The atmosphere is permeated with tension and unrest, which rears its head, every now and then. For instance, at a dinner party hosted by Lenny's parents there are heated arguments between their Sikh neighbours Mr. Singh and Mr. Rogers, the Inspector of Police. Lenny's father, however, normalizes the situation. However, this disharmony doesn't permeate the villages as is evident when the towns man Imam Din broaches the topic of Sikh and Muslim trouble, the villagers erupt in protest—"We are brothers. How can we fight each other?"[20] and "If needs be, we'll protect our Muslim brother's with our lives" (p. 56).

However, things in Lahore go on worsening and everywhere the talk centres on India going to be cracked. Lenny too perceives the change all around her "Ayah is no longer just my all-encompassing Ayah—She is also a token—A Hindu" (p. 93). The Ayah starts visiting temples, Imam Din and Yusuf attend to their prayers very religiously and even the Christians get infected: "...they looked down there noses upon the Pens who are Anglo Indian...who looked down upon all non-Christians" (p. 94). Even the jokes are categorized—as "Hindu, Parsi Muslims and Christian jokes" (p. 95). Only the group around the ayah remains unchanged. Hindu, Muslim, Sikh, Parsi "are as always unified around her" (p. 97). Lenny isn't allowed to play with Sikh children and as the time of Partition draws closer, Lenny notices a lot of hushed talk. With the sun of British Empire setting over Indian subcontinent, the people become more and more active. The scenes of communal riots that follow are shocking to the children. Like Lenny, tears apart the legs of her doll with the help of her brother and ends up sobbing unable to bear it she was actually re-enacting a scene from the riot which she had, witnessed.

Finally India is divided and Pakistan comes into existence. Lahore goes to Pakistan, and is, therefore an unsafe place for Hindus and Sikhs. Either they have fled or are blinded by communalism ready to knife each other. Only Ayah, among all Lenny's friends stays behind in Lahore. She doesn't go because Masseur had assured her of safety there. However, after the Masseur is murdered by Ice Candy Man and his body is found in a sack, the ayah is shocked. Ice Candy Man, further, abducts *ayah* and she is *gang* raped and then taken to Hira Mandi where she is sexually exploited by even Imam Din. Ice Candy Man marries her and renames her Mumtaz. However, ayah is rescued by Lenny's Godmother and sent to her home in Amritsar leaving the Ice Candy Man a mad fakir. The Parsis thus emerge as the Messiah of the Hindus, Muslims and Sikhs engrossed in a communal violence.

Cracking India highlights the atrocities committed in East Punjab against Muslims and by reappraising the personality of Jinnah suggests that the British were less than fair to him as well as to Pakistan. As Sidhwa says: "And I felt, in Ice Candy Man...a very grievous wrong that had been done to Jinnah.... They've dehumanized him, made him a symbol of the sort of person who brought about the partition of India.... Whereas, in reality he...tried to do everything by the British standards of constitutional law."[21] The novel presents, therefore a dispassionate account of the Partition, moving from political planning to reality; viewed from three perspectives—of a Pakistani, a Parsee and a feminist: "Through her various marginalised narrators and through the experiences of the many marginalised characters in her first-three novels, Sidhwa gives voice to hither to silenced groups of India and Pakistan and in doing so tells other version of her country's history."[22]

In her next novel, *An American Brat* she shifts the predominant locale of her fiction from Lahore and Pakistan in various cities across America as she explores the Parsi/Pakistani diaspora. This novel with its focus on diaspora is a logical extension of the interest in displacement and the clashes between communities which is present in all her previous three novels. *An American Brat* tells us about Feroza Ginwalla, a descendent of the Junglewalla clan portrayed in her previous novel, *The Crow Eaters* but, whereas the latter tells the rollicking tale of Faredoon Junglewalla's rise from rags to riches, *An American Brat* is a sensitive portrayal of the impact of modem America on a new arrival—Feroza, a pampered, protected, sixteen year old Pakistani girl sent to America by her parents who are alarmed by the rising tide of fundamentalism overtaking Pakistan and their daughter. Her family decides to send her to her uncle Manek, a graduate student at MIT, who though only six years older to Feroza, is a veteran in the ways of America. It's he who turns her three month visit to US into a four years stay. Hoping that a few months with her uncle would soften her rigid thinking, Feroza's parents get more than they bargained for—Feroza enthralled by the American culture and her new freedom, insists on staying. While attending college in Denver, Feroza falls in love with a Jewish student. After hearing that they intend to marry, her mother Zareen sets out for America hell bent on changing Feroza's mind. Zareen tells her angrily—"You can't just toss your heritage away like that. It's not in your bones,"[23] and regrets having sent Feroza to US—"I should never have let you go so far away. Look what it's done to you, you become an American Brat" (p. 279). Zareen explains to her the risks of marrying outside her faith. She would be thrown out of the community and wouldn't be allowed to enter the Parsee places of worship, nor attend the funeral rites of her grandmother, or her parents. But over the next two weeks, suddenly Zareen starts enjoying the freedom in US and even liking David. In the third week of her visit, many letters from Pakistan arrive reminding her of her mission and so do the two pamphlets titled "warning" and "notice" from a Parsee Priests' community in Mumbai and Bombay Zoroastrian Committee respectively.

Zareen tries her best to cause estrangement between Feroza and David and finally David does come to realize that Feroza's culture is quite different from his own to which he couldn't adjust to—"He felt inadequate wondering if he could cope with some of the rituals and behaviour that despite his tolerant and accepting liberality seemed bizarre" (p. 309). David's feelings for Feroza are no longer the same and he leaves for California for a job and Zareen goes back to Lahore. Though shocked, Feroza like all female characters of Bapsi Sidhwa doesn't ever give up. She bounces back to life and decides to live in America. She decides to marry, whoever she likes irrespective of the fact whether he is a Parsee or not. Thus, Feroza reflects the modem multicultural predicament, trying to strike a balance between tradition and modernity. Besides, Sidhwa has added a new dimension to the expatriate experience by exploring the cultural differences which alienate a person in his own country. Sidhwa's novel, *An American Brat*, is "an exceptional novel funny and memorable."[24]

Thus, Sidhwa's works cover a large range of topics, from history to contemporary reality. Talking of Bapsi Sidhwa, Sara Suleri Goodyear rightly remarks, "On a sociological level Sidhwa's work is crucial to an understanding of the cultural complexities of post-independence Pakistani cultures, and the diaspora they have occasioned. On a literary level Sidhwa's novels are constructed with grace and written with an exquisite sense of humour.... No writer has equalled Sidhwa's capacity to address grim historical realities with both precision and affection...the brilliance of her writing deserves to be honoured by the widest possible readership."[25] Bapsi Sidhwa's latest novel *Water*, based on the script of Deepa Mehta's controversial film about the lives of widows in 1930s Benaras, is a powerful book that not only complements the film but also holds up well as an independent work. It was not easy for Sidhwa to work on such a project: "I was hesitant because I had never written within the confines of a structured story before"[26]—said Sidhwa. Discussing the process of turning a film script into a novel, Sidhwa said,

"I have never worked so hard, but it was for me a new and exhilarating experience."[27]

Water is the third in Deepa Mehta trilogy; the novel based on the film, is Bapsi Sidhwa's fifth novel about the subcontinent. It is set in 1938, when the traditions of colonial India were being threatened by the modern ideas of Mahatma Gandhi. Focusing on a very young widow, *Water* introduces us to eight year old Chuyia, transported from a child's carefree life and a loving family to a widow's Ashram on the fringes of society, as the husband of her arranged marriage unexpectedly dies. According to the Hindu tradition of the time, she is discarded to a widow Ashram, her head shorn, and her life given over to penitence. Still years away from a proper understanding of the ways of the world, she is told that she no longer exists as person all because of the sudden death of a husband, she had barely met. "Once widowed, a woman was deprived of her useful function in society—that of reproducing and fulfilling her marital duties."[28]

Inside the widow Ashram, Chuyia encounters the strong and the weak, the corrupt and the honest, the victims and the victors. There, this impish girl disrupts daily life in the Ashram and becomes a catalyst for change in the lives of the widows, including her friend, the beautiful widow prostitute Kalyani, and her protector Shakuntala, who discovers her hidden power. Slowly, Chuyia overcomes her sense of dislocation, makes friends with other women in the ashram and stirs a few hackles with her directness in situations where others simply follow the letter of ancient texts: "Where is the house for the men widows?" (p. 81) She innocently asks at a gathering, producing instant shouts of outrage: "God protect our men from such a fate" (p. 81).

However, Chuyia's words have an effect on the middle aged Shakuntala, who tries to conquer her own inherent conservatism by questioning the scriptures. Mean while, a progressive minded young idealist named Narayan falls in love with Chuyia's friend, Kalyani, a beautiful widow whose earnings as a sex worker help in running the Ashram. Madhumati, the Ashram head who has forced Kalyani into prostitution ironically says, "We must live in purity, to die in purity" (p. 144). We are never allowed to forget that though they have their own self sustaining little community, where at times life does not seem too bad after all, they are forced into a life of compromise. All the women, Chuyia, Kalyani and Shakuntala are victims of a cruel unthinking tradition.

The overall restraint, the ability to make a point without underlining it, makes a stronger impact in the disturbing moments of the novel. Even Madhumati, variously compared to a "beached whale" (p. 47), and a "satiated sea—lion," and despicable in her treatment of Kalyani, too has a human side. She too was a young girl with dreams, who has turned a parasitic monster. Sidhwa creates pasts for all her widows to give them humanity in their stripped and primal state: "In fact a happier past is the one thing that keeps each widow from despair." *Water* has trademarks of Sidhwa's finest writing, most notably, her book *Ice Candy Man*. Those trademarks include nuanced but economical characterisations and the infusion of gentle humour into even bleak situations. Her humour and compassion glow in this novel. The brightly dressed eunuch Gulabi declares, "This Gandhi is going to sink India." Yet Gulabi realizes that if Gandhi believes the untouchables might be children of God, "then eunuchs are His step children" (p. 104). Her description of the street scenes of India is very realistic. She vividly recreates the grey, destitute widow ashram, the ghats and the chaotic crowds attending Gandhi's appearance. Sidhwa's stories may be simple but there subtexts are richly instructive. The angry doctor in *Cracking India*, scolds an ineffectual father—"You all want Pakistan! How will you govern a country when you don't know what goes on in your own house." Here in *Water*, a Brahmin husband rages at his wife: "a women's role in life is to get married and have sons. That is why she is created: to have sons! That is all!" (p. 8).

The novel concludes with a flicker of hope. As Gandhi's train passes through the village, the prospect of rescue from punishing Hindu traditions seems conceivable. The growing influence of Gandhi does in fact seem to indicate a better future for the victims of traditions. What is remarkable is the relevance of the story even today? The violent protests against Deepa

Mehta's film remind us once again that the unthinking adherence to traditions is still palpable, still very much alive. Talking of *Water* Sidhwa says, "Besides, being a gripping story, the plot also deals with the oppressive hold that traditions have on women and tells of oppression and constraints that govern even a girl child's life in a patriarchal society."[29]

Whether, it is introducing an unfamiliar segment of Indian life—the Parsees in *The Crow Eaters* or viewing realistically the abuse against women with a feminist stance in *The Pakistani Bride* or the poignant expression of the story of partition told from a neutral perspective or the acute portrayal of American life seen through the eyes of a perspective young immigrant in *An American Brat* or else a realistic picturisation of the life of a child widow, a victim of the unthinking adherence to tradition in *Water*, Bapsi Sidhwa emerges as a born story teller who writes with amazing authority, flair and ease.

Sara Suleri Goodyear beautifully sums up the unsettling quietude that the novel evokes: "Sidhwa historicizes the images, lends greater poignancy to faces and provides speech where the film must leave the woman silent."[30]

NOTES AND REFERENCES

1. *Los Angeles Times*, 9 August, 1992.
2. Quoted in Introduction: Sidhwa OUP Omnibus D 2001.
3. Sidhwa, Bapsi in an interview with Julie Rajan.
4. Sidhwa, Bapsi says in an interview with Bachi Karkaria, *The Times of India*: 19th Feb., 2005, Lucknow, ed: 4.
5. Sidhwa, Bapsi in an interview with Julie Rajan.
6. *Publishers Weekly*.
7. Baltimore Sun.
8. Cane, Ralph. J: "A Passion for History and for Truth Telling." The early Novels of Bapsi Sidhwa.
9. Sidhwa, Bapsi in an mterview with Julie Rajan.
10. Sidhwa, Bapsi: *The Crow Eaters*. Delhi: Penguin, 1990, p. 21.
11. Faiz Ahmad Faiz: "Pak Reviews": Review Excerpts £1: Om India Pakistan (2000-02, 9th July, 2004).
12. Kumar, Raj: Tribune, Nov. 29th 1980.
13. Sidhwa, Bapsi: *The Pakistani Bride*, Delhi: Penguin, 1990.

14. Gutman, Ruth: "Visiting Professor's Novel to be in Film"—(27th Feb., 1997) 4th para.
15. Sidhwa, Bapsi: "Writer in residence Bapsi Sidhwa Takes Laughter Seriously" (28th March, 1997) 6th para.
16. Sidhwa, Bapsi: "New Neighbours," 11th Aug., 1997.
17. Graeber, Laurel: "The Seeds of Partition"—Review of Cracking India. New York Times Book Reviews, 6th Oct., 1991.
18. Sidhwa, Bapsi in an interview with Julie Rajan.
19. Sidhwa, Bapsi in an interview with Feroza Jussawala and Reed Way Dasenbrock, ed. Interviews with Writers of the Post Colonial World. Jackson and London: University Press of Mississippi, 1992: 198-21.
20. Sidhwa, Bapsi: *Ice Candy Man*, Delhi: Penguin, 1989, p. 56.
21. Sidhwa, Bapsi in an interview with David Montenegro—"Bapsi Sidhwa: An Interview." The Massachusetts Review Winter, 1990, pp. 513-33.
22. Cane, Ralph. J: "A Passion for History and for Truth Telling." The early Novels of Bapsi Sidhwa.
23. Sidhwa, Bapsi: *An American Brat*, Delhi: Penguin, 1994, p. 279.
24. *Los Angeles Times*.
25. Goodyear, Sara Suleri in Bapsi Sidhwa's Omnibus edition by OUP (2001).
26. Sidhwa, Bapsi admits in her Acknowledgements, p. 200.
27. Sidhwa, Bapsi discussing the translation of a novel into film, 2005. Milkweed editions.
28. Sidhwa, Bapsi: Water, Penguin Books, India, 2006, p. 24 (All quotations from this book refer to this edition only.)
29. Sidhwa, Bapsi in an interview.
30. Goodyear, Sara Suleri: written in the blurb of Water.

'Triumph of the Human Spirit' in Tehmina Durrani's *My Feudal Lord*

> "Society, being codified by man, decrees that woman is inferior; she can do away with this inferiority only by destroying the male's superiority."
>
> —*Simone de Beauvoir*

Post-colonial literature addresses the issues of history, identity, ethnicity, gender and language. An important consequence of post-colonialism has been the acknowledgement and reappearance of women's experience after being concealed from the histories of colonial societies. Contemporary writings tend to reject the fixed representation of the images of women. Women writers today are incorporating their experiences to make new empowering image for woman. Their writings go beyond "hearth and home," redefine their experience and affirm the constructive power of women. The change that has taken place in Indian society so that new women will tell their own stories is beautifully explained by Anees Jung, a writer in quest of new images for women: "Not long ago a woman who spoke about herself was considered a loose woman. To voice a pain, to divulge a secret was considered sacrilege, a breach of family trust. Today, voices are raised without fear, and we are heard outside the walls of homes that once kept a woman protected, also isolated. Some of the women who speak here have stepped out, others who have not are beginning to be aware, eager to find expression. But let them speak for themselves."[1]

All across the world, especially in the Indian sub-continent, the act of writing is for a woman essentially an act of breaking her silence and the most recent books explore an educated woman's search for identity and meaning in an autobiographical form as in Kamala Das' *My Story* or in Sara Suleri's *Meatless Days* or combining autobiographical and ethnographic form as in Anees Jung's *Unveiling India: A Woman's Journey*. Sara Suleri, encapsulated memories of her Lahore childhood in her creative memoir, *Meatless Days* (1989), at the heart of which were the tragic accidents that killed her mother and sister. Kamala Das' *My Story* exemplifies recent texts in which South Asian women authors make the self interested qualities so condemned in earlier fiction become liberating, positive and creative forces. Kamala Das tells of intensely personal experiences, including her growth into womanhood, her unsuccessful quest for love in and outside marriage, and her living in matriarchal rural South India after inheriting her ancestral home. Taslima Nasrin, known as the "angry young woman" of Bangladeshi literature talks in her autobiography about her sexual assault by her relatives and other men in her early years. Focussing on the ideological significance of her first person technique, Taslima herself explains: "Time and again, I come back to my stories, and I intend to because I'm a woman. I speak to every woman through my experience, my awareness and my vision."[2] It is not surprising that Tehmina Durrani be included in the category of writers like Jean Rhys, Anita Desai, Buchi Emacheta, Olive Senior, Nadine Gordimer, Grace Nichols and Arundhati Roy who have placed women at the center of history, as makers and agents of history, not mute witnesses to it. Durrani's writings too, represent a distinctive and original contribution to all oppressed voiceless classes of women around the world and provide an extraordinary insight into the vulnerable position of women caught in the complex web of patriarchal society, establishing new directions for the women's movement in South Asia. Until now a primarily masculine intellect and spirit have dominated in their interpretation of society and culture, but now these writers have captured the gynocentric perspective to reverse phallocratic culture and bring about a transformation in lives of all oppressed women, the world over. By constructing and articulating their own as well as other women's experiences of humiliation, abuse and discrimination, they have found the power to break free from their shackles and rise to a different plane of survival.

As has been rightly remarked—"If Alice Walker's *Colour Purple* could create reverberations in Black American Society; If Lalithambika Antherjenam's *Confessions* could shake the confines of the Namboodiri illams; If Arundhati Roy's *God of Small Things* could send a tremor down the spine of the placid Syrian Christian community of Kerala, then surely Tehmina Durrani's *Blasphemy* and her novel *My Feudal Lord*, along with Taslima Nasrin's *Lajja* and critical writings in the *Selected Columns*, have torn the veil of ignominy which for centuries shrouded the lives of women in South Asia. The long vigil over, their march to freedom has begun."[3]

Tehmina Durrani's autobiographical account, *My Feudal Lord* was written to expose her complex ridden feudal landlord turned Pakistani politician husband, Mustafa Khar. Durrani wished the book to serve as a mirror for Khar, so that he might see in it the reflections of the man, the husband, the father, the leader and the friend that he actually was. Through this book she wants to reveal the deep rooted deficiency in the feudal value system, and provide an insight into the subservient position of women caught in the complex web of Muslim society. The book has made her a household name, not just in Pakistan, but also in Europe, where the book was a bestseller. *My Feudal Lord* describes Tehmina's traumatic marital life with Gulam Mustafa Khar, an important politician in the Zulfikar Ali Bhutto government, who later became the Chief Minister of Punjab. The book is neatly divided into three parts, aptly entitled Lion of the Punjab, Law of the jungle and Lioness. Throughout these sections we can see the progress of Tehmina from an ordinary elitist housewife to an emancipated human being contesting for equal rights and women's empowerment.

Whereas, Taslima Nasrin challenges the unassailability of Bangladeshi patriarchy and unveils the patriarchal agenda of subordinating women in Bangladeshi society, Tehmina attacks the Pakistani society, where the Muslim patriarchs dominate and the entity of women is that of inferior beings both intellectually and socially. Her main raison d'etre seems to be an instrument for the satisfaction of the man's sexual desires and perpetration of the species. Like Taslima again, Durrani hurls her more scathing attack against women themselves, against whom she lashes out quite forcefully. She writes: "The women in our circle did not seem to look beyond their raised noses. They chattered endlessly about disobedient servants, clothes, jewellery and interior decorations.... Many a day in the lives of these women was completely devoted to the topic of what to wear that evening"[4] (p. 65).

Tehmina too, like these women continued to move in best social circles and learned how to keep up the public facade as a glamorous cultivated wife and mother of four children. She moulded herself mechanically to cater to her husband's preferences be it in appearance, attire or makeup: "I now dressed for Mustafa. I had been raised to operate on the principle that appearances are paramount. I sampled all the collets that had been gathering dust in my wardrobe..."[5] (p. 65). What attracted her to Mustafa was the fact that he was "authoritarian, conservative and overpowering" (p. 58). He also "articulated her thoughts that buzzed in her brain since childhood." As she says: "I was a product of the powerful, privileged class but I had been a misfit, an underdog in my own surroundings understood the seal, for I was a rebel in search of a cause. Mustafa Khar defined the cause for me" (p. 58).

Besides, under the guardianship of her mother she realised that she "was being raised to be schizophrenic; an appearance of perfection was more important than genuine feelings. There was no question of discovering oneself. Identity and individuality were crushed. Personality failed to develop. My mind became a sanctuary for secret thoughts of escaping from that household. But for that, there was no other goal in life but marriage" (pp. 29-30). But her marriage to Mustafa Khar soon turned into a nightmare. The first part of *My Feudal Lord* discusses Mustafa as a man who revels in the total subjugation and repression of his female counterpart. Tehmina's conventional upbringing conditioned by her patriarchal social environment, in which she lived, made her accept her husband Mustafa's physical assaults and sexual brutality enduring these attacks as a part of her destiny. As Tehmina remarks: "A Pakistani woman will endure almost anything in order to hold a marriage together. In our society, marriage may be purgatory, bur divorce is hell" (p. 77). She further remarks: "According to feudal tradition, a wife was honour-bound to live her life, according to her husband's whims. A woman was like a man's land..." (p. 107). "There was not a day that Mustafa did not hit me for some reason; the food was late, his clothes were creased. With a shudder, I realized that I had become just like the now-discarded Sherry...this was a feudal hang-up: his class believed that a woman was an instrument of a man's carnal pleasure. If the woman ever indicated that she felt pleasure, she was a potential adulteress, not to be trusted. Mustafa did not even realize that he had crushed my sensuality. I was on automatic pilot...responding as much as was important for him but never feeling anything myself. If he was satisfied there was a chance that he would be in better humour" (pp. 106-07). Surprisingly, when Tehmina becomes pregnant Mustafa takes a lot of personal care of her. However, a close reading of the novel makes us realize that it is not out of love for her but in the hope of a male heir that Mustafa was attending to Tehmina. It was the social ethos which inculcated itself into her being and makes her perpetuate her marriage bond with Mustafa, realizing fully well that in a society, a divorced woman commands no respect.

Nayantara Sahgal too, like Durrani challenges orthodox thinking which enmeshes a woman's identity: "A woman is not allowed to be a woman in orthodox thinking. She has to be 'good' and good means virtuous in the sense of chaste. Uma is a woman with appetites that her husband couldn't satisfy, so she indulged elsewhere. Men do it, and there's no comment."[6] The second part describes the politically turbulent atmosphere—"the army had moved against Bhutto; Martial law was declared" (p. 110). General Zia had assumed power. "He said that the politicians were being held in protective custody, but would be freed soon" (p. 111). Mustafa convinced his leader Bhutto "to flee the country, and asked permission to do so himself to live to fight another day" (p. 16). Bhutto granted permission to Mustafa and he goes to London via Mecca along with Tehmina. Once Mustafa reaches London, his dilemma is resolved and he decides to remain loyal to the Bhutto government and so he starts contacting all possible exiles there. In London, Tehmina and Mustafa with all his perversions and atrocities start living in an apartment owned by Tehmina's parents who want their daughter and son-in-law to live happily together. They also urge the two not to file for divorce. Her father tells her: "You can only leave his home in a coffin" (p. 126). Tehmina finds herself in an ironical situation: "At first I found irony in situation: I had escaped from the domination of my master by climbing into the loop of a tyrant."

Mustafa's behaviour became the same as before and to make matters even worse he starts seducing her younger sister Adila, while physically assaulting her regularly. Tehmina camouflaged her bruises and buried her humiliation. Her mother advised her: "If a husband behaves in a strange or unreasonable manner, you should treat him like a sick human being, like someone who needs medical care and treatment. Deal with him like a psychiatrist" (p. 130). Tehmina was always acting and pretending so that the truth about her loveless marriage doesn't get exposed. She was perpetually in a state of paranoia: "It was schizophrenic existence. The humiliation of not being able to keep my husband happy and of falling short of my mother's definition of the ideal wife was becoming more frightening than the beatings...it simply affirmed my inadequacy" (p. 131). Finally, overcome by his physical assaults, Tehmina voiced her resentment and stunned Mustafa: "This is my father's house and I do not think that you should dare to lift your hand on me here!" (p. 134). However, her protests become feeble as she realizes that she will not receive support of her family or from anybody else for that matter. She says: "I dreamed of release, but reality stood in front of me like a stone wall. Divorce was just not possible.... A prisoner ultimately settles into a monotonous routine. Anger recedes, senses dull. The spirit is crushed" (p. 143).

After the execution of Bhutto in 1979, Mustafa started

travelling the entire continent, mobilizing support from those in exile. A champion of democracy in public life, he was still an inveterate wife—abuser in his private life. Tehmina started believing that he was working for the liberation and betterment of her homeland and would free her country from the military rule imposed by President Zia. However, emboldened by her silence he starts an incestuous relationship with Adila. Tehmina wanted to prove that the man whom she had chosen was honourable, and that Adila was to be blamed for the affair. She wanted to save herself the degradation of Mustafa not wanting her. Her ego couldn't accept the incestuous affair. But Mustafa batters her with the butt of his double barrelled shotgun and forces her to walk naked. This incident completely shatters Tehmina and she breaks down: "This episode would cripple my spirit perhaps beyond salvation. From this movement forward it would be nearly impossible for me to function as an individual. There was not one iota of self-esteem left. The shame had burned it down to ashes" (p. 165).

However, she retorts furiously when he next tries to hit her: "The next time you raise your hand on me—I will pick up a knife and kill you" (p. 188). She adopts a new way of torturing Mustafa: "I tortured him with indifference. I did not sulk. I demanded no apology. He tried to offer one, but I brushed it aside with the admonition.... Now my composure upset him, my silence weakened him" (p. 190). She visits the Holy Shrine of Ajmer when she goes to India with a diplomatic mission. She prays to God: "My two shadows were at my side as I entered the shrine. Their Hindu presence disturbed my Islamic prayers.... I asked God to curb Mustafa's bouts of violence and insanity. I want a normal home with peace and harmony" (pp. 233-34). After returning from India they file for legal separation under the court of law in London. After the separation, Mustafa tries to revoke the agreement but Tehmina was adamant that she wanted a divorce. Her children were made wards of court, Mustafa was granted to take three older children out every Sunday morning and ordered to return them by evening. In her desperate and compulsive desire to get rid of her hair—"this talisman of Mustafa's desire" (p. 235). She decides to snip away her incredibly long hair signifying that she didn't want to return to him. As she says: "Mustafa soon heard and understood its significance. He knew that I had finally decided not to return to him, ever again. Otherwise I would not have done away with what he loved most about me. Without my hair, he was a weak Samson" (p. 236).

However, Mustafa begins wooing her back with a vengeance and finally an ideological affinity makes the two return together to Pakistan. Mustafa is arrested at the airport and Tehmina for the first time is accepted as the leader to the people. She visits him regularly at jail and tries to mobilize public support for him. On his birthday, he forces himself on her in jail, even though her wounds had not healed. This makes Tehmina apply for the Islamic "khula" or divorce. Mustafa once more brainwashes her into believing that he was a champion of democracy and Tehmina starts to campaign for his release. She believed in Mustafa's words: "I tell suddenly in love with a noble idea—the return of the exiled leader. My original love for Mustafa was replaced by faith in his mission" (p. 242).

But when he emerges from jail his real self is revealed—a selfish, jealous, egoistic and possessive man. He becomes jealous of the public support that Tehmina commands and resumes his illicit relationship with Tehmina's younger sister, Adila. Tehmina is no longer the submissive tolerant person that she was earlier. As she tells Mustafa in presence of all: "Your marriage according to Koran, was over years ago when you slept with my sister. I have been living with you in sin. The contract stood null and void long ago" (p. 362). Tehmina decides to complete the divorce proceedings and also begins to write an autobiography. The new emancipated Tehmina decides to write her autobiography and break the traditional silence: "Silence condones injustice, breeds subservience and fosters a malignant hypocrisy. Mustafa Khar and other feudal lords thrive and multiply on silence. Muslim women must learn to raise their voices against injustice" (p. 375). Similarly, through her protagonist Jaya in *That Long Silence*, Shashi Deshpande too breaks the silence, that had been at the root of all the troubles in her life: "I will have to speak, to sister, I will have to erase the silence between us."[7]

After exposing the atrocities on women by Pakistani feudal masters in *My Feudal Lord*, Tehmina's second book *Blasphemy* generated a similar excitement as it dwells on a topic much talked about but almost never written on. The novel is about the life of a Pir, or a religious leader and custodian of a shrine, based on a real life character who Durrani says she met while she was "seeking guidance" when her husband was jailed by the Zia regime. *Blasphemy* has virtually defrocked the Mullahs and Maulavis. She sarcastically unveiled the debauchery of the so called religious Maulavis who misuse their sacred authority for personal gratification. The novel touches on incest, child abuse, prostitution and paedophilia. Durrani claims that her book aims at exposing the rot that the Pir system contains.

Set in South Pakistan, *Blasphemy* is an enticing novel by Tehmina Durrani. Angry and courageous in outlook, it establishes Ms. Durrani among the foremost writers of the sub-continent. *Blasphemy* depicts the struggle of a Muslim Woman against all that is contrary to what Islam stands for. It is an amalgamation of fact and fiction, blending to disguise and protect the victims of a horrible human tragedy, while exposing the powerful religious imposters who prey on a wretched and powerless people. A shocking tale of cruelty, sex and violence and it gives a horrific account of how the custodians of religion are using their 'special knowledge' to exploit the illiterate masses. The central character, Heer, is one such victim of this form of designed oppression by the antagonist Pir Sain. Through Heer's experience the author brings out a blasphemous way of life, unknown to the layman, practiced not only by Pir Sain but also by his followers. Pir Sain's abstinence from going to his wife during Ramadan is the action of any orthodox Muslim. His beating of Heer for missing her prayers further secures his image in front of the extremists. But then there is his demand that Heer aborts their child so he may satisfy his carnal desires, demands immediate retribution. Despite all his vices, he is holy and almost divine by his followers. *Blasphemy* is a tale where Heer exposes the evils of these 'holy-men'—first to herself and then to us.

It should not surprise anyone if the oft-debated Pakistani writer, Durrani, matches the enviable position of the Bangladeshi writer, Taslima Nasrin. Taslima in her novel, *Lajja* advocated the cause of the minorities in Bangladesh and has attacked Muslim orthodoxy. Tehmina too, in her novel, *Blasphemy* has exposed the Pakistani Maulanas and shown to the world how they exploit the masses behind the facade of Islamic religious traditions. Just as Taslima earned the wrath of the Islamic fundamentalists, who blamed her for allegedly blaspheming the Koran and issued a death threat against her, Tehmina too, may be a target of all the ire of the Muslim clergy as *Blasphemy* exposes the powerful religious imposters who prey on powerless people.

Whether the spokesperson is Taslima Nasrin or Tehmina Durrani, building a strong case for indictment against marriage, Vedic diktats, and social mores for women, lusty Pirs and holy men, the essence of all they want to speak is not much different to what Jonathan Swift has said: "We have just enough religion to make us hate, but not enough to make us love one another."

NOTES AND REFERENCES

1. Jung, Anees: *Unveiling India: A Woman's Journey* (New Delhi: Penguin Books, 1988), p. 109.
2. Nasrin, Taslima: Quote in Column, 102.
3. An article on Durrani by a lecturer from Chennai.
4. Durrani, Tehmina: *My Feudal Lord*, Corgi edition published, 1995 (Transworld Publishers), p. 65.
5. *Ibid.*
6. Arora, Neena; Nayantara Sahgal and Doris Lessing (A Feminist Study in Comparison), New Delhi: Prestige, 1991, p. 119.
7. Deshpande, Shashi: *That Long Silence*, Penguin Books India (Pvt.) Ltd., p. 192.